HOME WITHOUT WALLS

RELIGION AND AMERICAN CULTURE

HOME WITHOUT WALLS

Southern Baptist Women and Social Reform in the Progressive Era

Carol Crawford Holcomb

THE UNIVERSITY OF ALABAMA PRESS TUSCALOOSA

The University of Alabama Press
Tuscaloosa, Alabama 35487-0380
uapress.ua.edu

Typeface: Garamond

Cover image: WMU Good Will Center, Louisville, Kentucky; courtesy of the Southern Baptist Historical Library and Archives, Nashville, Tennessee
Cover design: Michele Myatt Quinn

Cataloging-in-Publication data is available from the Library of Congress.
ISBN: 978-0-8173-2054-6
E-ISBN: 978-0-8173-9289-5

For Mom and Dad

Contents

Acknowledgments

More people than I can possibly name have aided me in the creation of this book. My formative years were spent in church mission programs, Vacation Bible Schools, and Sunday school classes taught by Baptist women. Their stories are inextricably woven into the fabric of my life and writing. Others have influenced my academic work more directly. It is difficult to find enough words to express my gratitude to my mentor Bill Pitts, professor emeritus at Baylor University, who has supported this project from its inception to its completion. He set a very high bar for his students with his scholarship, work ethic, and his unfailing kindness. Bill and his wife, Dr. Ruth Pitts, have been my teachers, my tour guides, and my friends.

Wayne Flynt, professor emeritus at Auburn University, initially solicited the manuscript when he was the Religion and American Culture series editor for the University of Alabama Press. Dr. Flynt encouraged me to write this book. He read my early drafts and urged me to persevere. His interest in my work has given me the confidence to see this project to completion. I am indebted to Elizabeth Flowers at Texas Christian University for her careful reading of the manuscript, her insightful critiques, and her friendship. My friends and colleagues in the Baptist Classics Seminar, sponsored by Mercer University, have enriched my work. We have been meeting together annually for nearly two decades to read primary sources in Baptist studies. These colleagues have served as my sounding boards over the years and have sharpened my thinking through dialogue and debate. I would also like to express my gratitude to the editorial team at the University of Alabama Press, especially Dan Waterman, for his support of this project.

This project would not have been possible without the summer grant, sabbatical, and other support provided by the University of Mary Hardin-Baylor. Anne Price, Kathy Harden, and Teresa Buck, librarians at the Townsend Memorial Library at UMHB, have been generous with their time and graciously helped me search for the smallest details. Special thanks, also, to Jennah Hopper, for her cheerful work on the index. I would like to express my gratitude to other libraries and archivists that made my research possible and productive, including the Woman's Missionary Union Archives in Birmingham, Alabama; the North Carolina Baptist Historical Commission in the Smith-Reynolds Library, Wake Forest University; Musick Museum and Alumni Center, University of Mary Hardin-Baylor; North Carolina WMU Offices, Baptist State Convention of North Carolina; the Texas Collection at Baylor University; and the Texas Baptist Historical Collection in Waco, Texas. I could not have completed this book without the exceptional work of Bill Sumners and Taffey Hall, archivists at the Southern Baptist Historical Library and Archives in Nashville, Tennessee. In addition to being gracious hosts when I visited Nashville, they shared their considerable knowledge of Southern Baptist sources and accommodated all of my inquiries—large or small. Special thanks to *Baptist History and Heritage* and the *American Baptist Quarterly* for giving permission to include some of my earlier articles. Portions of chapter 2 were previously published by the University of Tennessee Press in *Reimagining Southern Baptists: Women, Gender, and the Politics of the Past*, edited by Elizabeth H. Flowers and Karen K. Seat.

My family has also been incredibly supportive of my writing. My three boys, Ben, Andrew, and Daniel, have been patient as I covered the dining room table in books, notecards, and scribbled outlines. They traveled to scholarly meetings with me and have even feigned interest on occasion while I talked about my research! I am proud of their accomplishments and look forward to hearing all the music they will create in the years ahead. Finally, I wish to express my appreciation to my husband and best friend, David Holcomb. In the midst of his own hectic academic schedule, he has read each chapter and offered invaluable and kind critique. I am unbelievably fortunate to have a partner who is so generous with his time and patient with my "process." There are no words to express my gratitude and love. You are still the best person I have ever met.

HOME WITHOUT WALLS

Introduction

In 1914 Lulie Wharton, a Woman's Missionary Union leader and social worker, described her vision of social engagement in a missionary journal. "No one can deny that her [woman's] work is primarily home keeping, care of children and ministry to the sick and helpless. The fact is that her house cannot be kept clean unless the neighborhood is clean; . . . that the moral standard of the vicinity of her home affects the character of her children. . . . These facts are forcing women to reach out and take her [*sic*] share in preparing the 'home without walls.'"[1] Like other southern women in the early twentieth century, Wharton accepted the prevailing domestic gender ideology that defined women's lives at that time. She believed women were responsible for the home—for the safety and care of children, for healthy food, moral training, and care for a neighbor in need. What makes her vision distinctive is that Wharton merged her commitment to domesticity with southern progressivism. The result was a more holistic social ethic. If mothers take their responsibility for home protection seriously, then the social environment outside the home must come under the purview of women. Women must not be content to nurse the sick at home; they must stop the spread of the disease in their communities. If children need uncontaminated milk, women must investigate how milk is processed and distributed. Wharton encouraged women to be proactive such that the boundaries between home and community become fluid. Southern Baptist women like Lulie Wharton accommodated their assumptions about gender to their growing concern for social reform during the Progressive Era. The publications and programming of Woman's Missionary Union, Auxiliary to the Southern Baptist Convention (WMU), at the turn of the twentieth century reveal that WMU leaders were southern progressives who developed a distinctly feminine social ethic shaped by the social gospel. *Home without Walls* examines the ways progressivism shaped the social ethics of Baptist women in the South.

Southern Baptist women in the Progressive Era stepped out of their place very cautiously. For Baptists in the nineteenth century the very existence of a female-led organization posed a threat to the status quo—particularly in the South. It had been a herculean task to form a female missionary society within a patriarchal denomination. As a result, WMU leaders struggled to maintain a balance between asserting their power and maintaining their credibility with their constituents. They carefully distanced themselves from the women's rights movement and never publicly endorsed female suffrage until after the ratification of the Nineteenth Amendment. They did so because missions were the priority and advocating women's rights would have destroyed their connection to Southern Baptists. On rare occasions, Southern Baptist women expressed their frustration with the limitations imposed on women. Lulie Wharton expressed her opinion on this subject in 1925. "The world needs the contributions women can make to its welfare," she wrote, "and this contribution can never be given in full measure as long as the notion prevails that her thoughts, her feelings, and her actions are of real worth only when they have been strained through a masculine percolator."[2] WMU leaders believed that women had not only the ability but also the obligation to make significant contributions to the world in which they lived. They were practical feminists in their determination to provide a platform for women's views and a space for women to do meaningful work.

It is noteworthy that progressivism shaped Southern Baptist women because it ran counter to the prevailing conservative ethos of southern religion. Historians of the American South have accurately described the vast majority of white southern Protestants as rural traditionalists, defensive of local autonomy, suspicious of government interference, and fiercely independent. In spite of the cultural obstacles, progressivism did make its way south of the Mason-Dixon Line.[3] Southern progressives challenged the traditionalists who resisted government interference in local affairs. Progressives advocated for social legislation, touting the values of efficiency, democracy, social justice, professionalism, and data gathering. Reformers like Walter Hines Page worked tirelessly for improvements in education, health, agriculture, and the railroads. Edgar Gardner Murphy joined Page in the fight for graded public schools, and together they spearheaded the battle against child labor. Belle H. Bennett, Mary Helm, Sara Estelle Haskins, Lilly Hardy Hammond, and other Methodist women addressed immigration issues, industrial problems, and worked to improve race relations. George W. Cable and Robert T. Hill battled the convict lease system, and Seaman A. Knapp revolutionized agriculture with his work in the Louisiana rice industry. These and other progressive leaders struggled to impose their version of justice onto the New South.[4]

While southern social reformers during the Progressive Era worked diligently to ameliorate social problems, they were also captive to their culture. William Link's masterful analysis of southern progressivism noted critical "paradoxes" inherent to the movement. Southern progressives instituted hierarchies to champion democracy, adopted coercive measures to accomplish humanitarian reforms, and established programs for the "social uplift" of black and rural white people that were fraught with racism and classism.[5] Progressives in the North shared most of these paradoxical traits with their southern counterparts—including a commitment to white supremacy. In the South, however, race defined progressivism. The majority of southern progressives believed that racial peace and social order could only be achieved through segregation and disenfranchisement. The "racial settlement" of the last two decades of the nineteenth century was largely the work of southern progressivism. Southern progressives used and often authored Jim Crow legislation in order to advance their social reform agendas. Progressives funded white education at the expense of black students and deliberately removed black southerners from the political process in order to make changes in local and state government.[6] Progressives argued that disenfranchisement was the only way to "remove the bribery, vote buying, ballot box stuffing, etc. which had plagued the South since the Civil War."[7] Temperance reformers likewise viewed alcohol consumption as a racially charged issue and exploited racial stereotypes to promote temperance legislation.[8] Even the most progressive of the southern reformers like Walter Hines Page, who fought for equal rights for black southerners, believed the "Anglo-Saxon" myth.[9]

In 1912 Governor Ben W. Hooper of Tennessee founded the leading institutional expression of southern progressivism: the Southern Sociological Congress (SSC). Hooper issued an invitation to southern governors on February 6 to attend a meeting in Nashville in the following May. Governor Hooper intended the Congress to address a broad range of "social, civic, and economic problems."[10] The Congress met annually for seven years, hosting a parade of social gospel speakers such as Samuel Zane Batten, Graham Taylor, Walter Rauschenbusch, and Charles Macfarland, executive secretary of the Federal Council of Churches. Southern leaders represented both conservative and liberal theological positions. Leading southern clergy predominated in the leadership, including Atlanta Baptist John E. White, Methodist ministers James E. McCulloch and John A. Rice, and Presbyterian cleric Alexander McKelway among many others. Southern Baptist layman Charles Hillman Brough served as president of the Congress in 1916, the same year he was elected as a progressive governor of the state of Arkansas. The SSC adopted a social program very similar to that of the Federal Council of Churches with adaptations for southern social problems. One historian argued that its social program could be "rightly considered a distinctly Southern version of the social gospel."[11]

SOUTHERN BAPTISTS AND PROGRESSIVISM

Southern Baptists have often been characterized as the quintessential conservative southern Protestant. Southern Baptists were committed to biblical authority, evangelism, missions, white supremacy, and the status quo. In his work examining the social views of Southern Baptists from 1865 to 1900, Rufus Spain described the denomination as "relatively unconcerned about the problems of society during the period" or "at ease in Zion."[12] Social historian John Lee Eighmy acknowledged progressive influences and elements of the social gospel, but he affirmed that Southern Baptists were generally "captive to their culture."[13] Conservative theology did not mean that Southern Baptists callously ignored every social problem. Many Southern Baptists expressed social concern, but most firmly believed individual conversion to be the solution for societal ills. It was a "trickle down" approach to social change; if individuals are transformed then they will, in turn, transform institutions and structures. Most Southern Baptists expressed their social concern by helping individuals with programs such as orphanages and food pantries.[14] So, how do we differentiate between this "social concern" expressed by typical Southern Baptists and the social attitudes of southern progressives? Historian Robert D. Linder provided helpful categories nearly half a century ago. Linder used "social concern" as a broad term meaning "a general interest in society's problems." "Social ministries" referred to those activities carried out by Christians designed to "help . . . individuals harmed by adverse social conditions." Finally, he defined "social action" as "organized effort at any level—personal, nonpolitical, and political—which seeks to change social and economic conditions to conform more closely to principles laid down in the Bible."[15] Conservative Southern Baptists expressed their "social concern" through "social ministry" aimed at dealing with the effects of harmful social conditions. Southern Baptist progressives demonstrated their "social concern" through "social action" designed to identify and remove the causes of social problems.

Historians of the American South have not only successfully defended the existence of progressivism in the South, but they have also demonstrated conclusively that progressivism made inroads among Southern Baptists.[16] Southern Baptist progressives exhibited a profound optimism that the tools of efficiency, democracy, professionalism, and proper methods could produce social change. Southern Baptist women advanced the cause of progressivism among Southern Baptists in the early twentieth century.[17] Progressivism entered Southern Baptist communities in part due to the work of individual leaders of the WMU such as Fannie E. S. Heck, Maud Reynolds McLure, and Lulie Pollard Wharton. They introduced progressive ideas to Southern Baptist women through WMU literature and shaped WMU programs using progressive methods. WMU leaders studied the social teachings of Methodist women, visited social settlements like Jane Addams's Hull House, embraced the work of the Woman's Christian Temperance Union (WCTU), and participated in the SSC.

The temperance movement served as the gateway for most southern religious leaders into Progressive Era reforms. By far, temperance garnered the most support among Southern Baptists in the latter part of the nineteenth century. Before the Civil War, Baptists largely classified drunkenness as a personal moral failing.

Alcohol consumption in small quantities met with general acceptance. One Virginia Baptist minister wrote wistfully about former days when a preacher could "take his julep to prepare himself for the duties of the pulpit or his toddy to brace up his wearied powers after the services were over."[18] In the 1850s, Baptist state conventions began endorsing total abstinence from alcohol, thus ending the minister's hope of finding courage in a mint julep.

As the decades of the 1880s and '90s progressed, temperance reformers began to advocate legislative solutions to the problem of alcohol. Baptists resisted the move early on by appealing to their long-held conviction that the church should not participate in political activism. Ultimately, however, they became convinced that alcohol constituted a social problem because it was responsible for family violence, poverty, racial conflict, and a host of other evils. Where alcohol was concerned, Baptists were willing to solicit help from outside the local congregation for solutions to problems that affected their communities. Beginning in 1886 the Southern Baptist Convention (SBC) endorsed prohibition and urged their constituents to cooperate in dismantling the liquor industry. In 1908 the SBC established a permanent committee on temperance. The temperance committee provided Baptists with current information on the status of legislation and urged them to participate in the political process with both their vote and voice.[19] Temperance activism allied Southern Baptists with other denominations in the fight to stamp out "demon rum." Through such organizations as the Prohibition Party, the WCTU, and the Anti-Saloon League, Baptists learned the methods and message of progressivism. The WCTU and the Anti-Saloon League received widespread support from Southern Baptists. The first three superintendents of the Texas Anti-Saloon League—Benjamin F. Riley, J. H. Gambrell, and Arthur J. Barton—were Baptists. In addition to serving as chairman of the SBC temperance committee, Barton also served on the national executive committee of the Anti-Saloon League, chaired the committee that drafted the national prohibition legislation in 1915, and represented the US government in an international conference on alcohol consumption.[20] Green Clay Smith, the National Prohibition Party's presidential nominee in 1876, was a Southern Baptist. Texas Baptist leader James B. Cranfill served as the Prohibition Party's vice presidential candidate in 1892, and Baltimore native Joshua Levering, a three-time president of the SBC, led the Prohibition Party in 1896. Levering was also the first cousin of legendary Woman's Missionary Union (WMU) corresponding secretary Annie Armstrong.[21] Both liberal and conservative churchmen joined in the temperance crusade and rubbed shoulders as they marched.

Southern Baptists' approach to temperance also reflected the racism, classism, and xenophobia endemic to southern progressivism. Baptists not only promoted temperance legislation as a solution to racial conflict but also promoted disenfranchisement as an essential strategy for abolishing the liquor traffic. As one Alabama Baptist association stated: wisdom demanded that they "use every means to keep whiskey from the negro" in order to "preserve our civilization and to minimize the danger of race conflict."[22] John E. White, pastor of the prominent Second Baptist Church in Atlanta, Georgia, prepared the article on temperance for a multivolume work called *The South in the Building of the Nation* in 1909. White defended the strategy of disenfranchisement, insisting that it was necessary for temperance reform and for the well-being of black citizens. "The fact that the negro constitutes a child-people element in our population and that the great mass of negroes are ignorant and weak, and therefore are to be protected from the perils of liberty, is an ascending idea in the legislative scheme of the South. The moral basis of the disenfranchise movement was here. Thousands of men—the justest of men—went with this consideration of the true welfare of the negro race, their thought being that through such limitation only could the discipline of citizenship become possible."[23]

White argued that depriving black citizens of their vote had reduced racial tension and led to a decrease in lynchings from sixty-seven in 1906 to fifty in 1907. "Disfranchisement of the Negro by law was the first great result of this return of social reason in the South," he insisted. Furthermore, without any hint of irony, he opined that disenfranchisement would restore the "sacredness of law" and the "integrity of Democracy" by freeing the "white people" from racial conflict so they could reconstruct their civilization and enact prohibition.[24] Even as it touted the benefits of disenfranchisement for reducing racial tension, southern temperance propaganda fanned the flames of racial violence by constantly alluding to the dangers drunken black men presented for white women. "The feeling of insecurity in the rural sections of the South on account of vagrant and drunken negroes had become a contagion among the country women," insisted White.[25] White supremacy infused and energized the temperance movement in the South.

Temperance activism illustrates this paternalism because the movement played a major role in the plans of white Baptists to "save" and "help the Negroes." Temperance "is the opportunity to emphasize our recognition of the South's responsibility for the negro's moral welfare," explained John White. "Anglo-Saxon supremacy should thus be exercised in consideration of our kindly concern about his development in our midst."[26] Some Southern Baptists encouraged benevolence toward black southerners because paternalism would demonstrate and prove the supremacy of the white race. "In saving and helping the Negroes to their best self expression as a race, we shall save Anglo-Saxon supremacy," claimed a 1912 SBC report. "To do the opposite, to seek artificially to repress the Negroes from the attainment of industrial efficiency and to neglect their moral and religious training is to call in question the superiority of our own race and open the door for its degeneration."[27] Southern Baptist women exhibited the same racism, classism, and xenophobia as other southern progressives in their reform work. *Home without Walls* explores some of these paradoxes with attention to the ways attitudes of white supremacy limited cooperation between white and black women.

THE SOCIAL GOSPEL

A few Southern Baptists progressives identified fully with the social gospel.[28] While this book is not about the social gospel per se, the social gospel was pivotal in shaping the ethics of Southern Baptist women during this era.[29] Whether accepted in full or in part, the social gospel served as a goad that pressed into conservative religious assumptions. The social gospel was a catalyst for social reform, even for those who remained committed to individual conversion.[30] John Lee Eighmy observed that "social gospel ideology broke through the conservative solidarity of nineteenth century Southern religion much as it did in the North."[31] Eighmy's revision of social gospel scholarship is important for several reasons. First, his work acknowledged the progressive elements of southern religious expression, overthrowing the reigning perception of the Southern Baptist as a "provincial hardshell, enemy of the flesh, heaven-bound defender of the faith."[32] Eighmy's work also provided a model of balance for scholars who struggle to narrate the story from "inside" the religious tradition by providing an unvarnished portrait of Southern Baptist attitudes. Finally, Eighmy maintained the liberal theological distinctives of the Social Gospel Movement while expanding the list of specific issues to which they might be applied.[33]

Denominational historian Catherine Allen laid the foundation for research on Southern Baptist women and the social gospel.[34] Historians Paul Harvey and Elizabeth Flowers have also pointed to the existence of a social gospel and progressivism among Baptist women.[35] *Home without Walls* builds and expands on this scholarship by focusing on issues that shaped the social ethics of WMU during the Progressive Era. WMU leaders embraced the ideals of southern progressivism including democracy, efficiency, data gathering, and social uplift. Again, they also exhibited the paradoxes of progressivism such as racism and classism. Early WMU leaders were typically well-educated, upper-middle-class women. They represented the Southern Baptist elite and as such had the time to read, write, and discuss ideas with other southern progressives. They rubbed shoulders with Methodist and Presbyterian women in clubs and ecumenical missionary meetings. Baptist women studied the missionary publications of these other denominations and adapted their ideas for a Southern Baptist audience. Some WMU leaders read social gospel theologians and attended their lectures. WMU leaders toured social settlements, joined social reform societies, and received professional training in social work. At the end of the nineteenth century, Southern Baptist women carved out a distinctly feminine space within a patriarchal denomination and developed a social ethic to sustain their work.[36]

METHODOLOGY AND SOURCES

Home without Walls is a social history of Baptist women and as such represents a cross section of fields from religious history to cultural studies. This work employs a variety of methodologies to explore the social ethics of Baptist women. The chapters dealing with WMU's attitudes on race and gender could best be characterized as cultural studies. The contributions of Annie Armstrong, who still casts a long shadow in Southern Baptist life, required a full biography. Although Armstrong was not the most progressive theologically, she used the tools of progressivism such as efficiency, professionalism, budgeting, and innovative financial planning more effectively than any other Baptist woman involved in WMU. The chapter on Baptist social settlement work uses case studies, and the analysis of the social gospel draws heavily on the fields of theology and religious history.

My research began at the WMU archive in Birmingham, Alabama. The Annie Armstrong notebooks are particularly important. Armstrong made scrapbooks of the articles that she cut from contemporary newspapers and magazines. She added personal notes and pasted handwritten devotionals and lectures to use as sources for her speeches when she traveled. The Southern Baptist Historical Library and Archive (SBHLA) in Nashville, Tennessee, is the primary repository of Southern Baptist materials. A collection of Fannie Heck papers can be found at the North Carolina Baptist collection, housed at the Z. Smith Reynolds Library, Wake Forest University, in Winston-Salem, North Carolina. Scholars can also find sources on Heck at the North Carolina State Convention office in Cary, North Carolina, and at the North Carolina State Archives in Raleigh. The Nannie Helen Burroughs papers are in the Library of Congress in Washington, DC.

The first chapter of *Home without Walls* traces the development of the women's foreign missionary movement and explains the rise of the Woman's Missionary Union, Auxiliary to the Southern Baptist Convention. It highlights the resistance Baptist women encountered as they initiated missionary work. Women in nearly every Protestant denomination established a missionary society in the nineteenth century. Southern Baptist women studied and celebrated the work of their Protestant sisters and saw themselves as part of a vast movement to spread Christianity around the world. Chapter 2 discusses the ways in which WMU leaders understood gender. WMU leaders accepted Victorian views of women but interpreted piety, purity, submissiveness, and domesticity in ways that allowed them greater freedom. They particularly embraced the idea that women should be in charge of a separate domestic sphere but expanded the definitions of "house" and "home" in ways that included all of society.

Chapter 3 introduces one of the most formidable women ever to be associated with WMU: Annie Armstrong. She uniquely modeled the pattern of using domesticity as a wedge to open doors for women. Under Armstrong's leadership the organization grew exponentially in size and influence. She developed WMU into a quintessential Progressive-Era institution using data gathering, efficiency, professionalism, publicity, innovative financial strategies, and gritty determination. Chapter 4, "Unreliable Allies," highlights the contact between Annie Armstrong and her counterpart in the National Baptist Convention, Nannie Helen Burroughs. Although WMU leaders provided monetary aid and mission support to black Baptist women, they ultimately failed to be allies on the issue of race. Southern Baptist women during the Progressive Era shared the racial views of other white southerners, paternalistic at best and virulently racist at worst. Most of their references to race in WMU periodicals served only to reinforce racial stereotypes. In spite of her friendship with Burroughs, Annie Armstrong failed to acknowledge the systemic racism that characterized the South. At times WMU writers encouraged members to seek racial justice in a generic sense. On occasion they called white supremacy into question, but there is no evidence that WMU publications ever challenged segregation. Southern Baptist women and National Baptist women did work together, but these instances of cooperation did not lead Southern Baptist women to question the system of Jim Crow that violated the human rights of millions of black southerners.

The fifth chapter defines the social gospel and explains how WMU leaders encountered both the social gospel and southern progressivism. WMU expressed its commitment to "modern thought" by creating a department in WMU dedicated to "Personal Service." Like other WMU programs, the Personal Service Department created an impressive administrative structure that stretched from local churches, to associations, through state conventions, to the national offices of WMU. Through these channels, the national WMU urged women to study social problems and practice social reform on the local level. The national office provided forms in hopes that women would report and catalog their work. Chapter 6, "A Gospel for All of Life," explores how WMU introduced local women to the social gospel. References to the social gospel, direct or implied, appeared most often in the Personal Service columns of WMU magazines. WMU also developed study guides, handbooks, and manuals to help train lay women in social reform. Many of these introduced social gospel theologians and recommended their writings in bibliographies. Finally, Southern Baptist women created a formal training school designed to prepare women for missionary service. The WMU Training School (WMUTS) emphasized social work methods and gave women access to professors who embraced the social gospel.

Chapter 7 describes how WMU established social settlements across the South that were later named Good Will Centers. Although critics have rightly pointed out that these social settlements functioned primarily as missions, WMU leaders stated that they were indeed creating social settlements. Regardless of how conservative these programs appear compared to the broader settlement movement, Baptist women at the time believed that they were marching in lockstep with the most current trends of the day. They established a model social settlement in Louisville, Kentucky, in connection with the WMU Training School. At the WMUTS Baptist women learned social work theory, and the model social settlement provided a laboratory for practical experience. The social settlements and other social service programs promoted by WMU in turn provided jobs for graduates.

The leaders of the Southern Baptist WMU from 1888 to 1920 were southern religious progressives. They developed an institution controlled by women and from that separate sphere molded much of Southern Baptist life throughout the twentieth century. They wove the values of southern progressivism, with all of its paradoxes, into the institutional structure of WMU. While the social gospel emphases faded in the 1920s, the effort to transform the social conditions that harmed the lives of individuals (particularly women and children) remained through the social work programs of WMUTS in Louisville, Kentucky. The training school educated generations of female missionaries and social workers, many of whom accepted paid positions in institutions created and largely financed by WMU. While they perpetuated the ideology of southern womanhood, Baptist women redefined the public and private spheres. In a world where male-dominated institutions excluded women, WMU created an independent parallel space and exercised power by generating the majority of the denominations' funds. Unequivocally, the main purpose of Baptist women was to further the cause of missions and bring the entire world to a saving knowledge of Christ. But in order to be "co-workers with Christ,"[37] they had to create a place to work. WMU carved out that space, funded missions, educated women, created jobs in social work, and became a powerful lobby for a feminine approach to social ethics within the denomination.

CHAPTER ONE

They Feared God More Than Men

The Birth of the WMU

IN 1900 ANNIE W. ARMSTRONG published the pamphlet *Women as Helpers in God's Kingdom*, narrating the history of women's work in missions. She began with the story of Adele Fielde—a young woman who set off for China in 1865 to marry her fiancé and share his life as a foreign missionary. When she arrived in Bangkok, Fielde was met with the "crushing news" of her fiancé's death. Setting aside her grief, Fielde remained in China to continue the work he had begun. Unfortunately, her methods aroused the suspicion of the American Baptist mission board, so they sent a commission of "earnest, thoughtful men" to investigate.

"Miss Fielde," they began, "we understand that you have taken upon you to preach the gospel."

"I will tell you what I do," she replied. "In the day I go under a tree, gather a group of native women, read the New Testament and explain it to them. If that is preaching, I suppose I preach."

"Well," they answered, "have you been ordained to preach?"

"No," Fielde answered. "I have never been ordained to preach, but I was foreordained." For Annie Armstrong, Fielde's answer summarized the key impulse of Protestant women's missionary work: it was a work initiated and ordained by God. Armstrong went on to explain that the organization of women's boards of missions had harnessed the "power of Christian women." There could be no doubt, she pronounced, that "Woman's Work may be said to be a force foreordained of God."[1] Armstrong firmly believed that women in mission work received their authority and their commissioning from God. This "ordination" from God superseded any authority that human beings—of either gender—could bestow. Baptist women were willing to challenge the established gender mores of southern culture, to redefine the meaning of "women's work," and to restructure the boundaries of the domestic sphere because they feared God more than men.[2]

Southern women faced tremendous opposition from Baptist men and struggled to gain acceptance from the Southern Baptist Convention. When they finally succeeded in establishing the Woman's Missionary Union (WMU) in 1888, Reconstruction had been over for ten years and the southern economy was gradually recovering from the devastation of the Civil War. The "true woman" of the antebellum South was evolving into the New South woman—armed with education and the experiences of the Civil War. WMU leaders were among these New South women who redefined domesticity in their own terms. They agreed (to a point) that the genders belonged in separate spheres, which is precisely how they defended the need for WMU. Women needed their own place to work. It just so happened that their work involved spreading the Gospel around the globe. Through service in WMU Baptist women developed invaluable skills in leadership, fund-raising, bookkeeping, organization, record keeping, public speaking, editing, publishing, and more. The high calling of the Gospel required skilled workers. WMU happily provided on-the-job training.

By embracing the entire world as their proper sphere, they created a powerful women's organization that would be the financial engine of Southern Baptists for over a hundred years. WMU functioned as the development and educational arm of the Southern Baptist mission boards, raising millions of dollars, publishing hundreds of thousands of missionary pamphlets, and providing missions education for women and children across the South. While it is true that WMU leaders carefully crafted their public image in terms of demure southern womanhood and had virtually no political voice in the Southern Baptist Convention, the power they did exercise amounted to more than moral suasion. As corresponding secretary of the WMU, Annie Armstrong secured about one-third of the revenue that flowed into the mission boards. She never let an opportunity pass to emphasize this to SBC leaders. Her letters paint a portrait of a deeply religious, fiercely driven woman. Since God had called her to support missions, she believed it was her responsibility to make sure the money was collected and expended in the most efficient, effective manner possible. She gave the male leadership clear instructions about how this should be accomplished. Most Baptist women wielded their power with more delicacy than Armstrong, but in every case the traditional gender relationships were nuanced by the women's conviction that they were embarking on a divine mission. The millions of dollars WMU programs poured into Southern Baptist coffers served only to illustrate that they were, in their view, a force ordained by God.

PROTESTANT WOMEN'S MISSIONARY BEGINNINGS

The following pages briefly trace the origins of the Protestant women's missionary movement and early Baptist women's missionary societies.[3] The broader women's missionary movement provides the backdrop for the development of the Southern Baptist missionary society that Annie Armstrong and her colleagues labored so dutifully to birth. One of the earliest women's missionary societies in America was formed on October 9, 1800, at the behest of Mary "Polly" Webb.[4] Webb encouraged Baptist and Congregationalist women to join together in the Boston Female Society for Missionary Purposes. Boston's example influenced women throughout the country. In 1812 Mary Webb published an advertisement in the *Massachusetts Missionary Magazine* inviting other women's societies to correspond with her. Over the next two years forty societies responded.[5] Protestant women's enthusiasm for missions was bolstered by the winsome, colorful letters of Ann Hasseltine Judson. Ann and Adoniram Judson, the first American foreign missionaries, set sail for India in 1812. On the way to the mission field, both of the Judsons converted from the Congregationalist faith to become Baptists. Their friend and colleague, Luther Rice, also decided to become Baptist when he arrived in Calcutta. The Judsons eventually established a Baptist mission in Burma. American women were thrilled by Ann Judson's vivid descriptions of the Burmese people and the exotic city of Rangoon. Judson's piety and passion challenged her readers to greater faith. Women in America empathized with Judson's loneliness in a foreign land and shared her grief after the death of her six-month-old baby. During her 1822 furlough Judson was greeted as a celebrity in each place she visited. Judson died in 1826 after heroic service to her husband and colleagues during the Anglo-Burmese wars. Ann Judson's life of sacrificial service inspired generations of young women.[6] When Luther Rice returned from India in 1813 to solicit support for the Judsons, he recorded information concerning every Baptist woman's missionary organization he could find. In 1817 the Baptist Triennial Convention reported 110 women's missionary societies working in cooperation with the national body for missionary purposes.[7] These local societies prepared the soil for the independent women's missionary boards that would be planted after the Civil War.

Why did Protestant women join the foreign mission movement in such unprecedented numbers during and just after the Civil War? Helen Barrett Montgomery, a northern Baptist, suggested four reasons for the growth of separate women's missionary agencies. First, she noted the emergence of women's academies and colleges. Next, Montgomery pointed to the experiences of women during the Civil War. Third, she explained that women in America were moved to action by their concern for women in foreign lands. Fourth, Montgomery credited the woman's rights crusade for providing women with greater freedom to organize.[8] Montgomery was a suffragette and felt a personal debt to the women of Seneca Falls. She narrated her history of women's missionary activity as a part of a larger story of women's rising status in American culture.[9] Montgomery viewed Seneca Falls as a watershed event and described the ensuing women's rights movement in glowing terms. She noted in 1912 that all of the goals of the crusade had been met except suffrage, and she believed that this movement had been directly responsible for the growth of missionary boards. The majority of Montgomery's missionary colleagues at that time did not share her views about women's rights. Historian Patricia Hill observed that the "women who took up the cause of foreign missions after the Civil War were explicit in their rejection of egalitarianism and felt compelled to dissociate themselves and their movement from the woman's rights crusade."[10] Susan Hill Lindley agreed that missionary leaders avoided connections with the women's rights movement but insisted that women's desire to control their missionary work lay at the center of the issue of separate boards. "It was," said Lindley, "a power issue. Women wanted more say in how the money they raised was spent—who was sent where and to do what."[11] Women who might not have openly lobbied for woman's rights did express a desire to wield power over their mission work. In the South, evangelical women were willing to assert themselves in cases where they believed they had received a divine commission. As Annie Armstrong illustrated in her pamphlet, a call from God superseded everything.

EARLY MISSIONARY BEGINNINGS FOR SOUTHERN BAPTIST WOMEN

Taking her cue from Montgomery, Southern Baptist leader Fannie Heck explained that Southern Baptist women formed societies because of education, the Civil War, and concern for women in foreign lands. She completely omitted Montgomery's discussion of women's rights. Heck made the connections between Baptist women's education and the missionary enterprise in her 1913 history of woman's missionary work called *In Royal Service*. She described education as a new day for women. "When the day begins to break, be it ever so faintly, many turn to the light with eyes of hope, though sunrise is yet far away," she mused. "So it is with the beginning of higher education for women."[12] Heck believed education played a pivotal role in the development of Southern Baptist female leadership, and she documented the schools that she felt had been influential. "It is claimed," she began, "that Judson Baptist College is the oldest Baptist college for girls in the world, and the 'oldest college for girls in the South having an unbroken record of work.' . . . Founded in 1838, it began work on January 7, 1839 with nine pupils." Judson College in Alabama was founded by Milo P. Jewett, a newly converted Baptist who later founded Vassar College. Judson's antebellum curriculum resembled Mount Holyoke's. The earliest catalog noted that the trustees had acquired a building, a library, and "specimens of natural science."[13] Alabama Baptists designed a school to provide women with a liberal arts education, though many Baptists hoped that the school would bolster denominational (and regional) causes. An 1853 editorial in the *Alabama Baptist* "looked forward to a time when education for women would produce enough teachers, authors, and publishers to eliminate all Northern influence in the South."[14] Heck named other schools for women established in the South before the Civil War. Bessie Tift College, established in Georgia in 1847, was the successor of Monroe College. Hollins College for women was founded in Roanoke, Virginia, as part of the coeducational Valley Union Seminary in 1842. This institution became an exclusively female college in 1852. According to Heck, Richmond Female College and Greenville College in South Carolina both opened in 1854. All of these colleges she deemed "centers of missionary training."[15]

Heck's list was not exhaustive. There were still more Baptist colleges for women established in the South in the first half of the nineteenth century that Heck omitted. Georgia Female College at Macon, chartered in 1836, is older than Judson College. Baylor Female College (now the University of Mary Hardin-Baylor) was founded in 1845 as part of Baylor College at Independence, Texas. Although the college was initially coeducational, in 1866 the women's department was organized under a separate charter. In 1886 the women relocated to Belton, Texas. Chowan University of Murfreesboro, North Carolina, traces its origins to 1848 when Chowan Baptist Female Institute was established as a four-year women's college. Nearly a dozen Baptist women's colleges were founded in the three decades leading up to the Civil War.[16] It is easy to understand why Fannie Heck described this period as the dawning of a new day for women.

Most WMU leaders were educated in these denominational women's colleges and private academies within the heart of Dixie. By the eve of the Civil War, a generation of women had been trained in Baptist women's colleges across the South—colleges that promoted true womanhood, but that also trained women in literature, science, languages, fine arts, history, mathematics, and music. For example, during the Progressive Era, Baylor Female College offered a curriculum similar to Vassar's. The Baylor College catalog of 1878–79 listed courses in Algebra, Latin, Botany, Natural History, Natural Philosophy, Physiology, Chemistry, and French or German.[17] These studies were served along with the critical evangelical assumption that women should "be useful" in God's kingdom.[18] Little did these college graduates know that they would soon be enmeshed in the bloody practicum of a civil war that would test their newly minted degrees.

The Civil War has been described as an "important trigger to the formation of separate women's mission boards."[19] Southern Baptist women in the late nineteenth and early twentieth centuries identified the Civil War as a contributing factor in their missionary expansion. Heck published her history of women's missionary work two years after Montgomery and repeatedly described the Civil War as not only a time of suffering but also a time when women accepted new roles. Although Heck preferred the phrase "baptism of fire" over Montgomery's "baptism of power," she nonetheless agreed that it was "no accident" that "the decade following the close of the Civil War . . . saw the launching of scores of organizations."[20] Baptist men also attested to the changes the Civil War had wrought in the roles of women. Texas Baptist leader J. M. Carroll asserted: "During the war period our women had to act as men for our people. No historian will ever be able to tell how gloriously this was done by our brave Texas women."[21] Tennessee Baptist A. C. Dayton boasted about the women in his state as he urged Baptists to persevere during the war. Dayton narrated a conversation he had with a Baptist woman who stayed behind to run the plantation. "Then you really wish your husband to go?" asked Dayton. The woman replied: "I do not like to be separated from him. It is a terrible trial, but some must go. And between submission to the North and the short separation from my husband it is easy to choose. I can't go and fight but I can stay and take his place on the plantation while he is gone. Let him go and do his duty. I will stay and do mine." Dayton concluded: "Tennessee and all the South is full of just such women." Although Dayton celebrated such "noble women," he was quick to caution that their work did not in any way challenge traditional roles. "During the war, southern women play a prominent role on plantations and in churches," he explained. "Yet they do so without stepping outside of their traditional role as subservient to their husbands.[22]

Fannie Heck insisted that wartime experiences tempered the character of southern women. It made them strong, resourceful, and resilient. She described in detail the various skills the women developed—organization, administration, nursing, distribution of supplies, and so on.

> Burdened with personal griefs and anxieties almost to breaking, the women at home were nevertheless in training for wider religious services—societies for making and gathering supplies for the soldiers were formed in town and country. Even the school girls took part in the work of mercy. Many others besides the girls of Central Female Society, now Hillman College, Mississippi, which did excellent mission work before the war, now did much to relieve the suffering of the soldiers by making clothing, nursing, scraping lint, writing letters, and reading to the convalescents. Aided by the women of the town, they sent boxes of supplies even so far as the quartermaster at Richmond. In places which were hospital stations, like Raleigh, North Carolina, the women of the town were organized into relief associations, and the town districted into wards from which in turn they visited and carried supplies to the hospitals.[23]

In addition to all of these skills, women learned to act independently of their fathers and husbands. In the absence of the men, women discovered self-expression. Heck explained that because of the suffering the women were "finding their voices in public prayer, as they met from house to house and poured out their sore hearts in cries for mercy to the God of war." After the war ended, these same women "gathered with tear dimmed eyes" and organized once again, "in their Memorial Associations."[24] The Civil War helped Southern Baptist women "find their voices" and forced them to forge new relationships. Through flexible, effective networks they essentially served as military support staff—shipping food, clothing, and supplies to the battlefront. The postwar surge of civil religion that venerated the idle southern belle could not erase women's experiences gained beyond the confines of hearth and home. When the Civil War ended, Southern women turned their eyes toward the future and directed their considerable talents toward waging a new war—the "triumphant war for world-wide righteousness."[25]

Like other Protestant women, Southern Baptist women were also motivated by a concern for the salvation of foreign women and by the conviction that the male boards were not sufficiently addressing women's spiritual and social needs. The first Baptist women's missionary society was called Woman's Mission to Woman, and the appeal of working for the conversion and "uplift" of women around the world remained a constant in WMU work. Southern Baptist women believed that God had commissioned American women to share the Gospel with women of foreign lands and had uniquely equipped women to accomplish this assignment.[26] As Fannie Heck observed, "The impulse which was moving the women's hearts so deeply would not be stilled. The sorrow of heathen womanhood was pressing heavily upon the hearts of American women everywhere. They felt within them the power to answer the cry, which God had opened their ears to hear."[27]

WOMAN'S MISSION TO WOMAN

Although Southern Baptist women had been leaders in the early mission society movement, they trailed behind other denominations in forming a national organization. Annie Armstrong said they were "very conservative. They hesitated to advance, lest they might go beyond the quiet path marked out for women."[28] Fannie Heck recalled that they struggled not only with opposition from men but also from the economic and emotional crises created by the war. "The impulse moving among Southern women encountered also the depression, sorrow and poverty which followed in the track of devastation left by the war. It is not surprising," Heck reported, "that this movement advanced so slowly in the South."[29] In spite of these considerable barriers, a call for organization sounded from Baltimore. When the Southern Baptist Convention met in Baltimore in 1868, Ann J. Graves invited the messengers' wives to gather in the basement of Seventh Street Baptist Church. Graves's son was a medical missionary to China who had persuaded his mother that the women of China could only be reached by women. He urged his mother to rally women to raise money to employ native Christian "Bible women." In response, Ann Graves led a group of women from several churches in Baltimore to form an interdenominational women's missionary society.[30] In October 1871, Baltimore Baptist women constituted the all-Baptist missionary society called Woman's Mission to Woman (WMW). WMW committed to "give light to the women that sit in darkness because of Bible destitution, by taking the gospel in their homes, through the agency of native Bible women."[31] Throughout the South women who were still reeling from the devastation of the Civil War empathized with the suffering of women overseas. "Amid these unwanted cares and deprivations the new calls of woman to women" grew louder, reflected Fannie Heck. In those days "Mother and daughter and the young granddaughter" often spoke of "Woman's Mission work," which was becoming "a distinct feature in the lives of Christian women everywhere."[32] The sincere belief that women's lives abroad were filled with spiritual darkness, poverty, illiteracy, oppression, and unspeakable suffering fueled the passion for missionary work.[33]

The leaders of WMW followed through on their commitment to introduce Christianity to women through the agency of women. Their first missionary effort provided financial support for the native Bible women who helped Dr. Graves. In 1872 the organization agreed to support missionary Lula Whilden, prospective superintendent of the Canton Bible women.[34] In December 1872, WMW sponsored the salary of a Signorina Rosa Guerizini in Rome. They also agreed to help support a "Women's Working Society," an industrial training class, organized by Jane Norris Graves in China. "The main object of this," explained Graves, "would be the women's improvement in spiritual matters, but would include also instruction in needlework, and aid in securing employment." In 1876, they adopted a Canton girl's school, supported mothers' meetings, and agreed to buy rice for two women who wished to engage in full-time biblical study in order to become Bible women. Ten years later, Maryland women appropriated $1,400 to purchase land and erect a building for a training school for Bible women in Canton.[35]

WMW dispersed the monies on a case-by-case basis, sometimes sending the finances directly to the field or to the Foreign Mission Board as a designated offering. When the corresponding secretary of the Foreign Mission Board suggested they donate their gifts undesignated to the board, the women declined.[36] Even when pressed, the women politely refused to be bullied. For example, a new director of the Italian mission, Dr. George Taylor, suggested the salary of Signorina Rosa Guerizini be discontinued and the money ($16 per month) be applied to his theological students. The society abided by his decision but agreed to pay only $3 for soup for Taylor's theological class. On hearing their decision, Dr. Taylor quickly decided to reinstate Signorina Guerizini.[37]

A shift in leadership at the Southern Baptist Foreign Mission Board (FMB) also helped WMW achieve its goals. Henry Allen Tupper became secretary of the Foreign Mission Board in 1872 and remained in that role until 1893. Tupper led the Foreign Mission Board to respond more positively to the requests of the Baltimore women and to change its policy regarding single women in the mission field. Fannie Heck commented that the women finally had "a friend at court." In his first report Tupper asserted that "the sisterhood of our Southern Zion should be aroused to the grand mission of redeeming their sister-woman from the degrading and destroying influence of Paganism." During his first year, the board commissioned Lula Whilden of South Carolina and Edmonia Moon of Virginia as missionaries to China. Moon was the first single female missionary among Southern Baptists since 1848. During Tupper's tenure the FMB consented to three key policies regarding women: (1) to keep separate records of the women's contributions, (2) to encourage the organization of women's work across the South, and (3) to emphasize the evangelization of women. In return, the Baltimore women encouraged other state women's organizations to send their contributions directly to the Foreign Mission Board of the Southern Baptist Convention.[38]

In 1873, Tupper's second year as secretary of the Foreign Mission Board, a dedicated young woman from Albemarle County, Virginia, boarded a ship for China as a Southern Baptist missionary. Her name was Charlotte "Lottie" Diggs Moon. Lottie Moon studied at the Virginia Female Seminary (later Hollins College) and the Albermarle Female Institute (connected to the University of Virginia) where she received a diploma in Latin. She continued her studies for a fourth year at Albermarle and distinguished herself as a linguist, mastering not only Latin but also Greek, French, Italian, and Spanish. On her graduation the trustees of the University of Virginia determined that five women had completed studies so advanced that they should be awarded Master of Arts degrees. Lottie Moon was one of those five women. After graduation she opened a school for girls in Cartersville, Georgia, with her sister Edmonia Moon. Once she arrived in China, Lottie Moon established a school for girls, but soon came to believe that she should adopt other strategies for converting the Chinese people to Christianity. In the early 1880s, Lottie Moon began her "country work" by traveling to remote villages to teach the gospel. "Not having the school to fill up my time and thoughts, I have decided to devote myself to country work and city visiting," she reported in a letter to the Foreign Mission Board in 1884.[39] However, rural evangelism proved both physically and emotionally exhausting. By 1900 Lottie Moon returned to her work educating Chinese girls. Throughout her career, Moon wrote precise, detailed letters to the Foreign Mission Board (FMB) and to women's missionary magazines describing China in vivid detail. She frequently pleaded with the FMB to send more single women to the mission field. Moon also urged Southern Baptist women in America to form an organization to support mission work.

Back in the States, the Maryland women were also encouraging Baptist women to organize. Ann Graves embarked on a writing campaign promoting her plan for missionary societies in each state in the South. She sent mite boxes to state organizations to encourage deliberate, consistent giving. Local branches of Woman's Mission to Woman began to appear throughout the South in the decade of the 1870s.[40] In 1872, South Carolina women began systematically giving to foreign missions. Two years later, they organized a Woman's Mission to Woman Society. In 1874, the Foreign Mission Board issued a formal invitation urging women to form central committees to coordinate women's work in each of the southern states. Within three years central committees were formed in every state in the convention.

Southern women's missionary societies were not without opposition. Even after the financial and missionary successes of WMW, the women encountered acrimonious debates on the floor of the 1872 Southern Baptist Convention. A motion to encourage the women in their work was met with rancor. Although the final votes favored the continuation of women's work, the fighting continued on the state level. For example, when North Carolina women organized a central committee in 1877 and elected Mattie Heck (Fannie Heck's mother) to the chairship, they were openly opposed by their state convention. When Heck reported "proudly" to the convention that the women had organized seventeen societies and had raised $300 for missions, they were greeted with such a "storm of dissension" from the convention that the "little bark, the unwitting cause of the storm, was crippled and soon sank from sight."[41] It took ten years for North Carolina women to recover their momentum. In Georgia, in the early 1880s, reports of women's work were ignored, and Kentucky pastors refused to give the Foreign Mission Board the names of women who might be interested in organizing. Fannie Heck reported that the men sat in "stony silence" when asked for women's names. "Not to be daunted," she explained, "the post masters were asked to send names of leading Baptist women. A number of good women were reached through the good offices of these officials."[42]

Opposition to women's organizations came from several quarters. First, some Baptists followed a pattern of rigid biblicism. Anything beyond preaching and a periodic business meeting within the church appeared too innovative and unbiblical to the rural Baptists. Societies and programs outside the church were typically met with suspicion. Furthermore, pastors and laymen resisted anything organized by women. As Texas Baptist women discovered, many Baptists considered women's missionary organizations "a menace to the integrity of the churches."[43] "Strange to say," reminisced the secretary of the Rio Grande Baptist Association in Texas, "the greatest hindrance to the advance of woman's work was the brethren, especially the preachers, and more especially, the deacons."[44] An early Texas WMU leader described the climate of opposition: "Even the more enlightened of [the ministers] were shy of women's societies. They were not sure that women knew how to carry on alone, not realizing their women had wonderful training in managing their homes, their children, and even their husbands, though the poor dears knew it not."[45] North Carolina women recalled a state meeting held in a church where the pastor was "violently opposed to women's work." The delegates from around the state plodded "through the rain to find the church cold and cheerless. A handful of women came in, shaking the rain from their skirts." After they were settled the delegates discovered that the "twenty or thirty" other women assembled in the church were not Baptist women, but Methodist and Presbyterians who had come "out of pity." The Baptist pastor had instructed his members not to attend.[46]

Biblical literalism also shaped southern attitudes toward women's organizations. The admonition in 1 Corinthians 14:34 for "women to keep silence in the churches" served as the guiding principle for women's roles in many southern churches. Women were forced to defend their work against those who wielded scripture to silence them. Mina Everett, a salaried mission worker in Texas, gently challenged the distinguished Texas Baptist pastor B. H. Carroll when he suggested that they should disband. "Someone rose and asked: 'Well, Dr. Carroll, do you not think that women can be serviceable in church work?' To which he answered: 'In my church I have the women divided into circles, and when I need a certain kind of work done I call on a certain circle, and if I have a different character of work to be done I call on another circle.' Whereupon Miss Mina, of courageous heart, spoke to him through his ear trumpet, without which he could not hear at all: 'Will you tell us, Dr. Carroll, by what Scriptural authority you direct your women's work?' Looking at her in quiet dignity, he laid aside his ear trumpet. Thus ended the discussion."[47]

As late as 1895, Baptist women lamented that key pastors continued to undermine their work by quoting scripture. Annie Armstrong found that some pastors who seemed supportive of women's work hindered their efforts by appealing to the Apostle Paul. She mentioned Dr. John Broadus, whose daughter was the president of the Central Committee of Kentucky, specifically. "I never heard him make an address on Woman's Work, or refer to it, that I did not feel sorry he had touched on it at all," she complained. "For while he spoke as approving of it, he always ended with a warning that we should not forget Paul's teaching—'let the women keep silence in the churches,' etc. etc." Armstrong noted that she always "hoped that Dr. Broadus would give our work his unqualified endorsement, but as far as I know, he never did."[48]

Conservative Baptists feared that any new role for women, even as mission workers, would put them on a slippery slope toward the pulpits. The Baptist newspaper, *Western Recorder*, stated this clearly in 1888. "We . . . fear that such an independent organization of women naturally tends toward a violation of the divine interdict against women's becoming a public religious teacher and leader—a speaker before mixed assemblies, a platform declaimer, a pulpit proclaimer, street preacher, lyceum lecturer, stump orator."[49] Women who organized missionary societies violated the "divine interdict" just as much as women who dared to speak in mixed assemblies. Another editor bitterly condemned "the effort to bring women to the front as public lecturers or speakers before mixed assemblies, or as ordained preachers of the gospel." He was determined it be "known *everywhere* that our people South, as a rule, are unalterably opposed to this thing."[50]

Some ministers feared that northern influences could bring not only women preachers but might also introduce an entire movement for women's rights. Southern religious leaders juxtaposed pure southern womanhood to jaded northern women—noble southern traditions to the corrupting influences of women's rights. Texas women recorded that the men "dreaded the spirit of 'woman's rights' taking hold of the women as a force. They feared insubordination of the women toward the brethren."[51]

In general Baptists worried that northern influences would lure southern women from their proper place. North Carolina women battled against accusations that they were attempting to take over men's work. "It is nonsense to speak of woman's usurping man's work! She does not want it!" declared a North Carolina mission leader. Women wanted no part of men's work, but they reserved the right to define woman's work in their own terms. This leader spoke for all mission-minded Southern Baptist women when she insisted that sharing the Gospel was woman's work, especially the effort to convert other women. A woman had no time to bother with a man's sphere because "she has sufficient responsibility devolving upon her in the performance of her own God-given duties. The condition of women in heathen lands is an irresistible appeal to Christian women."[52] In 1933 a Texas Baptist WMU historian described the prevailing attitude toward state central committees in the 1860s and spoke scathingly of the gender ideology behind it. "The ministry of the South largely opposed it," she recalled. "These ministers deemed it not at all proper for ladies to raise their voices in the churches. Southern aristocracy had placed woman on a pedestal. She was fair and beautiful and too frail for the storms that strong men must endure. Anyone knew that much. . . . So why be disturbed about the Gospel's progress?"[53]

This sardonic reference to woman's frailty was followed by a lengthy account of various pioneer women—including one who gave birth to her fourteenth child under an overturned wagon to protect it and herself from wild animals. The writer trusted her readers would see the irony in characterizing Texas women as frail females on pedestals. Furthermore, she insinuated that these attitudes were not only passé but also insignificant compared to the Gospel. Although "public opinion held sway" for the moment, "yet the Spirit called: 'Go ye into all lands and preach my Gospel to every creature.'"[54] The call of God's spirit to share the Gospel with the world compelled women to ignore public opinion.

WOMAN'S MISSIONARY UNION

As early as 1877, Baptist women began to dream of a south-wide organization, even as the Foreign Mission Board assured the hesitant Southern Baptist Convention that women were not in favor of a general committee for women's work. The first formal meeting of Southern Baptist women was held in Waco, Texas, in 1883 in conjunction with the Southern Baptist Convention. Baptist women of Texas, under the leadership of Fannie Breedlove Davis, invited women to join their husbands at the annual meeting, assuring them that "Waco was a paradise where the men, their wives, and their daughters could be entertained free of charge."[55] At this meeting Martha Crawford, Baptist missionary to China, was the first woman ever to address a formal assembly of men and women at a Southern Baptist Convention. Excitement radiated through every session of the program. Baptist women went home emboldened to form missionary societies in their local churches. Later, the *Baptist Argus* reflected that the meeting "sent a thrill all through the South."[56]

Baltimore's WMW hosted the second south-wide women's meeting, which met concurrently with the 1884 Southern Baptist Convention. Adele Fielde, the missionary to China commissioned by the American Baptist Home Mission Society, spoke to a mixed assembly. Fielde's northern Baptist affiliations were almost as shocking to the Southern Baptists as her claim to have been "fore-ordained." Fielde's address on Chinese women apparently fascinated those present. She was "cheered by leading members of the convention."[57] Meanwhile, at the men's meeting nearby, Joshua Levering (cousin to Annie Armstrong) made a motion that the Home Mission Board should appoint a woman to superintend women's work. His motion drew harsh criticism from the enemies of women's work. J. William Jones, the "evangelist of the lost cause," insisted the proposal marked the "entering wedge of Woman's Rights or platform speaking."[58] Levering's motion was referred to the Home Mission Board, where it was tabled.

As the tensions mounted between the convention and the women's organizations, the mission boards feared the women would establish an independent board. With nearly one-third of their financial support hanging in the balance, denominational officials hastened to demonstrate their good will before the next year's meeting. However, the next year proved even more disappointing to the women. Mary Oldham Eagle and Margaretta Dudgeon Early presented themselves at the 1885 meeting as messengers to the Southern Baptist Convention. The convention quickly appointed a committee of five men to study the situation. This committee returned a report stating that the language of the constitution did not prohibit women from serving as messengers. In response, the male delegates amended the constitution, substituting the word "brethren" for "messenger" to officially prohibit women from participating in the convention. This wording remained in the constitution for thirty-three years. "This was the voice of the Southern Baptists," commented Baptist historian H. Leon McBeth, "against the entire feminist movement."[59] If formal exclusion were not offensive enough, the convention vented their hostilities on H. A. Tupper, secretary of the FMB, who had been supportive of the women's organizations. They removed the administration of central committees from the Foreign Mission Board and placed administration under the jurisdiction of state conventions.[60] Many of the women's committees languished under hostile state leadership. "By 1887 the women's contributions to the Foreign Mission Board had slipped by 33 percent."[61]

Ultimately, Baptist women did not allow the hostility to dampen their missionary zeal. Ethlene Boone Cox later commented that "the action of the Convention in excluding women as members left the women of the Convention territory in an uncertain status." Women, however, had made too much progress to be turned from their course, explained Cox. She related the event with triumphalist glee: "They could not go back! All the glories of mission history rose up to bar such a retreat. They could not deny their heritage of Lydia, and of those 'certain women—Mary Magdalene, Joanna and Susanna, and many others who ministered unto them out of their substance' [Luke 8:1–3]. They could not forget Ann Hasseltine Judson and Henrietta Hall Shuck. For a time, these youthful missionaries had seemed doubly dead in that they had died so young, but lo, their dauntless spirits of immortal youth were alive and triumphant in these women!"[62]

Baptist women, encouraged by men like H. A. Tupper, believed they had a "mandate" from God to organize for missions. Tupper advised the women: "Refuse to be discouraged by opposition. No good thing has ever failed to arouse opposition."[63] He insisted that women should continue to serve as missionaries and work in mission societies even if the men felt threatened by it. No matter how much trouble mission work may cause between men and women, "so long as their combined effort falls immeasurably short of the world's necessities, it is wiser to stimulate the men than to restrain the women," he said. "If one sex neglects our Lord's Great Commission, the other should not be compelled to do the same."[64]

In 1887 Dr. A. E. Dickinson asked Alice Armstrong to write editorials for the Virginia state paper, *Religious Herald*, under the pseudonym "Ruth Alleyn," to encourage women to organize.[65] She agreed and penned persuasive articles insisting that Baptist women were lagging behind other denominations in missions due to the lack of a central organization. She eloquently defended the Victorian view that women were uniquely fitted to share the Gospel. She enumerated their "innate" qualities such as tact, patience, and "nimbleness of perception." "Call it intuition, if you please, or quick wittedness, [it] is of large value in Christian work." Alice Armstrong insisted that these gifts should not be neglected since God himself had given them to women. She compared women to a rare, ornate sword forged with exceptionally strong steel. God, the master craftsman, designed this weapon to be used in battle, not to remain uselessly hidden in its scabbard.[66] Since women were *created* to be engaged in mission work, she insinuated, to remain idle would be an offense against God himself.

At the 1887 SBC meeting, the women came prepared to develop a strategy for a south-wide organization. Since the convention refused to create a central organization for women's work within the denominational structure, the women took matters into their own hands. In order to ensure the development of a solid, permanent organization, the women took great pains to involve as many states as possible, as formally as possible. Those attending the 1887 meeting decided that the various state committees should send official delegates the following year. On May 11, 1888, thirty-two delegates from twelve states assembled in Broadstreet Methodist Church, Richmond, Virginia, to "decide upon the advisability of organizing a general committee; and, if advisable, to provide for the appointment, location and duties thereof."[67] Fanny Stout, of South Carolina, and Alice Armstrong, of Maryland, read papers articulating the obligations of women to organize for missions and spread the Gospel. On May 14, 1888, ten states approved the organization of the Executive Committee of Woman's Missionary Societies, Auxiliary to the Southern Baptist Convention. In 1890, at the suggestion of Texas Baptist women, the word "societies" was changed to "union" and the organization was then known as the Woman's Missionary Union (WMU).

Meanwhile, at the convention a few blocks away, a "stormy" discussion was taking place concerning the women. "Again it was prophesied that one thing would lead to another," explained Fannie Heck. A loud voice of opposition insisted "the women would first assume control of the money of the church, then of its deaconship, then of the pulpit, then of the convention." Another delegate stood and asked for the floor. He proceeded to tell a story of a little girl who went down to a well and did not return in a timely manner. Worried, her mother went to find her and found the little girl in a heap near the well, sobbing. "What is wrong?" exclaimed the mother. "'Oh, Mother,' she sobbed, 'suppose when I grow up I should be married, and suppose I should have a little girl, and suppose I should send her to the spring, and suppose she should fall in, and suppose she should be drowned—what would I do?'" Before he could finish, the audience understood his point. The delegate successfully painted the opposition as silly little girls, alarmed over imagined dangers. According to Heck, "The objections [to women's missionary work] died in a roar of laughter."[68]

The organizational structure adopted by WMU bowed to traditional views of gender. WMU's relationship to the Southern Baptist Convention is clearly reflected in the phrase "auxiliary." The women created an autonomous organization in voluntary cooperation with the work of the denomination, deliberately emphasizing their submissiveness to the male leadership. The financial agreements WMU reached with the mission boards illustrate the relationship. WMU did not receive money from the churches. All funds were directed to the mission boards. Alice Armstrong explained how the financial relationship operated: "The sinews of war, the necessary money for printing, postage, expressage, etc. was readily promised and equally furnished by the Home and Foreign Boards, as all collections went direct to their treasuries through state channels, reports only reaching the Executive Committee." Furthermore, she explained, "From the first, all moneyed compensation for service or traveling expenses was declined by the officers."[69] In other words, state WMU organizations sent all the funds they raised directly to the mission boards of the denomination. Then, the state officers sent their financial reports to the executive committee of WMU. The executive committee kept meticulous records, documenting receipts and expenses to the penny. WMU submitted an annual operating budget to the mission boards, though as Alice Armstrong stated, early officers of the WMU refused salaries or reimbursement for traveling expenses.[70]

When WMU was organized in 1888 the executive committee included the president, vice presidents, corresponding secretary (later executive director), recording secretary, and treasurer. By tradition, the vice presidential positions were held by the various elected state WMU presidents.[71] The two most influential positions within WMU were the president and corresponding secretary. Annie Armstrong held the position of corresponding secretary for the first eighteen years of the organization's existence, and Fannie Heck served as president (off and on) for fifteen years between 1888 and 1915. Although these two forceful personalities clashed, they both left a permanent imprint on WMU that defined its essential character and mission.

The delegates unanimously chose Baltimore as WMU headquarters with Annie Armstrong, of Baltimore, as corresponding secretary. On the recommendation of Annie Armstrong, the women selected Martha McIntosh, of South Carolina, to be the first president of WMU.[72] Vice presidents were selected from each of the cooperating states, while all the members of the executive committee hailed from Maryland. Until 1901, the executive committee managed WMU between annual meetings. The result was a tremendous concentration of power in the hands of the Baltimore women.[73] The Baltimore location was extremely important because it placed the leadership of WMU in the midst of a heavily industrialized port city with a large immigrant population. "By 1911," asserted a social historian of Baltimore, the city was "in the mainstream of the social reform movement."[74] Thus, the women's missionary activity of a predominantly rural, southern denomination operated from within the heart of a bustling metropolis, surrounded by progressive reform movements.

WMU LEADERSHIP

WMU historian Catherine Allen contends that the founders of WMU represented "the aristocracy of the white South."[75] If a photo had been taken of all the women it would show "wealth, white skin," and "soft hands."[76] WMU leaders were the wives and daughters of prominent white Baptist pastors, editors, missionaries, and Baptist college presidents. All of the corresponding secretaries from 1888 to 1920 were born into wealthy families, and all three remained single during their terms. The first corresponding secretary of WMU, Annie Armstrong, was the daughter of a wealthy Baltimore merchant and philanthropist. His estate was assessed in 1850 to be worth $37,000, roughly equivalent to $1.2 million dollars in 2019.[77] Edith Campbell Crane, who followed Armstrong as corresponding secretary, also grew up in a wealthy Baltimore family with deep Baptist roots. Kathleen Moore Mallory, who served as WMU corresponding secretary for thirty-six years, grew up in Selma, Alabama. Her father, Hugh Mallory, "was a prominent lawyer, progressive gubernatorial candidate in 1910, state Baptist convention president, and advocate of woman suffrage."[78]

WMU president Fannie Exile Scudder Heck also hailed from a wealthy southern family. She received the name "Exile" because at her birth in 1862 her family was "exiled" from their home in Morgantown, North Carolina, due to the Civil War.[79] Heck served as the second, fourth, and seventh president of WMU, totaling fifteen years of service in that role. Her father, Jonathan McGee Heck, earned a law degree from Rector College in Pennsylvania. He established his practice in Morgantown, Virginia, and joined the Confederate Army after Virginia seceded from the Union. After the war, he built his family a mansion in Raleigh, North Carolina.[80] In Raleigh, Fannie enjoyed all the benefits of leisure and education in southern aristocracy. In addition to serving as WMU president, Heck led the North Carolina WMU as president for twenty-nine years, was chair and founding member of the Associated Charities of Raleigh, vice president of the Wake County Betterment Association, president of Raleigh Women's Club, member and second vice president of the Southern Sociological Congress, and founder of the North Carolina Conference for Social Service. Also, Heck promoted relationships with Northern Baptists. In 1907 she presided over a joint meeting of Northern and Southern Baptist women at the Jamestown Exposition. She also delivered an address to Baptist women of the world at the Philadelphia gathering of the Baptist World Alliance.[81]

In addition to their affluence, WMU leaders were typically better educated than the average Southern Baptist. Although we do not know the details of

Annie Armstrong's training, she and subsequent corresponding secretaries had some form of higher education. Edith Campbell Crane, who took the helm of WMU after Armstrong, graduated among the first ten from Bryn Mawr College near Philadelphia in 1900. After graduation Crane worked for six years as the secretary for the Bryn Mawr School in Baltimore, then for one year at the New York State YWCA before accepting the position at WMU.[82] Kathleen Mallory graduated in 1902 from Goucher College in Baltimore with majors in Latin and history. After graduation she returned to her home state of Alabama where she became corresponding secretary of the Alabama WMU. When the national WMU offered her the position of corresponding secretary in 1912, she moved back to Baltimore.[83] Described as a "masterful tactician and fundraiser," Mallory mobilized two hundred thousand women and children to support Southern Baptist missions. When Mallory retired in 1948, gifts through WMU to Southern Baptist causes totaled more than $8 million.[84]

All of the six presidents of WMU from 1888 to 1920 graduated from women's colleges except the first president, Martha McIntosh, who attended St. David's Academy in Society Hill and a private boarding school in Charleston. After her term as president she married Theodore Percy Bell, who had been denied an appointment as a foreign missionary in 1881 for holding "unacceptably liberal views about the nature of the Bible."[85] WMU president Fannie Heck was "educated at the seminary in Raleigh conducted by Prof. F. F. Hobgood, and at Hollins Institute, Virginia."[86] Apparently she was "a crack shot; an expert horsewoman; an accomplished needlewoman; a skilled wood-carver; an artist with brush, pen, and scissors; and an inventor of at least two items."[87] Like Annie Armstrong, Fannie Heck never married, but instead brought all her energies to bear on mission work and community service.

Abby Manly Gwathmey accepted the presidency of WMU for the year 1894–95. She was born in Tuscaloosa, Alabama, and educated in Virginia.[88] She was the daughter of Basil Manly Sr., who was president of the University of Alabama and leader in the formation of the Southern Baptist Convention. Her brother Charles became president of Furman University, and her brother Basil Manly Jr. was one of the founding professors of Southern Baptist Theological Seminary in Louisville, Kentucky. She married William H. Gwathmey, a physician trained at William and Mary and the University of Pennsylvania. He became the president of the Richmond and York River Railroad.[89] Lillie Barker, president from 1903 to 1906, graduated from Chester Female Institute in 1887 and sailed for Bahia, Brazil, in 1888 to serve as an SBC missionary.[90]

Minnie Kennedy James was the last president to serve in the time frame of this study. A native of Texas, James studied at Sam Houston State Teachers College and married W. C. James in 1894. She served as WMU president from 1916 until 1925, during the SBC's tumultuous 75 Million Campaign. This inaugural fund-raising venture seemed successful initially because Southern Baptists pledged to give over $92 million. Unfortunately, the Great Depression prevented most Baptists from fulfilling their obligations, and the SBC actually collected just under $59 million. To compound the disappointment, many of the boards had based their spending on pledges rather than receipts, creating a financial crisis for Southern Baptists. The Woman's Missionary Union pledged $22,360,000 to the campaign. In the final tally, WMU gave $15,025,000—a remarkable accomplishment on the eve of the Great Depression. In addition to navigating difficult financial challenges, James also called on the SBC to give women equal representation on denominational boards. Although her requests were not granted, James took a stronger stance on denominational women's rights than any other WMU officer had before—perhaps stronger than any have since.[91]

The relative wealth and education of WMU leaders distinguished them from the average Southern Baptist. The majority of Southern Baptist churches in the last decades of the nineteenth century were in rural areas with poor, uneducated members. In addition to the obvious advantages that wealth and education provided, wealth translated into time. The WMU leadership could devote hours to their missionary work that most local women simply did not have the luxury to give. Although Baptist women could finally boast of a south-wide women's missionary organization, the fact that opposition had been overcome at the national level did not dissolve local barriers to women's work. Fannie Heck noted in her history of WMU that the battle for WMU still had to be won in local churches and in state conventions. "Everywhere it was the same story," she reported. "While the leaders in the general convention had ceased to question the beneficial effects of woman's work, the committees must meet hand to hand the opposition of many of the pastors and indifference of many of the women." The progress of the WMU had to be accomplished "one by one, woman by woman, church by church." Furthermore, the local women rarely had full-time workers such as existed on the national level. Instead, said Heck, "the work was voluntary and without equipment" and had to be conducted without funding. "The fallacy, not yet dead, that woman's work is cheap," she wrote, "had full sway." Instead, the work had to be done "by busy mothers after the babies were put to bed; by tired housewives in the small hours of the night," and by "hard-worked teachers."[92] In short, all the dreams and plans of a well-educated national leadership depended on the scarce labor of thousands of local Southern Baptist women.

In spite of these challenges, local Southern Baptist women joined WMU and worked diligently to carry out the mission as outlined by the national organization. Together they raised millions of dollars and built an extremely efficient missionary empire. Their innovative fund-raising campaigns, systematic planning, and meticulous bookkeeping stood in stark contrast to the men's "haphazard" approach to denominational work.[93] The male-dominated boards and agencies benefited immensely from the women's work and willingly adopted the majority of their suggestions. As a result, WMU initiatives, such as a week of prayer for foreign missions, Christmas offerings, a week of self-denial, and graded mission study courses filled the Southern Baptist calendar. WMU programs produced a flood of material culture. Pamphlets, tracts, mite boxes, Christmas pageant programs, prayer calendars, study guides, mission journals, and missionary "star cards" were made available for every local woman's society. Eventually, graded mission programs guided Baptist boys and girls through studies published by WMU. Many children attended summer camps staffed by WMU members, and generations of young women developed their leadership skills through WMU programs. The Union fostered close networks of women, then provided them with leadership opportunities as mission speakers, Bible study teachers, and society organizers. Through WMU local women learned to orchestrate fundraising campaigns, gather statistical data, file financial reports, conduct business meetings using parliamentary procedures, and a host of other leadership skills. Local women participated in WMU for all of these reasons. Ultimately, WMU was successful because the women held a single belief in common. From the well-educated to the barely literate, whether from old money or humble birth, Baptist women were convinced that they were fulfilling a divine call through WMU work. Annie Armstrong spoke for Southern Baptist women when she proclaimed that women's missionary activity was "fore-ordained."

CONCLUSION

As WMU grew in strength it developed into a distinctly feminine institution operating parallel to the other Southern Baptist entities. For the most part, the story of the Woman's Missionary Union resembles the growth and development of other Protestant women's mission organizations. Those same forces that compelled evangelical women to form independent missionary boards—higher education, the Civil War, and the plight of women in "foreign lands"—proved to be instrumental in the founding of WMU. Southern Baptist women shared the missionary perspective of other nineteenth-century American evangelicals who believed world evangelism hinged on the conversion of "heathen" mothers. Victorians assumed that women were uniquely fit to reach the women of the Far East. Mothers could best reach mothers. Their mission philosophy placed the burden for world evangelism on women. Protestant women shouldered the responsibility and launched a gender-based mass movement that "eclipsed the Student Volunteer Movement and the Laymen's Missionary movement in size" and mobilized more women for service than any other woman's movement in the nineteenth century.[94]

Early WMU leaders fought tirelessly to establish a missionary organization in the face of tremendous opposition from both Southern Baptist pastors and laypersons. They insisted that God called women to aid the cause of missions, and this divine call must take precedence over any objection that mere mortals might raise. After years of struggle, Southern Baptist women finally established their missionary organization in 1888. The leaders represented the aristocracy of the South. WMU corresponding secretaries and presidents in the Progressive Era, almost to a person, hailed from wealthy, influential Southern Baptist families. They were well-educated women, well versed in the methods and rhetoric of the Progressive Era. Wealth and education distanced them from the vast majority of the Southern Baptist women they hoped to lead.

Annie Armstrong freely invoked the call of God to expand the arenas of women's work. She did not demand equality as a human right or reject subordination on principle. She asserted women's authority, like Adele Fielde, on the grounds of "fore-ordination." Even when WMU became financially independent, Baptist women chose to remain an auxiliary of the denomination because they believed Southern Baptists could and would win the world for Christ. As a result, the contributions of Baptist women continued to be subsumed under male agendas. This is the critical irony: WMU's commitment to Southern Baptist piety provided the rationale for them to organize and act independently while simultaneously keeping them tethered in a separate, subordinate sphere. Their piety both liberated them and bound them.

CHAPTER TWO

The Reconstruction of True Womanhood

WMU and Gender

In 1913 Fannie E. S. Heck, the president of WMU, described the "typical" southern woman in the 1830s and compared her to a "modern" woman of the early twentieth century.[1] "To be a girl [in 1830] was to have the best of everything; to be the pet whose beauty was admired, whose accomplishments were extolled, whose favor was sought." Heck's model antebellum woman was "mistress of a large household, rising early, directing every detail of a family of many members and many servants." The role of this southern woman was "to be mother to her own large flock; model, guide, physician, provider, teacher, priestess to the slaves on the plantation or around the big city home."[2] The woman Fannie Heck described led her entire life within the domestic sphere, under the authority of the male members of her family. "Though full of care she would always be protected and admired; shielded from the rough winds of business, all contact with any but those chosen for her friends, her father, brothers, husband standing between her and the big world of which she must only know the beauty and to whose rude side she must be blind. Such, she had been taught, was the birth-right of Southern women."[3]

Heck deliberately emphasized the role of the southern belle as the beautiful, sheltered woman with little access to education, with limited knowledge of the world at large, with few professional options, and no access to business. She painted this portrait as a foil for the "modern" woman of her own generation in the second decade of the twentieth century. Heck's modern woman stood in stark contrast to the protected southern belle. In the last chapter of her history of Southern Baptist women's missionary work, Fannie Heck wrote: "How shall we sketch the woman of today? Shall we typify her in cap and gown; with the thermometer and scalpel; with book and globe; with ledger and adding machine;

with cuffs and apron; with notebook and typewriter; before a flying loom; or both mistress and maid at home?"[4]

This modern woman possessed an "outspoken reliance on herself," Heck wrote, and was prepared to "make that reliance good by incursions into any honorable profession, all of which have been forced open at her demand." Heck believed that the accomplishments of her generation marked a new day for southern women who boldly entered a new century as college graduates, doctors, teachers, businesswomen, and writers. Moreover, Heck believed that women's missionary societies had facilitated this transformation from true womanhood to new womanhood. Twenty-first-century women may view Heck's optimistic portrait of her "woman of today" with a great deal of skepticism. Nevertheless, Heck and her colleagues at the turn of the twentieth century touted their progress—not just as Christians but also as *women*—and were conscious that they were moving beyond the earlier accepted boundaries of domesticity. Baptist women took the basic assumptions of antebellum domesticity and reconstructed them into a New South "lady" who would, according to Heck, "demand . . . recognition in all walks of life."[5]

Southern Baptist women reconstructed their definition of womanhood during the Progressive Era. Their reshaping of true womanhood ideology enabled participation in southern progressivism and accommodated social gospel theology. WMU's idea of a New South lady justified new professions for women from social work to medicine. What exactly was true womanhood ideology and how did WMU reconstruct it? This chapter examines three key movements or ideologies that shaped a southern version of true womanhood: Victorian domesticity, the southern belle, and evangelicalism. Then, the chapter explores how WMU in turn reshaped three key characteristics undergirding southern womanhood: piety, domesticity, and submission. The reconstruction of gender enabled WMU to fashion a broader social ethic and to embrace the social gospel.

A cursory reading of Baptist women's literature may lead one to doubt that WMU leaders sought to exercise power in their denomination because there are so few overt challenges to the status quo. Read within their historical and denominational context, the literature reveals a more nuanced portrait of women quietly seeking to expand their influence.[6] It is true that WMU leadership did not publicly endorse the suffrage movement. WMU historian Catherine Allen states that WMU's commitment to missions overrode every other allegiance. "No national WMU officer is known ever to have expressed an opinion," reports Allen, "much less campaigned in public, for suffrage."[7] Yet Southern Baptist women felt compelled to distance themselves from the women's rights movement in order to forge any society at all. Male antagonism toward the movement erected barriers to the women's efforts to organize a national missionary society.

Their mission activities were sharply curtailed at times by the fear of "women's rights" within their denomination. That is why Fannie Heck made no reference to the women's rights movement whatsoever in her book, *In Royal Service*, whereas Helen Barrett Montgomery features it prominently in *Western Women in Eastern Lands*. Heck crafted her book for a southern audience, and Montgomery wrote for the North. The presence of women lecturing about the South raised a specter in the hearts of many Southern Baptists that remains a source of contention within the denomination to this day: female preachers. Because they did not openly endorse suffrage or advocate for legislation protecting women's rights, it is tempting to paint these women as indifferent to the status of women. Yet an influential cadre of WMU leaders fostered a feminine consciousness among Baptist women—promoting education, encouraging leadership, fostering business skills, and paving the way for women to enter into a variety of typically male professions. The writings of Fannie Heck and her colleagues reveal that WMU leaders often interpreted "true womanhood" in ways that broadened their sphere and challenged the status quo.

THE MAKING OF A SOUTHERN BELLE

"Victorian domestic ideology" (also called the "cult of true womanhood" or the "cult of domesticity") is a term that describes the constellation of middle-class gender assumptions that emerged in the wake of the Industrial Revolution. Women's magazines, religious literature, novels, etiquette books, professors, and preachers alike described the ideal woman in terms of four basic virtues: domesticity, piety, purity, and submissiveness. The language of "true womanhood" punctuated the discourse of the period.[8] Victorian ideology divided the world into separate spheres. The public sphere of economics and politics belonged to men. Women were assigned to the private, domestic sphere of the home. This emphasis on domesticity idealized the role of mother and placed the responsibility for child rearing completely on women. Writers frequently quoted the words of William Ross Wallace: "The hand that rocks the cradle is the hand that rules the world." All women were presumed to possess a "mother heart" that loved children and placed the interests of children above all else.

According to Victorian gender ideology, women were innately more pious than the men who had to brave the cold, cruel world of commercial capitalism. True womanhood assumed that women were born more pious than men and that piety was essential to their identity. Virtuous women infused the home with kindness, compassion, and charity—a counterpoint to the crass public squares of economic warfare inhabited by men. A cultural expectation emerged that "real men" would be sexually aggressive, while "true women," would be either ambivalent about sexual passion or blatantly asexual. Female submission to male leadership (by no means a new concept) permeated Victorian literature as well.[9]

In the northeastern United States the occurrence of what scholars have termed "true womanhood" or the "domestic ideal" can be traced to the economic shifts at the beginning of the nineteenth century. Social historians typically attribute the emergence of a "domestic domain" to the rise of industrial capitalism.[10] Domesticity was one of many "wide and deep-ranging transformations" occurring in all facets of American culture between the years 1780 and 1830.[11] At the beginning of the nineteenth century, the majority of families still worked together on the family farm or in family businesses. Women made an essential contribution to the family income, whether in the shop or on the farm. By the last decades of the century, industrialization had removed the urban worker from the vicinity of the home. Middle-class women were no longer expected to make an economic contribution.[12] The shift to an industrial system divided society into public and private spheres necessitating the creation of a meaningful social function for the home and the women who remained there.[13]

A different variety of domesticity, adapted to the uniqueness of the southern climate, took root below the Mason-Dixon Line. The exact relationship between the idea of a "southern belle" and true womanhood ideology as it existed in the North is unclear.[14] Suffice it to say that whether we are speaking of the industrialized North or the Plantation South, gender stereotypes were remarkably similar. Southern women were encouraged to find their primary identity in family relationships—as daughters, wives, and mothers.[15] Southern culture held marriage to be the apogee of a young woman's ambitions. The virtues of domesticity placed tremendous pressure on a young woman to marry—and marry early. Fannie Heck affirmed this in her description of a typical 1830s girl: "Already though but seventeen she [the typical girl] was quite old enough to be thinking of marriage. Indeed her older sister had been married on her seventeenth birthday and her mother a little earlier still." After finishing school, what but marriage "was left for a girl of 1830 to desire?"[16] The accuracy of Heck's general description is borne out in women's journals of the period.[17] Southern women learned quickly that the goal of their lives was marriage and marriage meant submission.

Married women relinquished not only their hearts and their trust but also surrendered their property, monetary assets, and wages. Most southern states maintained legislation to this effect until well into the twentieth century. Wives in Georgia were not granted control of their earnings until 1943.[18] Married women in some states could legally engage in business with their husband's consent, but this was not considered "proper" behavior for a lady. Furthermore, women, it was thought, did not possess the mental capabilities to conduct business. In spite of the reality that southern women ran households and in many cases entire plantations in their husband's absence, popular culture portrayed women as intellectually deficient. A short column published in an 1870 edition of the *Texas Baptist Herald* vividly illustrates this negative view of women's capabilities. The writer disparages women's intellectual, creative, and artistic abilities then soothes the insult with a backhanded compliment:

> Not equal to man in the rude strength of bone and muscle, not equal in steady grasp of intellect; but in fineness and uncomplaining, suffering, how superior! She has not, she cannot, write a poem like Milton but she can live out, as Lady Franklin did, an epic of nobler elevation than any painted picture of imagination. She cannot paint such as manly genius can do, but she can, all unobserved by the great world, paint upon her soul the immortal virtues of faith and piety, and have a purer Madonna than Raphael ever painted, impressed upon her heart; Which is greater? The one who expresses what others have done, or the one who does it himself?[19]

The myth of true womanhood asserted that ladies ought to be weak, dependent, illogical, and mentally incapable of operating outside their sphere.

In truth, there was no "place" for southern women beyond the sphere of domesticity. The South provided no culturally accepted role for unmarried daughters. "Old maids" were looked on with pity, depicted as "forlorn damsels who make the midnight air echo with plaintive bewailings."[20] If single women were fortunate enough to own property, common law viewed them as having the same ownership rights as men. Unfortunately, spinsters customarily received no independent income from their parents but were "farmed out to sibling households and expected to sacrifice themselves for the needs of their reproductive kin."[21] Undoubtedly the "reproductive kin" welcomed extra help, for married women typically bore a child every other year. It was common for children to be born as little as thirteen months apart.[22] Studies of rural women at the turn of the twentieth century reveal that the birth rate for farm families exceeded that of townspeople. Reformers in the blackland prairies of Texas were often astonished "at the number of women who had to stop and count to determine the number of children they had."[23] Married women typically spent their entire reproductive lives in an endless round of pregnancy. Childbirth was an extremely dangerous event for both mother and child. A twenty-four-year-old woman from Ellis County, Texas, reported in 1900 that she had been married at age sixteen. In those eight years of marriage she had given birth to "six children and buried three."[24] The experience of Elizabeth Perry, who became pregnant ten times in as many years of marriage, resulting in four live children, two stillbirths, and four miscarriages, was not all that unusual.[25] Fourteen percent of southern women died before age thirty-five, while only 8 percent of northern women died before that age.[26] Whether married or single, the domestic expectations placed on southern women exacted a tremendous price.

The southern plantation system added a sinister dimension to true womanhood ideology as well.[27] Patriarchal authority necessitated the subordination of women as a corollary to the subjugation of slaves. After 1831, apologists for slavery increasingly based their arguments on the "positive" effects of slavery, including its effect on white women. Writers alleged that slavery relieved white women from strenuous work, protected their purity, and contributed to a harmonious social order.[28] Whether "protected" or subordinated, women were central to the patriarchal defense of slavery.[29] Southern writers took for granted the subjugation of both women and slaves to white men. The rebellion of either women or slaves would pervert the natural order. "Each planter is in fact a Patriarch—his position compels him to be ruler in his household," explained a lecturer in 1851. The patriarch offered "protection" in exchange for obedience. William Harper stated the exchange more bluntly. "Women, like children, have but one right, and that is the right to protection. The right to protection involves the obligation to obey. A husband, a lord and master, whom she should love, honor and obey, nature designed for every woman."[30] Harper's sentiments lend credence to the assertions of historians that true womanhood ideology "was self-consciously used to justify the domination of both Southern Ladies and slaves by elite white men."[31]

Throughout the first half of the nineteenth century, southern women experienced increasing pressure from every cultural institution to adhere to a very narrow definition of womanhood. Southern slave culture combined with southern religion to reinforce the hierarchical social order. In the rising tide of southern nationalism prior to the Civil War, the ideal of the southern lady became more intense, fanned by the flames of sectional pride. The external threats to the South heightened the need to diminish internal threats to social stability. Southerners often equated any change in the role of women or in the institution of slavery with the downfall of the family and the consequent demise of society.[32] Southern men rallied to the aid of the Confederacy to defend hearth and home and to accomplish their "protection" of women on the battlefield.

The virtues of piety, purity, submissiveness, and domesticity defined the ideal southern woman. This mythology depicted women as the fulcrum of hearth and home, the inspiration for a Confederate knight's quest. After the Civil War ended, southern mythmakers imbedded the image of the "southern belle" into the religion of the "lost cause."[33] Ministers regaled their congregations with the heroic deeds of southern women during the war, carving the mystical pedestal with flowery rhetoric. "Her life was one long act of devotion," wrote Thomas Nelson Page in 1897, "devotion to God, devotion to her husband, devotion to her children, devotion to her servants, to the poor, to humanity." In short she was a saint, indispensable to her family and her church. "Her word" to both her children and her servants "was law . . . and they worshipped her."[34] Protecting the "lily white" purity of their women became the symbolic means of restoring a southern white manhood emasculated by military defeat.[35]

Ironically, the Civil War altered the roles of white Southern women. As men answered the draft, women assumed their vacated positions and responsibilities in order to survive. The desperate circumstances of war eased social constraints on women, giving them greater access to centers of male power such as banking and commerce. Confederate sympathies also raised women's interest and participation in politics. Conditions after the war made it very difficult for men or women to return to the status quo. The death of thousands of Confederate soldiers left families devastated and a generation of single women without marriage partners, further disrupting traditional spheres. The Civil War destroyed the plantation system and weakened the gender mythologies that inhabited it. All the "lost causism" of the postwar era could not fully reconstruct it. To be clear, domestic ideology did not disappear overnight; on the contrary, the vestiges of true womanhood still cling to the hems of many southern women's garments.[36] The New South dawned on women trapped in many of the same cultural expectations as before, but the seeds of change had been sown.[37]

Nineteenth-century evangelicalism reinforced true womanhood ideology by sanctifying both the home and the women's role in it.[38] Methodism served as a conduit for Victorian ideology in the South by preaching the gospel of "domesticity" along with revival religion.[39] Since Methodism dominated the southern religious landscape from the antebellum period until the turn of the twentieth century, Methodist domesticity buttressed the gender ideology of plantation culture. Responding perhaps to the overwhelming majority of female congregants, ministers emphasized domesticity and piety as the feminine contributions to the cause of Christ. Pious mothers shaped the faith of their children and held the potential to transform their husbands through quiet submission. Rev. Richard Allestree, in one of the most widely read collections of sermons in the South, advised women: "the worse the Husband is, the more Need there is for the wife to carry herself with that Gentleness and Sweetness that may be most likely to win him."[40] Methodist preaching fastened a religious imprimatur on the prevailing views of southern womanhood.

Southern Baptist ministers marched in lockstep with their evangelical counterparts in embracing true womanhood ideology. Southern Baptists affirmed that women had an innately pious nature. Preachers and editors alike argued that God had designed women to operate in a separate sphere. "We have profound respect for woman," asserted the Virginia Baptist *Religious Herald*, "and it is because we have, that we desire to see her moving in the sphere to which her Creator has assigned her, and for which her physical, intellectual and moral qualities eminently fit her. As the friend, companion and solace of man all her rights and interests are secure."[41] Conversely, women who rejected domesticity and obedience were tainted as impure and impious. "As the rival of man, in the struggle for place, power and prominence, she as the 'weaker vessel' is doomed to defeat." The woman who dared challenge traditional roles would emerge from the fray, "not with modesty, delicacy and loveliness which impart a charm and influence to her sex, but soiled, dishonored and disappointed."[42] Baptist men repeatedly recorded their disapproval of women who strayed from the domestic sphere and expressed pointed distaste for the woman's movement. "When . . . woman becomes *emancipated* from the care of the young and the making of the home, she has entered into the worst of all bondage, which comes always to every one who disregards the law of his life. They only 'walk in liberty' who have learned to obey the divine precepts, as written in their being."[43] Because they viewed true womanhood as a divine imperative, Baptists viewed the rejection of domesticity as a transgression against God. If it weren't bad enough that they offended God, Baptist editors insisted that such women encroached on the rights of men. "There is no genuine assertion for woman's rights; there is actually *abandonment* of these, with an unseemly claim for *man's* rights."[44] Baptist men opposed any formal organization for women's rights and were highly suspicious of any change in the traditional role of women. For an activity to be approved by the male-dominated culture, it had to be clothed in the garb of domesticity.

In a sermon published in May 1871, J. T. Zealy compared the private sphere that women inhabited with the public realm occupied by men. He assigned women unlimited power within the confines of the home. "And now look at this influence in the homestead. Home! This is woman's kingdom. Here she sits upon the throne of empire. Man's sphere—by the rougher constitution of his nature—is the more public one; that of woman—by her delicate organization—the more private, but not the less honorable, or requiring the less ability. Yes, her home, is woman's place of duty and power—that sweet realm still spared of man's forfeited paradise, out of which go influences that govern the world." He characterized the home as an Eden, a paradise of virtue and peace. Although women theoretically controlled this "empire," the purpose of this "sweet realm" was to make life easier for men. "In that sweet empire, in the sanctuary of domestic life, amid the tender devotion and gushing sympathies of home, man finds repose from his tormenting cares, his feverish anxiety for wealth, his restless ambition for distinction, and from all the excesses of human passions. Woman is the presiding spirit in this dearest spot on earth."[45] In Zealy's view the power women could rightfully wield was designed to benefit husbands who would find respite from the "tormenting," "feverish," "restless," and ambitious world of business.

The home was the domain of women, and it was also a sacred place where woman reigned as priestess and queen. Fannie Heck alluded to this when she referred to her "southern lady" as a "priestess to the slaves."[46] Yet the emphasis on women's identity as spiritually superior to men did not negate submissiveness to male authority.[47] This spiritual leadership extended only to their households, where she would use her pious influence to transform husbands and children. "Woman from her throne in the Christian home has made Christ the king of her husband and children and servants," argued Zealy.[48] Whether "malignant or benign her influence spreads itself from centre to circumference, a blessing or a curse," he opined. "Her constant presence in the homestead gives her opportunity to exert influence which the husband and father never has." With vivid imagery of separate spheres, Zealy explained the responsibilities of men and women. "While he is mingling with the outside world, taxing brain and muscle—following the plow, wielding the sledge, shoving the plain [*sic*], or pursuing some of the higher callings of life, she is imparting a character to those around her at home which will continue, either in dark or splendid lines, when our world shall be burned up, and the sun and stars shall have gone out."[49] While men were "mingling with the outside world," women were responsible for the moral character of the entire family. Zealy asserted that a woman would be ultimately held accountable for the spiritual life of her household. "Upon her it will depend whether the curse of the Lord shall be in her home, as it is in the house of the wicked, or His blessing, as it is in the habitation of the just."[50] Zealy's portrait of woman, if taken at face value, poses all sorts of problems—not only for women's rights but also for evangelical theology. In his mythological home, women's work is eternal, yielding blessings or curses. She becomes a Christ figure who mediates salvation for those around her. This sharply counters an evangelical message of individual conversion and personal accountability before God. As a result of this tendency to equate Christlike virtues with the feminine, women often found themselves cast in the role of the suffering servant.[51] One WMU magazine article suggested specific qualities mothers needed to influence their households. "What blessings should we ask for the mothers? What do they, and we ourselves need? Unselfish love, infinite patience, wisdom and insight, tact and sympathy, health to bear the daily strain, quiet nerves, a sense of humor that smoothes rough places, a sweet strong cheerfulness, a likeness to Christ that shall be reflected in the lives of all the household."[52] Female qualities and those of Christ were so often equated that women came to be regarded as inherently religious—the female character more readily conformable to the image of Christ.

It is important to keep in mind that for the vast majority of women, "true womanhood" was simply not true. It was a myth, albeit a powerful one. The only ones who could conceivably fulfill the obligations of the "southern lady" were a handful of middle- to upper-middle-class women. The antebellum women who fit Heck's description of a "pet whose beauty was extolled" represented a small percentage of privileged white women with the leisure time to practice their piety and to care for their homes exclusively.[53] This excluded the vast majority of southern women, slave and free, black and white, who worked in the fields and farms across the rural South. The majority of white Southern Baptist women were not wealthy southern belles before the war, nor were they among the elite after the war. Most Baptists in the South during the Progressive Era were poor and lived in rural areas. According to the census of 1890, 96 percent of Baptists lived in rural areas.[54] Rural Baptist women worked hard and had very little leisure time, even for education. The corresponding secretary of the Education Board for the Southern Baptist Convention commented that "since the Baptists predominate down South much of the ignorance and illiteracy revealed during the War is Baptist ignorance and Baptist illiteracy."[55] Nevertheless, domestic ideology persisted as the standard for evangelical women, the majority of whom had little hope of embodying its virtues. As Anne Scott so astutely observed, the myth of the southern lady never derived its power from reality, any more than had notions of "omnipotent men" or "satisfied slaves."[56]

RECONSTRUCTING TRUE WOMANHOOD

Fannie Heck, Annie Armstrong, and other Southern Baptist leaders shared many of the assumptions about the nature and role of women that pervaded Victorian culture. Their seamless transition from southern belle to the New South lady was accomplished by appropriating accepted cultural definitions of womanhood. They still believed that the ideal woman should be pious, pure, submissive, and responsible for the home. Although leaders of the Woman's Missionary Union affirmed these virtues, they interpreted them in ways that gave women more freedom. Half a century ago, Barbara Welter noted that this gender ideology, which she called "The Cult of True Womanhood," carried within itself the "seeds of its own destruction." If women took seriously the virtues of the cult of true womanhood, the virtues themselves would undermine separate spheres. "For if woman was so very little less that the angels," explained Welter, "she should surely take a more active part in running the world."[57] The writings of WMU in the Progressive Era illustrate Welter's point beautifully. Baptist women appropriated the language of piety to defend their missionary organizations. God had called women to improve the spiritual conditions of their homes and the whole world. Baptist women used domesticity to justify their social ministries, calling them "homes without walls." Southern Baptist women insisted that when they organized missionary societies, worked in the inner city social ministries, or even trained as doctors, they were being submissive to the preachers who urged them to obey the Gospel. Baptist women believed that the preaching of the Gospel inspired all of the accomplishments of Fannie Heck's "modern woman."

Southern Baptist women insisted women must serve in the forefront of the missionary efforts because they were, by nature, more in tune with Christ. They extended this belief to include all women around the world. Baptist women insisted that women in every culture were more pious than men and would be the key to converting other people and groups to Christianity. They assumed that Christianity was a liberating force and openly celebrated the benefits of Christianity for women. WMU leaders also agreed that women belonged in the home, but they reasoned that the home, therefore, belonged to women. They did not question the notion that women should be responsible for their children but expanded this idea to include all children. WMU encouraged women to embrace their maternal role completely and to address the social problems that adversely affect the lives of children *as mothers*. Ultimately, Southern Baptist women reconstructed true womanhood because they applied it—literally.

Piety as Christian Missions

The leadership of WMU appropriated Victorian ideology to defend their missionary activity and to reconfigure the boundaries of domesticity. WMU leaders accepted the idea that women were inherently more pious without equivocation. They sincerely believed that God had created women with an innate spirituality. When Baptist women in the South were struggling to form a denominational missionary society, the basis of their argument was that God would not have given women this unique spiritual nature unless he intended for them to use it. It was an argument based on design. Alice Armstrong stated this clearly in the first organizational meeting for WMU in 1888. "Should a naturalist see for the first time the wing of a bird, he could judge from its construction . . . that it was intended for easy and successful progress through the air. The fin of a fish is the best oar that ever worked in an oar lock. . . . The Gospel of Jesus Christ . . . was put into the hands of man and woman alike to be distributed to the sin-sick and dying. . . . [Nevertheless,] with a tenderer heart and keener sensibilities than man, she [woman] can take in a fuller measure of the love of Christ. . . . The same tenderness which draws her to Christ, widens her sympathies towards all whom she may help."[58] Armstrong concluded that these gifts were meant to be used. "Shall this Damascus blade, upon which the Divine Artificer has expended much of his cunningest workmanship, shall it be idly sheathed in its scabbard?"[59] Armstrong used an overtly masculine symbol to argue that women were the best tool in God's arsenal for sharing the Gospel with the world. The minutes of the Rehoboth Baptist Association echoed these sentiments in 1913, "We are sure . . . that God endowed women with special gifts." Therefore, women should show their gratitude by "service in the great fields of religious activity for which her special gifts so eminently qualify her."[60]

Some women did chafe at the equation of femininity with Christianity and took issue with accusations that Christianity appealed to women because they were the "weaker sex." Mary Hill Davis, president of the Texas WMU, gave her perspective on the feminization of Christianity in a speech in San Antonio in

1907. She implied that women accepted Christianity—not because they were weaker, but because they were smarter!

> Women and Christianity have ever gone hand in hand. Woman's quick and blessed response to the call of love divine has been the cause of the heaping of much opprobrium upon her devoted head. How often have we heard it remarked with withering scorn by scoffing, unbelieving men, that religion is only for women and children, implying that only the so-called weaker sex, and the plastic little lives entrusted to her guidance, could or would accept the simple, gracious, life-giving message of a Savior's atoning blood! But such an impeachment is not to the discredit of woman, but rather to her eternal credit. . . . When the veil is lifted, she shall stand erect in the light of a glorified womanhood. Rather than a reproach, it is the glory of Christianity that women preponderate on all occasions, and in all the forms of testimony to it.[61]

Davis argued that the "so-called weaker sex" accepted Christianity because it brought the "truest success" in life. Women heard a "simple," beneficial message and acted on it. The implication is that these "scoffing, unbelieving men" did not recognize a good thing when they saw it. Women should not apologize for the fact that they "preponderate" in the faith, but rather be proud of their numbers—assured that they will be vindicated in the end and "glorified" as women.

In spite of Mary Hill Davis's irritation with the idea, most Baptist women accepted the notion that Christianity held a unique appeal for women. Related to this belief were several other underlying assumptions. First, Baptists took it for granted that all women in every culture shared the same religious nature and could exert religious influence over their families. Zealy alluded to this in his previously quoted sermon. "If mothers were all Christians, and such Christians as they ought to be, a hope might be cherished that the world would soon be converted," he wrote. "O woman! Great is thy power," continued Zealy. "With thee is a lever strong enough to move the world and bring it back to God. In thy hands are seeds to be sown in the soil of humanity, which may yield a harvest to be garnered in heaven."[62] Mothers were the key to the salvation of the whole world.

Second, Southern Baptist women assumed that American women enjoyed a higher status and more freedom in their culture than non-Western women experienced in theirs. Evangelicals firmly believed that Christianity was responsible for this elevated position. In her letters to the United States in the early part of the nineteenth century, Ann Judson insisted that Christianity benefited women. Baptist and other Protestant women poured over her letters and held them up as the words of a saint. In a letter to the Female Judson Society of Richmond in 1823, Judson rebuked those who opposed mission activity on the grounds that there "were heathen enough at home" and insisted that American women had tremendous advantages over the Burmese.[63] WMU leaders shared Judson's perspective. An early WMU publication titled *Our Mission Fields* printed a poem by Laura S. Copenhaver written in the voice of a foreign woman pleading for help:

O women of the West that hear not,
O women dwelling in the blessed light,
O women of the West that fear not
The darkness deepening into endless night:

By lives that end when yours are just beginning
By babes that perish in our helpless hands
By mother joys we have no hope of winning
By nameless horrors which our law commands.

. . . .

They tell us that your lives are full of joys,
And best of all, that they are free—are free.
Yet we in bondage cry to you; the noise
Of wailing, can it reach from sea to sea?

The poem continues in this vein for several more stanzas urging American women who have "love and power" to help lives that "perish—hundreds every hour."[64]

Although the mission studies in WMU magazines were obviously designed to show the superiority of Christianity over other world religions, they still introduced young women in the rural South to world religions. It is fascinating that in the same edition that speaks of the horrors foreign women endure, of corrupt laws, and false worship, Baptist women printed a cheerful description of life in Japan—including an explanation of a Japanese god. "The god Jizo is especially the children's god. They think he takes care of little children who are dead," the writer explained. "As the children pray to Jizo they toss little pebbles toward the idol."[65]

Ultimately, Baptist women believed that Christianity was the key to improving the lives of women trapped within oppressive "heathen" cultures. Ann Judson appealed directly to Protestant women by suggesting that they would be as "degraded" as Burmese women if they had not heard the Christian message. "Had the commands of our Savior been limited . . . what would now be the situation of our own sex? What was our situation, and in what light were we viewed when Augustine, the first Christian missionary visited the shores of our ancestors? Were we not then as Eastern females now are—the servants, the slaves of the other sex, and viewed by them as almost destitute of intellect, and little superior to the brute creation? If, my beloved sisters, this change in the situation and circumstances of our sex has been effected through the instrumentality of the gospel, how great should our efforts be to enlighten those who are still degraded?"[66] In 1893 a North Carolina mission worker urged Baptists to consider the benefits of Christianity for women. "While we discuss what women are doing for missions, we may well consider what missions are doing for women, in developing the highest type of womanhood." She provided statistics concerning the oppression of women: "The condition of woman in heathen lands is an irresistible appeal to Christian women. There are 100,000,000 women in India in a state of almost brutal degradation."[67] Mary Hill Davis, president of the Texas WMU, echoed these sentiments in 1907.

> Has the Gospel of Jesus Christ been a friend to women? Look around you then think of barbaric Africa, benighted India, beclouded China, and the other lost nations of the earth, and contrast the condition of the women before the people had heard the blessed story with their state after the refreshing, life-giving message had come to them. . . . The resounding affirmative answer comes in glad notes that shall resound until the heavens shall be rolled together as a scroll. . . . From the beginning of the Christian era, women have been animated by the grateful and honest desire to do their part in the worlds' evangelization, and who would set bounds on their wonderful possibilities when they proclaim their redemption by seeking to lead those who dwell in darkness into the kingdom of life and light?[68]

Baptist women from Burma to Texas shared the belief that Christianity had improved the lives of Western women and would do the same for their "heathen" sisters. This concern for foreign women fueled the fires of missionary spirit. Women around the world needed Christianity, but many of these women could not be reached by traditional methods. American women recognized that women who were isolated from public life would need to be reached by other women. Thus, piety and separate spheres together provided the impetus for women to receive religious training in order to meet the needs of their own gender. Since Baptist men were not focusing their mission strategy on women, WMU did not perceive missionary work as a departure from their proper sphere. When religious women began to heed the preacher's call to exercise their spiritual authority, they embarked on a journey that would lead them away from hearth and home into the four corners of the world. Piety undermined domesticity.

Gendered concerns also compelled women into the field of medical missions. The spiritual and physical needs of women coalesced to affirm the role of female medical missionaries.[69] Male missionaries pointed out that female doctors were needed on the field because men were not allowed to attend women in many cultures. Helen Barrett Montgomery discussed this issue at length in *Western Women in Eastern Lands*. Montgomery noted that "the need for women physicians to relieve the physical sufferings of their own sex was first perceived and emphasized by missionaries."[70] She offered an example given by a male medical missionary in India. "Thousands of women die annually because such help as might be given them cannot be had on account of the restricted condition of their lives. A physician walking in the streets of India recently heard the screams of a woman coming from a fine native house. He asked a servant to say to the master of the house that a physician was passing by who would gladly be of service. The man returned an answer that he would rather his wife should die than be relieved by a male physician."[71] In spite of early pleas from the mission field, mission boards were reluctant to appoint female doctors. A laywoman of some influence organized a society to support female medical missionaries in 1851, but "the project aroused a storm of opposition and ridicule." Some opposed the project because they did not support any form of medical missions and believed only evangelism was necessary. "Then there was that awful bogy," commented Montgomery, "of woman going out of her *sphere*, even for the saving of life."[72] Eventually the argument that women needed physicians of their own sex to protect "separate spheres" and to further the work of the gospel won the day.

In 1913 a writer in *Our Mission Fields* openly pleaded with Southern Baptist women to support the training of female doctors and nurses. "In many of the mission fields the need and opportunity for women physicians is unparalleled. Medical women are the only ones who are permitted to enter the homes of millions of women. There are tens of thousands of sick women who would rather die than have a male physician attend them in sickness. And because there are no women physicians in many large districts they do die. . . . Let us heed the earnest requests for reinforcement and equipment that come from our own medical missionaries on the fields."[73] In this same edition of *Our Mission Fields*, a female doctor from India encouraged women to volunteer as medical missionaries. "My dream for the future is to have an army of medical women come to this country, to go out two by two to preach and to heal and to teach."[74]

It is unclear exactly how many Southern Baptist women responded to these pleas and received medical training in order to serve as missionaries during the Progressive Era. Southern Baptists appointed the female doctors and other health care workers between 1880 and 1920. Dr. Ruth McGowan was the first female physician appointed by the SBC. She was commissioned in 1885 to serve in China.[75] Jesse Pettigrew of Virginia, appointed in 1901 for ministry in China, was the first "trained missionary nurse." Dr. Hallie G. Neal received her training at the Woman's Medical College and the Illinois Medical College and was appointed in 1907 as a missionary to Mexico.[76] Kentucky native Claire Keith was appointed by the Foreign Mission Board in 1916. She was the first female registered nurse commissioned by Southern Baptists to serve in Africa.[77] Dr. Francis Hatchett earned her BA from Baylor Female College (now the University of Mary Hardin-Baylor) in 1879 and became one of the first women in Texas to earn a medical degree. She later served as a professor of medicine at the University of Pennsylvania. A pamphlet from the University of Mary Hardin-Baylor lists over a dozen women who received degrees in the medical field in the 1920s and '30s.[78] The 1926 *Album of Southern Baptist Foreign Missionaries* listed ten women working as nurses, two as doctors, and another twelve women as "medical workers."[79]

Southern Baptist mission boards paid women as medical professionals to serve on the mission field even while they clearly affirmed that women belonged at home. But the rationale for sending female doctors and nurses rested firmly on the pious nature of women and the needs of women in separate spheres. Female missionaries, doctors, and nurses were initially appointed *because* of the cult of domesticity, not in spite of it. This may explain the seeming contradiction of Baptist women's colleges and seminaries perpetuating Victorian assumptions about women while training women for professional vocations.[80]

Expanding Domesticity

The emphasis on domesticity and the incumbent maternal imagery were the most dominant features of Victorian gender ideology in WMU. Domesticity not only provided justification for organization and missions but also produced a distinctly feminine social ethic. Within the language of domesticity, WMU leaders discovered mandates for social action.[81] Baptist women were fully aware that they were expected to remain in a separate sphere—and even joked about it among themselves. In her presidential address of 1902, Sarah Jessie Stakely exhorted the women of WMU to create "a missionary atmosphere" in their homes. "You remember for a long time," she noted sardonically, "we have heard much about women's sphere in religious work—many were profoundly interested in getting us properly located, in helping us decide what we could and we could not do. But no one will deny that to us belongs the home."[82] Maternal interests contributed to the theological presuppositions of Baptist women. Women's everyday lives were consumed with issues of nurture—feeding those who were hungry, clothing the naked, and nursing the sick. As a result, women used practical, maternal images to advocate a more wholistic view of salvation and to advocate social reform.[83] This use of maternal imagery was common among female Progressives.[84]

WMU leaders also appealed to the maternal sympathies of Baptist women to enlist their service in evangelism and social service. "In the fullness of time God is sending forth His daughters, as well as His sons for the uplift of the world which so much needs mothering. Who knows but that woman has come to the Kingdom for such a time as this? Society needs woman's interpretation of life in every department of it. The world needs the contribution women can make to its welfare and this contribution can never be given in full measure so long as the notion prevails that her thoughts, her feelings and her actions are of real worth only when they have been strained through a masculine percolator."[85] Wharton, and many other leaders of WMU, believed social service gave women a personal mission in the Kingdom of God. Through Personal Service Southern Baptist women could move beyond the doors of their homes, and beyond the church doors, into the communities of the South, which so much needed "mothering."

Maud Reynolds McLure promoted mission work in the inner cities by pointing to the city children. "Innocent, bright-eyed boys and girls are these, just as beautiful as your children whose little feet are dancing along the happy paths of childhood, while these little ones are pattering over hard stones into the garish paths of sin."[86] "When we see the ill-kept homes," stated the WMU magazine, "the poorly prepared food and the shabbily dressed children, our hearts go out to them and we long to help them to a higher plane of living."[87] Rural ministry also appealed to the domestic concerns of women. "The making of the environment of the country girl and boy healthful, educative, attractive and uplifting is a crying need."[88] Social concern was merely the expansion of the role of mother to include all children and every home.

WMU periodicals also appealed to motherhood as an evangelistic strategy. WMU literature assumed that mothers were the key to converting and reforming the family and then the world.[89] "Find your way to the mother's heart," advised WMU writers, "and you will have touched the keynote of this family."[90] The Personal Service Committee urged local societies to establish Homemakers' Clubs, or mothers' meetings primarily to convert women to Christianity. The February 1915 edition of *Royal Service* stated: "Educated motherhood is the demand of today, not only in our own land but across the sea. It is a demand that will not be ignored; it is a Macedonian cry that refuses to be silenced. Consciously or unconsciously every true mother feels the spiritual development of her child is vital and important. . . . The greatest emphasis should be laid upon the fact that the aim of the club is to lead the mothers to Christ who alone can help them [children] through the hard places of life."[91] WMU programs of social service focused almost exclusively on women and children. Whether in work with immigrants, city dwellers, industrial workers, or concerns with public health, Baptist women tailored their efforts to reach women and children.[92] Ministry to mothers was a recurring theme in the pages of *Royal Service*. They believed women could become ideal mothers through an imitation of Christ. "The aim of Homemakers' Clubs is to help mothers to gain a sense of the value of Christ to every human being, young or old," insisted *Royal Service*. "What blessing should we ask for the mothers? What do they, and we ourselves, need? . . . [A] likeness to Christ that shall be reflected in the lives of all the household."[93]

Baptist women assumed that every single woman had an innate maternal instinct—whether she was conscious of it or not. They did not believe that every woman knew best how to exercise her maternal concerns. WMU leaders often asserted that women in poverty needed instruction. One objective of their programs was to educate poor and immigrant women in order to improve the social conditions of the family. "For mother love is, when aroused, the strongest; when enlightened the truest leaven in the hand of the social worker for elevating the home."[94] Mothers' clubs offered information on hygiene, sewing, first aid, and child care in addition to Bible study. WMU recommended methods they considered "the true ideals of home making and child training."[95] "Educated motherhood is the demand of today, not only in our land but across the sea," insisted Susan Tyler Pollard of Baltimore, Maryland. This education could be gained through "Homemakers' Clubs" where "problems of everyday life in the home are to be discussed; child welfare, training, care of infants, first aid to injured, household economies and problems of every kind."[96]

Practical education complemented the primary objective of missions. "The purpose of the club is not only to bring cheer to the lives of the mothers; it is to help them to solve the many difficult problems they meet in the care of their homes and their children, and especially to give them the message of Christ's love."[97] One society in North Carolina explained that at their mothers' club "we teach [the mothers] fancy work as well as plain sewing. An interesting program is prepared. These meetings are especially attractive to the tired mothers, they bring their babies and one of our young girls goes each time to amuse them."[98] "Cheer-All Clubs," devoted to helping young women working alone in urban areas, were also developed by WMU workers. "In Cheer-All Clubs girls are banded together to help, protect and encourage other girls and for the development and advancement of Christian young womanhood."[99] These clubs typically met on Friday evenings to entertain young women who worked all week. The meetings began with devotions and hymn singing then continued with various "bright and entertaining" programs. These might include games or stories read aloud while the girls worked on "embroidery, millinery, or basketry."[100] Baptist women believed that they could improve the lives of underprivileged women through domestic and religious education.

Like other women at the turn of the twentieth century, Baptist women continued to affirm domesticity, but they interpreted it in ways that blurred the lines between public and private.[101] If women were limited to the sphere of the home, for example, they felt it was reasonable to expect to control that sphere they had been assigned. The same Texas Baptist newspaper that published Zealy's sermon calling home a woman's "sweet empire" also published a reprinted article from *Harper's Bazar* that illuminates the subversive potential of true womanhood ideology. "We hear a good many sermons now a days from the text that the chief duty of woman is to render home attractive to her husband. No doubt any good wife will make this her crowning pleasure; but where duty is in question, there is another phase of the matter which is sadly overlooked—the duty of the husband to make home pleasant for the wife. As a very small portion of his waking hours is spent in the house where his wife's whole life is passed, it would seem quite as important that her convenience and tastes should be consulted as his." With a note of sarcasm, the writer insists that women should have unqualified authority over the temporal aspects of the household as well as the spiritual. "The home should belong to the wife; she should plan the house, arrange the furniture, lay out the garden, and order all the details. She knows from experience, better than her husband could possibly do, what arrangement best conduces to her housekeeping convenience. It would be just as absurd for her to undertake to be the architect of his warehouse and to place the desks, drawers and pigeonholes of his counting-room, as for him to divine from his omniscience the most convenient spot for her cupboards." She further argued that the wife should control which trees are cut, and how the flower beds are laid out. Finally, the author boldly demands that "the homestead should belong to the wife in fee-simple; she has a right to the nest in which she rears her young, and ought to be assured that it can never be torn from her by those reverses of fortune to which, in this country, all are so liable. Women all feel this, though they are apt to lack the courage to say it."[102] The call for "fee-simple" implied an absolute ownership of land whereby the owner could do whatever she wished with the property. This author from *Harper's Bazar* welcomed the idea that home was a woman's "kingdom" as long as she owned the deed to the castle. It is intriguing that a Baptist paper reprinted this article in the late nineteenth century. Although this may be indicative of a more independent spirit in Texas, it nevertheless illustrates cracks in the foundation of Victorian domesticity.

Some Southern Baptist writers interpreted domesticity as a mandate to become involved in broader civic activities and used the language of hearth and home to justify their actions. Concern for children could give women a vested interest in poverty, labor laws, prohibition, education, and economic justice. The March 1916 edition of *Royal Service* stated: "The standard which the best and wisest parent desires for his own child that must the state desire and provide for *every* child whether native, immigrant or negro."[103] In a 1914 article in *Royal Service*, Lulie Wharton clearly articulated this propensity for reconfiguring private and public spheres.[104] "Neither husband, wife nor child finds satisfaction or complete maturity in the family alone," Wharton explained. "Their ambitions and needs demand a larger opportunity—a wider circle. This circle is the community—the 'home without walls.'" Wharton then urged Baptist women to embrace "community realization" to foster a spirit of social reform in their neighborhoods. Anticipating conservative resistance to her proposals, Wharton skillfully noted: "Someone may urge that this is not woman's work. No one can deny that her work is primarily home keeping, care of children and ministry to the sick and helpless. The fact is that her house cannot be kept clean unless the neighborhood is clean; . . . that the moral standard of the vicinity of her home affects the character of her children . . . these facts are forcing women to reach out and take her share in preparing the 'home without walls.'"[105] Wharton's vivid imagery indicates that she, at least, comprehended the ideological shifts. Women were removing the walls that limited them to the domestic sphere and folding the public realm under the purview of the private.

Subverting Submission

Baptist women in the Progressive Era used true womanhood language to broaden both their personal and institutional power. WMU workers repeatedly denied accusations that they wished to trespass into masculine realms of power while they systematically carved out new arenas for female autonomy. For example, minutes of the South Carolina WMU written in 1892 stated: "It is nonsense to speak of woman's usurping man's work! *She does not want it!*" This seems pretty clear. Yet even this seemingly traditional North Carolina writer went on to explain that women did not want man's work because "she has sufficient responsibility devolving upon her in the performance of her own God-given duties."[106] Women did not have the time to bother with men's work because they were too busy taking control of their own finances and developing independent programs. The struggle to control their own money and determine the course of their own work lurks just beneath the surface in WMU literature and correspondence. In 1912 a WMU writer explained why the earliest women's mission work floundered. "The early scattering efforts . . . didn't fail for lack of fervor and interest, but because little money was in the hands of women then, and because once again they were resisted by the men of the denominational boards."[107] She goes on to demonstrate that the great success in missions began when women moved out from under male control and managed their own finances.

It is also true that Southern Baptist women often affirmed their submission to male authority in their letters and publications, yet their references to submission often, strategically, defend their religious work. For example, at the organizational meeting of WMU in 1888, Fanny Stout read a paper urging women to approve the south-wide missions organization in spite of opposition. "Much will depend on the spirit we show," Stout insisted. "The brethren are our guardians—and when they realize what we want to do, that we do not wish to wander in any dangerous ways, but are only trying to follow them as our leaders and trying to carry into practice what they have taught us from pulpit and press, their anxieties will cease."[108] Most likely Stout was being entirely guileless in her explanation, simply stating a belief in female submission to male leadership. She was also candidly stating the limitations of women's work. Their organization had to operate with a spirit of submission and obedience in order to win the approval of the male-dominated Southern Baptist Convention. Nevertheless, she pointed out that women were practicing what they had been taught from "pulpit and press." Husbands and pastors had no grounds to complain about female missionary activity because the women were merely being submissive and obedient to their instructions.

Privately, some Baptist women clearly chafed at the restrictive bonds of male authority. Southern Baptist missionary Charlotte "Lottie" Diggs Moon provided a leadership model that inspired Baptist women across the South. Lottie Moon served as a missionary to China from 1873 until 1912. She repeatedly argued that single women made more effective missionaries and insisted that the mission board respect her independence. From the beginning she proved to be an influential member of the North China mission. Southern Baptist Foreign Mission Board executives relied on Moon to provide them with concise, balanced reports on the religious progress of the work, on financial holdings, and business transactions. Lottie Moon corresponded frequently with Annie Armstrong, and it was Moon who encouraged Armstrong in her dream to establish a woman's missionary society. The women shared a passion for missions and a determination to see their ideas reach fruition.

In 1885 a conflict over mission board policy toward single women forced Moon to bluntly state her opinion about women's leadership. When rumors were circulated that single women might be prohibited from having a full vote in mission meetings, Moon wrote the board a letter clearly stating her concern. "Can you tell me—or rather will you tell me," she wrote to Dr. H. A. Tupper, "if the China committee proposes to make any changes in the status of unmarried women in the missions? Here in Tungchow the ladies have always been admitted to mission meetings on equal terms with the gentlemen of the mission." Moon went on to briefly narrate the history of the mission in Tungchow, including a reference to an earlier period of conflict. "At that time, as you know, the mission was left entirely in the hands of the women," she reminded Tupper, intimating that the mission may not have survived without the women. Ultimately, Moon made her feelings plain. "To exclude unmarried ladies would be a most glaring piece of injustice, in my opinion. To such exclusion I could never submit & retain my self respect." Moon did not shy away from the language of "rights" in this discussion. She explained how she had pitied Presbyterian and Anglican female missionaries "for the way in which their rights were ignored." Moon concluded with an ultimatum to Tupper and the China committee: "I presume the China committee is laboring under a misapprehension of facts. I suppose they are unaware that the ladies here, whether married or single, have always occupied precisely the same position as the gentlemen. Otherwise, I cannot see why they felt called upon to say that they 'do not endorse' my position. If it indeed be their real purpose to deny ladies of this mission rights that have never heretofore been questioned, then, sorrowfully, but as a matter of self-respect & duty there can be no course open to me but to sever my connection with the board."[109] Of course, the board did not accept Moon's resignation, nor did they exclude her and other single women from mission meetings in China.

In July1896, Annie Armstrong wrote to J. M. Frost about the limits of female power and seemingly agreed with the status quo. "I regard it as the sheerest nonsense for persons to claim that women can do men's work. We can go a certain distance and there we have to stop, and unless we have the support of our brethren, the work does not assume the proportions it should." Notice that Armstrong did not characterize the limitations as a deficiency in *women*, rather she was stating the harsh reality of her circumstances. Women could not do their work without the approval of men.

Armstrong did make clear statements about submission to male authority. She concluded that "our brethren are the God-appointed leaders."[110] Armstrong was notorious for affirming male authority, then expecting the heads of the mission boards to follow her detailed instructions. In other correspondence, Armstrong demonstrated her disdain for domineering males. She pleaded with R. J. Willingham to distract a certain Tennessee pastor while the WMU workers toured the state in 1903. Armstrong grumbled that the pastor named Golden "thoroughly, entirely, and fully believes in man's supremacy." She then noted with some exasperation that "[Golden's] wife (who is a really talented woman) seems completely overshadowed" and during their last visit "sat by almost as mum as an oyster."[111] In 1913 Mary Hill Davis, who served as president of Texas WMU for twenty-five years, commented about the relationship between men and women. "They [the men] seem very much to need us . . . and we need them—a little."[112] Her words were likely meant in jest, but if gender records on the mission field are any measure, her comment was entirely true.

Baptist women's efforts to expand their power were not always relegated to private correspondence. By the end of the Progressive Era some Baptist women understood that their power needed to be guaranteed in the governing documents of the denomination in order to be secure. In 1922, *Royal Service* magazine reported a very public effort the women made to expand their influence over denominational institutions. "Many of the women felt for a number of years that the work of the WMU would be greatly strengthened and helped if there could be a fair proportion of women as members of each of the Boards of the Convention," explained the writer. "Then, in view of the large contributions of women to the causes of the denomination it was thought fair that women have some proportionate part in the administration of these funds. . . . Accordingly in 1921 the WMU petitioned the SBC to amend its constitution so that there might be 9 women added to its Executive Committee and 12 women to each of its five boards." The petition failed when it was replaced by a substitute motion that the

Committee on Committees nominate "any brethren or sisters according to their personal qualifications."[113] A petition such as this would have needed broad support from WMU state leaders in order to be submitted to the convention in the first place. Even though this petition failed, the very fact that the women tried to gain an equal voice on institutional boards is remarkable. WMU leaders continued to be frustrated by their lack of power within the SBC. Lulie Wharton expressed her view of the problem in a 1925 article in *Royal Service*. "The world needs the contributions women can make to its welfare," she wrote, "and this contribution can never be given in full measure as long as the notion prevails that her thoughts, her feelings, and her actions are of real worth only when they have been strained through a masculine percolator."[114] Wharton's words suggest that WMU leaders were beginning to challenge not only the application of true womanhood but also the substance of it.

CONCLUSION

Southern Baptist women appropriated and internalized true womanhood ideology with its requisite emphasis on women's innate piety, purity, submissiveness, and domesticity. While they accepted the cultural expectations of women and took these very seriously, women interpreted these expectations to broaden women's roles rather than limit them. Baptist women embraced the idea that women were inherently more pious than men and concluded that women would be more effective missionaries and social workers. WMU leaders essentially agreed with domesticity—the teaching that women should be responsible for all matters relating to the care of the household and children. While they may have agreed that women should be in charge of children and home, they also argued that the barriers between public and private spheres were fluid. Maternal concerns led WMU leaders to visualize a new "home without walls" in which women actively worked to improve the lives of every mother and child. Baptist women repeatedly affirmed their belief in submission to male authority and insisted that the vast women's missionary enterprise was a direct result of their obedience to pastors who exhorted them to share the "whole gospel with the whole world."

As Baptist women reconstructed the boundaries of true womanhood, they in turn restructured their social ethics. Obviously, these ideological shifts did not occur in a vacuum. The social reform impulses of the Progressive Era and the social gospel profoundly shaped the development of WMU's social ethics. Arguably the transformed version of true womanhood, that Fannie Heck called the "modern woman," grew out of southern progressivism. For the quintessential expression of this New South lady, we should look no further than Annie Armstrong, the principle architect of WMU.

CHAPTER THREE

Professionalism and Administration

The Armstrong Era

Annie Armstrong once mused that if she had been a man, she would have been successful at business. "I believe I have some ability in this line," she stated.[1] Fannie Heck observed that Armstrong was "energetic, resourceful, persevering, trained in the management of large affairs, of masterly mind and a born leader." This was high praise indeed since there was no love lost between the two women. Heck said herself, "this is not idle flattery."[2] Armstrong was the financial and organizational "mastermind" behind WMU. Since women of her generation had virtually no access to business careers, Armstrong applied her considerable talent to the "business" of WMU.[3] She was the quintessential missionary professional. She used accounting, marketing, promotion, advertising, publishing, and mass communication to raise money and awareness for foreign and home missions. Baptist women contributed $45,765 to missions in 1888. In 1913, they gave $300,848, and in 1920 offerings to Southern Baptist mission causes generated by WMU totaled $2,418,924. The tracks for this growth—from thirty thousand to nearly two and a half million dollars—were laid by Annie Armstrong.[4]

Annie Armstrong is important to this study not only because she built the financial engine that drove missions but also because her life highlights many of the paradoxes inherent to Southern Baptist women's work in the Progressive Era. Armstrong was a model southern progressive. Her commitments to professionalism, efficiency, data gathering, and record keeping came directly from the progressivism playbook. Like other progressives her work was fraught with contradictions. On the one hand, she was a New South woman who looked toward a future of greater freedom for women. On the other hand, she used the tools of progressivism to build an institution that perpetuated Victorian ideals of separate spheres. She frequently acknowledged that women should be submissive to men while effectively functioning as the director of development for male officers of the Southern Baptist mission boards. Armstrong affirmed the essential piety of women while urging women to wield their piety in ways that would undermine both submission and domesticity. As explained in a later chapter, Armstrong transcended her culture at times to develop networks of missionary cooperation and genuine friendships with African American women. But in keeping with the pattern of southern progressivism, she remained mired in paternalism and never challenged segregation. Finally, while she may not have shared all of Fannie Heck's views on social reform, it was Annie Armstrong who built the infrastructure essential to making Heck's vision of personal and social service possible.

Annie Armstrong was born in Baltimore on July 11, 1850, and spent most of her life in a brick row house at 1423 McCulloh Street. Her father, successful tobacconist and philanthropist James Dunn Armstrong, died shortly after she was born. Although the 1850 census assessed James Armstrong's real estate holdings at $37,000, he experienced financial reversals just before his death. After his death, his estate was valued at $10,000. The care of Annie and her two older sisters fell to their mother, Mary Elizabeth Walker Armstrong. The older daughters, Mamie and Alice Armstrong, attended the Southern Home School for Girls at 233 North Eutaw Street, whose students gained notoriety during the Civil War for flagrantly wearing Confederate colors to irritate the Union soldiers occupying Baltimore. One biographer suspects that Mary Elizabeth Armstrong may not have sent her youngest daughter to the school because of the "lively" atmosphere. Annie's name does not appear on the school register, nor is it known where she received her education. She speaks of her training in letters, but does not name an institution. However, her articulate correspondence with literary references and occasional Latin phrases were the work of a well-educated woman. Her meticulous bookkeeping and detailed reports provide evidence of her skill in business and accounting.[5]

Mary Armstrong reared her children in a household imbued with missionary zeal. She was among the Baltimore women who responded to the call from Ann Graves to organize for missions and was present at the first meeting of Southern Baptist women in Baltimore in 1868. Mary devoted her days to missionary meetings, Bible studies, and prayer circles. The Armstrong women attended Seventh Street Baptist Church in Baltimore. Dr. Richard Fuller, a Yale graduate and Charleston native, served as their pastor. His persuasive sermons and thoughtful manner slowly won over the youngest Armstrong. He baptized Annie in December 1870 when she was nineteen years old. After her conversion, Armstrong enthusiastically joined her mother in mission work and social ministry.[6] Dr. Fuller left Seventh Street Baptist Church to establish Eutaw Place Baptist Church in the suburbs of Baltimore. In 1871 the Armstrongs and 130 others joined Fuller to become charter members of Eutaw Place. "Annie Armstrong would be an active member of Eutaw Place for sixty-seven years, until her death in 1938."[7]

Armstrong never married. Instead, she spent her life zealously advancing the cause of Christian missions and benevolence work both nationally and locally. Armstrong was a founding member and twenty-four-year president of the Woman's Home Mission Society of Maryland, corresponding secretary and chief architect of the Maryland Baptist Mission Rooms, and Corresponding Secretary of the Woman's Missionary Union, 1888–1906. In Baltimore, Armstrong established the Ladies Bay View Mission for poor women, sponsored mission and social work for immigrants, and helped establish two missions and an orphanage for African American families. She served as the manager of the Aged Men and Aged Women's Homes of Baltimore for twenty years. Armstrong resigned as corresponding secretary of WMU in 1906 in the wake of a disagreement over the WMU Training School and focused all of her energies on her church and social service ministries in Baltimore.[8] She never accepted another denominational post. In her 1913 history of WMU, Fannie Heck wrote that the Union owed its early growth to Annie Armstrong "more than any one person."[9]

A PUBLISHING EMPIRE

Armstrong pioneered a publishing industry of missionary literature before WMU was formally organized. Helen Barrett Montgomery called mission literature the "light infantry" in the "triumphant war for world-wide righteousness."[10] Armstrong persuaded Maryland Baptists to underwrite the Baltimore Mission Rooms in 1887, where she and a small staff of volunteers produced a flood of leaflets, pamphlets, and other missionary literature. This missionary publishing enterprise proved to be one of Armstrong's most important contributions to WMU culture. In Baltimore, Maryland, in the summer of 1886, Annie Armstrong lamented to her sister that Baptists needed more missionary literature. The Foreign Mission Board had only five leaflets describing their mission activities, and the Home Board had none at all. Armstrong's biographer related the conversation that followed.

> "Maybe," suggested Miss Alice, "the Convention will establish a department to meet the need for fresh literature."
>
> Annie threw back her head and laughed. "Sister Alice," she stated, "after observing the Convention when it met here in Baltimore, I cannot help thinking if the establishment of a literature department has to wait until *it* acts in the matter, many years will go by before the want is supplied."
>
> Then looking directly at her sister and emphasizing the words with the thrusts of her uplifted pen, she said deliberately, "If there is to be a distinctive literature for the fields occupied by the boards of the SBC, it will have to be created."
>
> "Yes?" queried Miss Alice.
>
> "Yes," stated Annie positively, "others have worked out a way of supplying

> missionary intelligence. In Philadelphia, the Baptist Woman's Missionary Bureau [North] was established last March, and the Presbyterian Mission Room has been working for a still longer time."
>
> Her face took on a thoughtful look. "There are," she reflected, "enterprising ministers in Baltimore who might do pioneer work."[11]

Armstrong enlisted "enterprising ministers" in Baltimore to underwrite a printing venture. The Baltimore Baptist Association voted in 1886 to establish a "place where books and periodicals may be found" to be directed by Annie Armstrong. Henry Wharton, editor of the *Baltimore Baptist*, offered space for the small library above his office on Fayette Avenue rent free and installed a new staircase to keep the women's petticoats from showing as they climbed the old ladder to the upper room. The Baltimore Association agreed to pay the printing and postage costs. The Maryland women's Home and Foreign missionary societies committed to furnish the room and staff the library. In essence, the men of Baltimore provided the women with a publishing house and a female voice to the convention. In March 1887 the Maryland Baptist Mission Rooms were officially opened.[12]

In that first year the Mission Rooms "poured out a very flood of free literature," including mission leaflets, "brick cards" for Cuban chapels, missionary prayer cards, Christmas programs, and envelopes for a Christmas offering. In all, the Mission Rooms published nearly 120,000 items in 1887.[13] When WMU organized in 1888, the Baltimore Mission Rooms became the headquarters for the mission work of Southern Baptist women. From this location, Annie Armstrong directed the work of the Union, published volumes of missionary literature, wrote thousands of letters, and launched hugely successful fund-raising campaigns. In April 1888, Armstrong reported eighty-six annual subscriptions at 30 cents; 315 packages mailed; 452 orders filled; 60,000 leaflets sold; and 1,000 envelopes prepared for the 1888 SBC meeting in Richmond.[14] Much of this literature was provided to Baptists around the country free of charge. On the tenth anniversary of WMU, Armstrong reported that the Maryland Mission Rooms had published a total of 109 leaflets and pamphlets, distributed 1,384,903 of these items, and prepared 616,055 Christmas envelopes for the annual Christmas offering during their first ten years.[15]

Armstrong recorded every item she published or mailed and made judicious use of the resources available to her. For example, at the first executive committee meeting of WMU, the leadership expressed the desire to publish a distinctive women's paper. Armstrong persuaded them to use the existing denominational mission journals, *Our Home Field* and *Foreign Mission Journal*, because she said Baptist women would only subscribe to a few journals. Before the meeting Armstrong had contacted the editors of those papers and secured permission to create a separate column for women's missionary work. Alice Armstrong agreed to edit the women's column in the *Foreign Mission Journal*, and eventually Annie became the editor of the column in *Our Home Field*. In addition to not wanting to flood the market, the corresponding secretary of WMU was fiercely loyal to the boards of the SBC, and she carefully avoided competition with their efforts. WMU did not launch its own periodical until 1906, after Armstrong left office.[16] Edith Campbell Crane, Armstrong's successor, reported $2,494 in periodical sales in 1906. This amount grew with each passing year. In 1920, WMU reported receipts totaling nearly $15,000 in this category. By the end of World War II, literature sales had become the bread and butter of the WMU operating budget.[17]

Annie Armstrong not only flooded the South with missionary literature but also with thousands of personal letters. Alice Armstrong reported that her sister wrote 600 letters in her first year as corresponding secretary and 2,700 in her third year.[18] In a ten-year summary of her work, Annie Armstrong reported having written 77,447 letters and manuscripts along with 3,402 postals (postcards). On average she mailed over 8,000 letters a year and roughly 674 letters per month. The secretaries of the Southern Baptist boards received the majority of Armstrong's correspondence. In these letters, she outlined her fund-raising plans, made suggestions to increase revenues, proposed articles and features for their periodicals, and supplied graphics for those articles. Armstrong recommended new missionary outreach methods, suggested resolutions to be introduced at the Southern Baptist Convention, solicited salaries for female missionaries, submitted budget reports, demanded detailed accounts of expenditures, and handled a myriad of other business matters. In a typical week, Armstrong wrote each of the three secretaries daily—letters that were often more than ten pages long.[19] Meanwhile, she penned a steady stream of correspondence to both home and foreign missionaries. On a trip out West in 1902, she encountered a missionary and "was surprised" when he told her "that he had one hundred letters from me." She thought he was exaggerating, but then, she realized she had been writing him for ten years.[20]

A FINANCIAL EMPIRE

Under Armstrong's leadership, WMU employed the fund-raising strategy that other Protestant women had pioneered with great success—mites from millions. As Susan M. Yohn explained in her study of the business methods of Protestant women's societies, the financial strength of women's organizations rested on the "small donations of millions."[21] Helen Montgomery observed in 1910 that women tended to focus on small gifts from large numbers of donors—drawing on biblical examples such as Ruth who gathered small portions of wheat behind the harvesters or the widow who gave her last mite. While the men sought out large donors, women cultivated humble, consistent givers. "The women started in as humble gleaners to pick up such scattering sheaves as their brethren might have left," Montgomery explained. The women asked for pennies and "astonished the world with their success."[22] Baptist women imitated their Protestant sisters and adopted the strategy of "mites" with equally astonishing results. The Baptist Mission Rooms distributed small boxes for women to place on their mantels as a reminder to give sacrificially. In her ten-year summary, Armstrong noted that her office had distributed nearly one hundred thousand mite barrels and boxes.[23] I. T. Tichenor encouraged her to see the United States as a "base of supply" to win the world for Christ, and she developed a business plan to tap that resource. Like other Protestant women's missionary agencies, WMU emphasized "systematic" giving over the amount of the donation. Armstrong insisted that Baptist women should practice "systematic, proportionate giving" out of gratitude to God "because we have freely received."[24]

To solicit and administer these large sums of money Protestant women developed "very highly specialized, subdivided, yet exceedingly simple organizations." The officers could reach from "headquarters to the remotest auxiliary, with appeal and information."[25] Annie Armstrong served as WMU's chief administrator and financial strategist. She directed a team of leaders in Baltimore who networked closely with women on the state level, who in turn worked tirelessly to rally local churches and associations to support programs outlined by headquarters. One of the first programs launched by the Maryland Mission Rooms was the Cuban brick card. Armstrong designed cards in the Maryland Mission Rooms in 1887 to help fund the building of new churches in Havana. Each card gave the name of a church with specific details about its history and the need for a building, along with a picture of a pastor or missionary involved with the church. WMU adopted the brick card initiative after 1888. Armstrong sent each of the State Central Committees samples of the cards and asked them to take orders for them from their local societies. The societies would receive the literature free of charge since the boards of the SBC paid for printing and postage while the women who designed and mailed them "donated" their time. From 1888 to 1898, WMU distributed nearly 140,000 chapel and brick cards.[26]

Also in 1887, after reading a letter from Southern Baptist missionary Lottie Moon, Armstrong proposed two additional initiatives to the Foreign Mission Board for China. In order to raise funds to send two women to China so that Moon could return to the states for a much needed rest, Armstrong suggested a week of prayer for foreign missions and a Christmas offering. "Armstrong wrote the 1,206 letters to the southern societies *by hand* to request the women give to the Christmas offering." Alice Armstrong credits these two projects with bringing in nearly $10,000 more than the previous year. The week of prayer for foreign missions followed by an offering during the Christmas season became permanent fixtures on the Southern Baptist calendar. In 1918, at Annie Armstrong's suggestion, the offering became officially known as the Lottie Moon Christmas Offering.[27] Through these early efforts Armstrong successfully raised thousands of dollars, highlighted the ministries of a woman, and financed the salaries of two more single women.

In 1899, Armstrong launched another fund-raising program called "star cards." Similar to contemporary baseball cards, these introduced Baptists to missionaries around the world. "The picture of a missionary will be framed in the star," Armstrong explained. "Around it, in the points of the star, will be one hundred small stars which will register gifts." One of the first two cards featured Marie Buhlmaier, a missionary to immigrants in Baltimore whose position and salary had been negotiated with the Home Mission Board by Annie Armstrong.[28] The other card highlighted the work of Rev. Peyton Stephens, a children's Sunbeam worker. The next three cards focused on women, Mrs. N. Maynard, Willie Kelly, and Claudia White. The cards "are, as you see, very dainty and pretty," boasted Armstrong. "It is hoped that they will 'take' with our young people."[29] Through these cards, she again accomplished several objectives: she raised money for missions, involved more young women in the work, and celebrated the role of Baptist women in missions. Armstrong rarely missed an opportunity to underscore the contributions of women.

Armstrong's considerable gifts also included financial planning. When a WMU member came to her wishing to give $4,000 to the Foreign Mission Board, $4,000 to the Home Mission Board, and $1,000 to the Sunday School Board, she helped facilitate what she called the "Annuity Plan." The money was given through Armstrong and the boards agreed to pay the interest on the gift to the donor as long as she lived. On her death, the capital remained with the boards. As she explained, "by the Annuity Plan the donor makes a simple transfer to the board; is relieved of all expense of taxes, insurance, repairs, etc.; avoids legal complications after death, and receives during life a regular income from the Board to which the gift has been made."[30] This initiative in particular demonstrated her aptitude for financial management.

WMU headquarters kept careful records on all mission gifts. Armstrong insisted that a monetary value be placed on all the "gifts in kind" that Baptist women provided and was adamant that these amounts be counted as part of the WMU contributions on official financial reports to the convention. The boxes that Baptist women sent to missionaries on the frontier represented the bulk of "in kind" gifts. In 1901 when the Home Mission Board (led by T. P. Bell) attempted to end the practice of placing a value on the boxes, Armstrong lobbied fiercely against his plan. She appealed to the other two boards, suggesting that the resolution was designed to hurt women's work and would threaten their financial receipts. "You may not know there is pending before the Home Board a resolution not to place a money value on boxes sent to Frontier missionaries," she explained. "You will recognize that this is part of the result of Dr. Bell's antagonism to WMU methods."[31] The 1913 WMU financial report to the SBC estimated the monetary value of the boxes shipped to the frontier over the previous twenty-five years at $471,000 with the total amount of gifts—including gifts in kind—at $2,908,748. Apparently, Armstrong won.[32]

Armstrong carefully documented every dime that society members contributed to the boards of the Southern Baptist Convention and was a fanatic about careful reporting and deadlines. She hounded the leaders of the state Central Committees to turn in their reports promptly and fumed if they were late. On April 21, 1899, she wrote a letter to J. M. Frost of the Sunday School Board complaining about the state leaders: "It is extremely aggravating though, to find how thoroughly wanting in promptness many persons are. About three weeks ago I wrote to every Central Committee asking them to be prepared to send their reports by April 20th and giving them minute directions how said reports should be prepared. . . . This morning, April 21st, I am about to send off four telegrams for four state reports that have not yet come to hand."[33]

When she said April 20th, she meant April 20th. Armstrong expected not only the women but also the secretaries of the boards to provide her with detailed, accurate, and prompt reports. She expected immediate responses to her letters and payment for services in full when the bill was submitted. "I now enclose bill for [Marie Buhlmaier's travel expenses] which amounts to $25.55," she wrote I. T. Tichenor. "As this money has been advanced, I will be glad to have it returned as soon as convenient." To R. J. Willingham she wrote: "May I now ask that you kindly let me have as soon as possible the amount received by the Foreign Mission Board since February 7th?"[34] She felt delays were discourteous. "I will assume the responsibility of extending the time for your manuscript to July 20th," she wrote A. J. Barton. "Be kind enough not to let anything prevent its coming by that date."[35] She valued thoroughness, promptness, and careful record keeping because she approached her work as a professional and expected this from others.

Armstrong's management style reflected the trend of other Protestant women's societies in adapting the practices of the for-profit corporate world to the work of missions. The everyday tasks of WMU took her far beyond the domestic sphere into the increasingly complicated world of business. She supervised secretaries, stenographers, and office girls including firing them with no hesitation if their work fell below her standards. She managed the payroll and contracted with printers, photographers, and artists to produce leaflets and other publications. The Mission Rooms' budget required a thorough knowledge of financial procedures and interaction with the banking industry. And as previously noted, Armstrong had more than a fair grasp of the intricacies of managing large estates when women wanted to give to missions.

The one point of departure that Armstrong made with the rising professionalism of religious work in the late nineteenth and early twentieth century was her refusal to accept a salary for her labor. She was intransigent on the matter, though the mission boards urged her to accept payment. Even when she experienced personal financial hardship, she refused remuneration. Her own family members argued with her about the wisdom of refusing a salary. "Eugene Levering insisted that I was not looking at things at all in the right light; that I had no scriptural grounds for the attitude which I had taken in regard to women's work, namely, no salaried officers. He said that the Bible plainly taught the workman is worthy of his hire and that those who preach the Gospel shall live by the Gospel. That the work that I am doing is parallel to the work of a missionary and that the Bible recognizes no difference between the man and a woman." She was not convinced. "So much for Mr. Levering's way of looking at things," she quipped. "For nearly fifteen years I have tried to teach the principle of women giving their work without remuneration, and for me to accept a salary would be inconsistent with these teachings." Consistency, to Armstrong, was sublime. But, it was more than stubbornness. She believed that if WMU workers accepted payment, it would increase WMU's operating budget at the expense of missionaries on the field. "It would open the door for State officers to expect payment for their services . . . thereby involving much expense." Furthermore, she understood that accepting a salary would make her more beholden to the boards and jeopardize her freedom. "I know I am peculiarly sensitive to criticism and I have felt that as I was not a salaried officer, I was in a measure independent."[36] Her devotion to missions, thrift, and love of freedom governed her resistance in the matter.

In spite of her opposition to accepting a salary, Annie Armstrong clearly understood the value of her labor. She viewed her work as a "donation" to missions and would probably have listed it as an "in kind" gift if the boards would have allowed it. She gently reminded the corresponding secretaries of their good fortune when given the opportunity. "I have decided to disregard the very earnest protest of some that I should not do so much work for the Sunday School Board," she confided to J. M. Frost in 1901, "as your board was perfectly able to pay for having that work done by others, which I have been doing for years, and supply the manuscript as usual."[37] Although she was absolutely correct in all of her reasoning, the freedom to donate their labors to the cause of missions was simply not an option for most women. It was not practical. She won the battle and never accepted a salary personally, but she lost the war. After her retirement, the office of the chief executive officer of WMU became a salaried position.

Armstrong listened to local women and implemented their ideas if she felt they were promising; nevertheless, under her guidance WMU operated from the top down. This is illustrated by a comment Blanche White made in her history of the Maryland WMU. "Miss Armstrong suggested that societies over the South plan their monthly programs in accordance with the topics listed on the cards sent from the Baltimore headquarters office."[38] Hence, Armstrong urged every society to adopt uniform programs, which she designed. Local women sent reports to their State Central Committees who sent them to Baltimore. Local women read editorials, pamphlets, and missionary news generated from Baltimore. Local women gave money through campaigns designed in Baltimore and, in so doing, felt they were part of the larger world. Baptist women believed God called them to look beyond local concerns and to join their southern sisters in a global mission. Although local societies of Baptist women maintained their autonomy and generally chose to implement only those programs that appealed to them, they still accepted the leadership of a national organization. As a result WMU helped to loosen the ties of localism, providing southern women with a broader perspective and paving the way for a stronger denominational structure in the twentieth century.

PUBLIC RELATIONS

Annie Armstrong was the point of contact between WMU and the boards and agencies of the convention for eighteen years. The force of her personality shaped the relationship between the women and male leadership during that time. Even though she was committed to the idea that women should maintain a "separate sphere," she firmly believed that women should control their sphere with an iron fist. Armstrong became such a formidable presence within the Southern Baptist Convention that some called her "Miss Strongarm" rather than Miss Armstrong.[39] She was a determined, driven, persistent, tireless workaholic. Because she felt that it was perfectly within her role as a woman to represent the interests of WMU in furthering the progress of the Gospel, Armstrong bluntly expressed her opinion to the secretaries of the Foreign, Home, and Sunday School Boards. Her letters were filled with detailed instructions, suggestions, proposals, and such, and she simply would not budge on an issue when she felt she was in the right. At one point J. M. Frost suggested that she mail a fund-raising letter directly to the superintendents of the Sunday schools from Baltimore on WMU letterhead. She wanted Frost to execute her plans through his office. "No, no, no!" she responded. "While I am perfectly willing to do the work for the three boards as I offered, I am by no means willing to make the appeal to the Sunday Schools. I have already had to bear too much unkind criticism for me to be willing to do anything which I consider unnecessary and which persons could criticize."[40] "Which I consider unnecessary" was the key phrase. Armstrong had clear ideas about what ought to be done for the management of the Mission Rooms and for missions in general that for her took precedence over any social mores. She either ignored, or was entirely unaware of, that Victorian gender ideologies might have prevented her from giving orders to the male leadership of the convention. She admitted that she should probably couch her sentiments in more subtle phrases. "I, perhaps, do not weigh my words as carefully as I should when writing to the Secretary of the Boards," Armstrong confessed. However, she expected them to be able to handle whatever she had to say. "I have an idea they know me well enough to appreciate that I would not say or do anything contrary to their wishes, unless I thought it was absolutely necessary, and when this is the case, they will be kind enough to allow me to exercise the right of private judgment without getting annoyed; in other words, we agree to disagree at times."[41] She would not dare contradict their wishes—unless she thought it was necessary. When this was the case, she expected them to be "kind enough" to acquiesce.

Armstrong respected intelligence and was openly contemptuous of those who failed to make good decisions. In 1904 Armstrong wrote to Frost telling him of the invitation the Baltimore Minister's Conference had extended to the Southern Baptist Convention to meet in their city in 1906. However, the city was still recovering from a devastating fire, and the church the men chose was logistically problematic. "The delegates attending the convention would have to go probably a mile or more to find hotels, as there are none in that section of the city. Well, well, well," she mused, "I suppose it shows enterprise, but indeed it seems to me it shows precious little common sense." She attributed the poor decision-making to their state secretary who can, she said, "*plan* large things," but obviously lacked the sense to implement those plans.[42]

As a quintessential overachiever, she refused to leave the work of the Mission Rooms unattended, even when she was ill. She confided in J. M Frost more often than the other secretaries. "I appreciate the force of what you have said in regard to my taking a rest for the sake of the work," she told Frost, "but it is perfectly out of my power to do so. Many and varied duties anchor me just where I am."[43] The following year she expressed the same unrelenting attitude toward her work. "I have not seen a physician, nor am I willing to consult one, for I am perfectly well aware what his advice, if not orders would be and these I *cannot* follow. When I did at last consent to let my family send for a physician during the attack of the Grip [the flu] I had last winter (I refused to see one until I felt I was largely over said attack as I knew he would not let me keep on directing the work at the Mission Rooms and dictating letters while I was suffering so much with my head) he told me that I must during the course of the next six months take great care of myself, etc., etc." But her stubborn dedication to her work was more than duty. "Work to me," she asserted, "as you probably know, is a perfect delight."[44] On a typical day she woke early in the morning to attend her "domestic responsibilities," arrived at the Mission Rooms by 9:00 a.m. and remained there until 6:00 p.m. She confessed that it was difficult for her to sympathize with those who did not attack their work with such enthusiasm. Armstrong's insistence on perfection made it particularly difficult to keep stenographers and domestic help. "Our domestic machinery has not of late been moving on smoothly—I have had to change servants," she wrote A. J. Barton. In 1899 she reported to the secretary of the Foreign Mission Board: "our stenographer is to leave, I am sorry to have to make a change, but I do not think it would have been right to have increased her salary," as was requested. In 1902, she noted: "I have notified the stenographer I would dispense with her services. She is so careless that I can no longer put up with her mistakes."[45]

Armstrong did not "suffer fools gladly," neither did she overlook a slight. She had a quick temper when she was crossed, and her apologies more often served to justify her position rather than express remorse. If she felt that the WMU had not received the deference she felt the women deserved, she could be extremely terse. Her initial dealings with the secretary of the Foreign Mission Board, R. J. Willingham, were anything but smooth. When he accepted the role near the end of 1893, he sent her a letter suggesting that he visit Baltimore to have a "free, easy talk" about the work of WMU and the Mission Rooms. However, he did not visit as soon as she had planned; and when he finally did make his way to Baltimore, the meeting was rushed and interrupted. On January 19, 1894, Armstrong wrote Willingham a blistering letter—often referring to him and to herself in the third person. She used the opportunity to remind him of the financial importance of WMU. "I did offer to come to Richmond if it was impossible for you to come to Baltimore, but it does seem a little strange that it is necessary for me to do this when the Cor. Sec. of the Foreign Board can take long trips to various State Associations, occupying days, when the money receipts from those States may be only a few thousand dollars and certainly not requiring the immense amount of work to secure same as is necessary to obtain the offerings made by Woman's Mission Societies." She insisted that he must come to Baltimore in order to confer with her, the corresponding secretary of WMU, unless he did not think their work was important enough for the trip. "I would now close by asking if you think I have been unreasonable in requesting that the Secretary of the Foreign Board should come to Baltimore at this time and remain sufficiently long to familiarize himself with the work being done for foreign missions by the W.M.U. and the Mission Rooms, and to let those who have these branches of the work in hand have the satisfaction of knowing his wishes so mistakes may not occur. . . . Should Dr. Willingham think that other work is more important and he cannot in justice to it spare the time to come to Baltimore, if he will let me know I will then consider if it would be well for me to leave the work at the Mission Rooms long enough to come to Richmond."[46] He wrote her an equally blunt response that infuriated her even further. He told her he had given her "more time than any other one person, not in this office, since I have begun the work." She was outraged. "I do not consider that Dr. Willingham has given *me* one fraction of a second of his time since he has been Cor. Sec. of the Foreign Board," she fumed in response. "He has taken the time necessary to write . . . 25 letters, 5 postals, and send one telegram, and have two hurried conversations with her." In that same amount of time (about four months), she continued, "I have had to send out 11,997 letters and 659 postals (this does not include the correspondence from the Mission Rooms)." She concluded with the remark that this had all been done "to advance the cause of foreign missions," and "it certainly does not place Dr. Willingham under any personal obligation." She let it be known clearly that "this work in which we are engaged, I do not regard as Dr. Willingham's work or the work of the Woman's Missionary Union. It is to me God's work." Annie Armstrong worked for God. Therefore, by extension, when Willingham worked for Armstrong, he was also working for God.[47]

The corresponding secretary of the Home Mission Board also received abrupt letters from Armstrong. In 1899 I. T. Tichenor solicited suggestions for improvements or change from leading Baptists concerning the work of the Home Mission Board. He made the critical mistake of not asking Annie Armstrong for her opinion directly, but instead asked her to send her suggestions to a "Mr. Dunson." She refused. Armstrong reminded Tichenor that WMU had provided one-third of the Home Mission Board's receipts the previous year. She expressed surprise that Tichenor had not bothered to contact her but welcomed suggestions from some state secretary who was not doing "one tithe" the work of the WMU. "It is quite evident that the Board does not desire any expression of opinion on that subject from the Corresponding Secretary, W.M.U." Armstrong wanted Tichenor to understand which side his bread was buttered on.[48]

Even her closest associates felt the sting of her temper from time to time. In 1900 Armstrong extended an invitation for J. M. Frost to stay with her family on a visit to Baltimore. He replied that he wanted to "establish other centers of acquaintance" while he was in the area. In other words, he wanted to stay somewhere else. Armstrong wrote him on October 8 and said, "I shall *never* again embarrass you by extending an invitation to our home," then went on with her business letter. Apparently, he wrote her back chastising her for her intemperate response. "While I cannot truthfully withdraw one thing that I said with the letter," she replied, "yet I now see that I ought to have had more regard to your and Dr. Van Ness' feelings. . . . I can now ask that you will excuse me for writing as I did on October 8th."[49] She must have offended Frost earlier in the year because in February she wrote: "It occurred to me as I read your letter of February 10th . . . that you felt a little hurt after receiving the one which I wrote you February 8th. I hope this was not the case, but if it was and you deem an apology necessary, please consider that it is offered."[50]

Although she seemed unaware that her apologies were half-hearted, she knew she had trouble controlling her temper. "My own temper has been in quite an explosive state of late," she wrote A. J. Barton, "and I have had so much difficulty in preventing others from discovering it."[51] Apparently, the secret was already out. T. P. Bell had written to J. M. Frost in December 1897 mystified about what he might have done to offend her. "As to the matter between Miss Annie and myself, I am in perfect ignorance of any cause of offense that she could have had against me." He went on to explain to Frost that he had "at her request" spent an entire afternoon "revising a manuscript" of a speech he had given. Then, he made all the changes she asked him to make, even when he did not think they were necessary changes. Nevertheless, "she just simply cooled, quit writing to me. . . . I am not going to bother about the matter, but let it work itself out. She gets in those fits occasionally and then gets out of them."[52] This was a gross miscalculation on his part. Armstrong did not easily change her mind about anything.

The letter reveals more important information than the news that Armstrong was mad at T. P. Bell. His letter illustrates how he responded to her requests. He did exactly what she told him to do. This seems to be the way the secretaries of the board generally responded to Armstrong. They followed her instructions. Frost even joked that he was "following in her wake." She devised new programs, literature, features, and columns in their publications. She identified women who wished to be missionaries and located areas that needed mission work. When missionaries wrote to her, she listened to their requests—particularly those of the women—and made every effort to supply their needs. More importantly, Armstrong could deliver the funds to implement the programs she believed in. For example, when she heard that a women's circle in a church in Norfolk had pledged to raise $375 for Lottie Moon's school in China, Armstrong led the WMU to "secure the money needed for all the schools in foreign countries." She wrote A. J. Willingham that "I am quite sure the plan will work well and I hope to be able to get the $14,000.00 needed for the school work largely from sources that heretofore gave very little, if anything, to Foreign Missions."[53] She did not say what those sources were, but Armstrong had already demonstrated her ability to locate untapped sources of revenue. It was this uncanny ability and her keen mind in general that earned her the respect of the male leadership and compelled them to do her bidding.

PARTING WAYS WITH WMU

Armstrong resigned from WMU in 1906 over the last in a series of conflicts with WMU president Fannie E. S. Heck. Armstrong and Heck clashed over numerous issues, mostly because of their equally strong personalities. Both wished to control the programs and plans of WMU; neither cared to compromise. Fannie Heck was one of the few people who challenged Armstrong's hold on the Union. Heck managed to irritate the corresponding secretary early on by failing to respond to her letters and turning in reports after Armstrong's deadlines. Reading between the lines, it is easy to see that Fannie Heck did not think her job as president entailed rubber stamping Armstrong's agendas or demurely taking orders.

In May 1898 Fannie Heck requested that Armstrong send her the Executive

Committee agendas in advance of the monthly meetings so she could respond to issues in writing. Since Heck lived in Raleigh and could not attend each meeting in Baltimore, she felt this was a fair request. Armstrong wrote her back with a quote from the WMU constitution stating that in the absence of the president, "the Vice-President of the State where the committee is located shall take her place." In other words, if she could not come to the meetings personally, they would carry on without her. Armstrong had no intention of allowing Heck to shape the course of the Executive Committee meetings from a distance. Both women appealed to the corresponding secretary of the Mission Boards for advice. Heck asked R. J. Willingham to reason with Armstrong. "Do you think," inquired Heck, "knowing her as you do, that this would have any effect other than to cause her to overawe the committee with a threat to resign the care of the whole work if her will is disputed, a threat she has used in time past on one or more occasion?"[54]

Ultimately, Armstrong called for a judge to interpret the constitution and arbitrate the dispute. The judge sided with Armstrong on the technical interpretation of the by-law, but urged her to supply the agendas out of Christian courtesy. As a compromise, Armstrong sent Heck the Executive Committee meeting minutes each month. Heck ignored her. "Not once during the course of the year has Miss Heck made the slightest acknowledgement of receiving the 'Minutes,'" Armstrong complained to I. T. Tichenor. Heck refused to respond to letters or conduct any business with Armstrong. The relationship became so strained that Armstrong finally declared "if Miss Heck will not resign, I must."[55] Fannie Heck did resign the office of president of WMU in 1899 in response to pressure from Armstrong.

In 1906 Annie Armstrong lost a battle with Fannie Heck and other WMU leaders over the establishment of a woman's missionary training school. Armstrong opposed it while many supported the establishment of such a school in Louisville, Kentucky. Armstrong felt betrayed because the women had engaged in what she perceived as "political wire pulling" in their efforts to garner support for the school on the state level without her knowledge. When it became clear that Fannie Heck would be reelected as WMU president, it was the last straw. Annie Armstrong resigned as corresponding secretary of WMU in 1906. She also resigned as president of the Woman's Home Mission Society of Maryland (a position she had held for twenty-four years), and she relinquished her leadership in WMU at Eutaw Place Baptist Church. Annie Armstrong never again held a WMU office—nationally or locally.[56]

CONCLUSION

In her last months in office, Armstrong worked more feverishly than before to leave things in good order. In addition to the routine work of the Mission Rooms, she endeavored to complete several key projects. One long-awaited dream was realized with the opening of the Margaret Home for the children of missionaries in Greenville, South Carolina. Because of the difficulty in securing an education for their children on certain mission fields, the Margaret Home provided a safe place for children to attend high school and college in the United States. Armstrong also introduced an "apportionment plan" using quotas for state committees—an idea that had been used with some success by Methodist women.[57] Two final capital campaigns occupied her last hours in office. First, she launched plans to fulfill a request of the Foreign Mission Board for $3,000 to add a new ward to a Baptist hospital in China. Second, she redoubled her efforts to discharge an earlier WMU commitment of $20,000 for the Tichenor Memorial Church Building and Loan Fund.[58] During Armstrong's tenure WMU developed from a gathering of thirty-two delegates in 1888 to an entity representing thousands of Southern Baptist women from over 20,000 churches. When her tenure was completed she handed over the reins of an organization with 4,387 state women's societies, 1,500 Sunbeam Bands for Children, and 618 Young Women's Auxiliaries. From 1888 to 1906 annual mission receipts more than doubled and the WMU operating revenue grew from $400 to $8,187.[59] WMU had become a fine-tuned network of women, with strong avenues of communication, capable of raising large sums of money in relatively short periods of time.

After ending her relationship with WMU, Annie Armstrong turned her attention to benevolence work in Baltimore and focused on the social uplift of those in need. She had long been a volunteer at nursing homes and orphanages in the city. When the Aged Men's and Aged Women's Home in Baltimore realized that she was available, they quickly offered her the position of manager, which she accepted. In spite of the new job, Armstrong continued to be an active member of Eutaw Place Baptist Church. She taught children's Sunday school and served on various committees. While studiously avoiding the home and foreign mission societies at Eutaw Place, she kept her position as director of the "mothers' meetings." At these gatherings neighborhood women, who typically "would not attend the Sunday services at the prestigious church," came to the church on Friday afternoons. In addition to Bible study, singing, and prayer, the mothers' meeting offered "a store" that "supplied yard goods at wholesale prices." They gave women fabric as needed. The program also boasted a "coal fund," and a "savings bank." Annie Armstrong's church provided social services for the community very much in keeping with a WMU Personal Service programs that are featured in a later chapter. Armstrong directed these mothers' meetings at Eutaw Place for forty-two years.[60]

Characteristic of Progressive Era reformers, Armstrong possessed an unassailable optimism about the future for women and for the world. Her vision for uplift always included equipping women and saving the nations in equal measure. Armstrong consistently celebrated the contributions of women and insisted that women could be powerful if they worked together. One of her favorite mottos for WMU was: "In Union is Strength." Armstrong reminded the Union in 1900 that before women's mission societies were formed, women's abilities were largely "undeveloped." Yet because of WMU "numbers of thoughtful women can now testify to a new estimate of life and its responsibilities; a better understanding of all Christian service, and closer fellowship with Christ."[61] Armstrong believed that the work of Christian service involved the development of women's talents. She called "thoughtful" women to take their faith more seriously, and she believed faith would compel them to take themselves more seriously. It might be tempting to dismiss Armstrong's appeal for women to mobilize and use their power as merely a means to her pious ends—since she never publicly endorsed suffrage or made any call for the rights of women in general. That assessment, however, misses something of Annie Armstrong's character and the depth of her religious belief. The core of her conviction was that God called *women*—to think, to work, to plan, to organize, to raise money, and to go to the ends of the earth on his behalf. This divine mission, she believed, would elevate women as worthy "co-laborers" with Christ and empower them to transform the world.

FIGURE 1. Annie Armstrong, corresponding secretary of the WMU. Photo courtesy of the Southern Baptist Historical Library and Archives, Nashville, Tennessee.

FIGURE 2. Fannie Exile Scudder Heck, president of the WMU. Photo courtesy of the Southern Baptist Historical Library and Archives, Nashville, Tennessee.

FIGURE 3. WMU Good Will Center, Louisville, Kentucky. Photo courtesy of the Southern Baptist Historical Library and Archives, Nashville, Tennessee.

FIGURE 4. First group of women to study at the Southern Baptist Seminary in Louisville, Kentucky, 1904. *Front row, left to right*: Miss Jenks, Nancy Weigel, Mrs. Weigel (house mother), Linda Weigel, Annie Allen; *Second row*: Rena Groover, Alice Huey, Ella Jeter, Mrs. Mahaffy, Clemmie Ford, Cynthia Miller, Emma Leachman. Photo courtesy of the Southern Baptist Historical Library and Archives, Nashville, Tennessee.

FIGURE 5. WMU workers at a $75 Million Campaign conference, Nashville, Tennessee, 1919. Photo courtesy of the Southern Baptist Historical Library and Archives, Nashville, Tennessee.

FIGURE 6. The WMU's first building, at 15 West Franklin Street, Baltimore, Maryland. Photo courtesy of the Southern Baptist Historical Library and Archives, Nashville, Tennessee.

Above: FIGURE 7. WMU leaders in 1902: *Left to right*: Eliza Broadus, Kentucky; Annie Kate Woods, Mississippi; Jane M. Ammen, Louisiana; Sarah Jessie Davis Stakely, Alabama; Mary K. Oldham Eagle, Arkansas; Abby Manly Gwathmey, Virginia; Mary Emily Wright, Georgia. Photo courtesy of the WMU Library and Archives, Birmingham, Alabama.

Right: FIGURE 8. Nannie Helen Burroughs, corresponding secretary of the Woman's Convention, National Baptist Convention. Photo courtesy of the Southern Baptist Historical Library and Archives, Nashville, Tennessee.

CHAPTER FOUR

Unreliable Allies

Southern Baptist Women and Race

ON JANUARY 28, 1939, NANNIE HELEN BURROUGHS, corresponding secretary of the Woman's Convention of the National Baptist Convention, wrote a letter to Eutaw Place Baptist Church in Baltimore, Maryland, eulogizing Annie Armstrong. "No woman in America has ever done more to encourage Negro Baptist women in their work than our recently departed friend, Miss Annie Armstrong," wrote Burroughs.[1] Armstrong and Burroughs shared much in common. Both women served as corresponding secretary of a Baptist female missionary society. Both women fought hard, private battles to carve out and preserve an independent female space in strongly patriarchal denominations. Both possessed forceful personalities that brought them into conflict with other female leaders. Both exhibited a keen business sense and wielded significant power within their organizations. In spite of all they held in common, at the turn of the twentieth century these kindred spirits faced each other from opposite sides of an immovable color line—mired in a caste system that oppressed black women and warped the ethical vision of white women. Although a considerable chasm divided them, Burroughs and Armstrong forged a relationship that, according to Burroughs, fostered "Christian, interracial understanding and cooperation between White and Negro Baptist women of the South."[2]

In *Righteous Discontent*, Evelyn Brooks Higginbotham described the cooperation of black and northern white Baptist women as an "unlikely sisterhood" but gave little attention to the relationship between black and white women in the South. Higginbotham did not mention Annie Armstrong, even though Burroughs referred to Armstrong as "my inspiration" and a "trailblazer in Christian cooperation between white and Negro Baptist women."[3] Undoubtedly Southern Baptist women were omitted because the vast majority of their encounters with black women served only to illustrate the common pattern of discrimination and bigotry. Still, there were a few notable exceptions of cooperation. These efforts of a handful of white southern women should not be overly lauded, nor do their contributions diminish the heroic work of black Baptist women to establish independent organizations. As Higginbotham so cogently stated, "Interracial cooperation . . . does not negate or minimize the importance of black self-help in developing attitudinal and institutional counterweights to the oppressive and debilitating racial climate of the late nineteenth and early twentieth centuries."[4] Black Baptist women deserve the credit for establishing their own programs. At times, they worked with southern white women to accomplish specific goals. Although they proved to be unreliable allies in the crucial fight against segregation, Southern Baptist women did aid black Baptist women in developing missionary organizations. These interactions led some white women to question their assumptions about race and to engage in limited programs of racial reform.

Cooperation did not indicate that WMU leaders embraced modern views of social justice. Leaders of WMU, including Annie Armstrong, held racial attitudes consistent with most white Progressive Era reformers. The majority of southern progressives were white supremacists who believed that racial peace and social order could only be achieved through segregation and disenfranchisement. Historian Dewey Grantham noted that the "racial settlement" of the turn of the twentieth century was a "fundamental component of southern progressivism." William Link concurred: "The twin convictions of black inadequacy and white paternalism formed a bedrock for the reform program."[5] Even the most progressive of the southern reformers, like Walter Hines Page, who fought for equal rights for black southerners, believed the "Anglo-Saxon" myth of white supremacy.[6] While Southern Baptist women like Annie Armstrong, Fannie Heck, Lulie Wharton, and Ella Broadus Robertson believed they had a moral and spiritual obligation to offer assistance to African American women, they did not express their views in terms of human rights or social justice. They were unable to transcend their culture on the issue of race. In spite of Nannie Helen Burroughs's repeated and pointed appeals, WMU leaders did not align themselves with black women to challenge segregation. Race divided them more profoundly than gender could ever unite them.

BLACK BAPTIST BEGINNINGS

The oldest black Baptist congregations in the South owe their existence to the ministry of a slave named George Liele, who was converted on a plantation near Savannah, Georgia, in 1772. Liele helped organize the Silver Bluff church whose members later merged into the First African Baptist Church of Savannah.[7] In spite of these independent beginnings, most black Baptists belonged to white churches before the Civil War. There were about forty thousand black members of white churches at the beginning of the nineteenth century.[8] The segregation of Baptist churches in the South began soon after emancipation. Church life offered newly freed slaves a ready opportunity to exercise their liberty and to create independent self-governing institutions. The Georgia Baptist Convention kept fairly comprehensive records of church membership that illustrate the exodus of black Baptists from white churches. In 1860 Georgia Baptists recorded 27,734 black members of white churches and no all-black churches affiliated with the Georgia Baptist Convention. In 1895 the record indicated thirteen black church members remaining in white churches and 206,267 members of black Baptist churches. Rufus Spain asserted that by 1895 the segregation of Baptist churches in the South was complete.[9]

In addition to independent congregations, black Baptists also stepped up efforts to form a national organization. In 1880 the Baptist Foreign Missionary Convention (BFMC) of the United States was founded in Montgomery, Alabama. This organization focused on foreign missions—primarily African missions—and resisted alliances with white Baptist missionary societies. Emanuel Love, who served as the most visible leader of the BFMC, believed that "our work as an organization will develop qualities and powers in us as a people that will not be developed if we go into another [white] organization."[10]

Six years later, a younger set of black leaders established the American National Baptist Convention (ANBC). James M. Washington asserts that this body "provided a much needed intellectual outlet for many of the younger and more progressive brothers and sisters who were graduating in large numbers from Northern sponsored black schools, such as Shaw University and Wayland Theological Seminary."[11] A young minister from Kentucky named William James Simmons provided vision and leadership for the ANBC. Simmons believed in higher education for women and endorsed women's right to work outside the home. Despite such beliefs he did not lend his support when women petitioned the ANBC to form an independent society in 1890 because he felt women should be integrated into the leadership of the ANBC.[12] Simmons and other key leaders soon began to work toward a merger with the BFMC, believing that a unified Baptist voice would improve the power and prestige of the race. As with most Baptists, unity proved somewhat of a challenge. Dissension over the creation of a national university birthed a third black Baptist organization, the National Baptist Education Convention (NBEC), in 1892. Although these internal conflicts made national solidarity seem remote, the need for unity became increasingly clear as violence against black citizens became more acute and white Baptists failed to deliver support.

After the Emancipation Proclamation, freedmen across the South were optimistic that they would be full recipients of all the benefits of American democracy. Legislation passed during Reconstruction fueled this hopeful vision. The Civil Rights Act of 1866 granted citizenship to all persons born in the United

States. The Fourteenth Amendment to the constitution (1868) was designed to secure these rights. Southern states were required to ratify the Fourteenth Amendment before being readmitted to the Union. The Fifteenth Amendment (1870) enfranchised black men, stating that no citizen could be denied the right to vote on the basis of race, color, or previous condition of servitude. The Civil Rights Act of 1875 guaranteed equal treatment in public accommodations. Unfortunately, after the passage of the act, northern activists and political leaders grew weary of the battle to protect the rights of black citizens and began to withdraw from Reconstruction both physically and theoretically. "The Federal Government," quipped historian James Melvin Washington, "experienced a failure of nerve."[13] By 1877 every former Confederate state had been returned to the control of southern Democrats. Black political influence plummeted. Frederick Douglass lamented the erosion of rights in his essay "The Color Line in America." "Without crime or offense against law or gospel, the colored man is the Jean Valjean of American society. He has escaped from the galleys, and hence all presumptions are against him. The workshop denies him work, and the inn denies him shelter; the ballot-box a fair vote, and the jury-box a fair trial. He has ceased to be the slave of an individual, but has in some sense become the slave of society."[14]

In 1883 the US Supreme Court abandoned the earlier gains in civil rights and opened the floodgate for Jim Crow legislation in the South. In 1890 the state of Mississippi adopted laws designed to remove black men from the voting booth. One after another, southern states followed suit, systematically disenfranchising black citizens and imposing rigid codes of segregation. The final barrier to segregation was removed by the Supreme Court in *Plessy v. Ferguson*. In 1892 a man named Homer Plessy boarded a train from New Orleans to Covington, Louisiana. Because Plessy was one-eighth black, he was legally considered a black man by the state of Louisiana. When he refused to relinquish his seat in a railroad car reserved for white passengers, he was arrested and jailed. Plessy filed suit, claiming that forced segregation was a violation of his constitutional rights. The Supreme Court disagreed; in 1896 it ruled against Plessy, giving legal sanction to the apartheid system deemed "separate but equal." Accordingly, black men and women were separated from white people on train cars, streetcars, and steamboats. Black Americans could not eat in the same restaurants, frequent the same theaters, or share the same public parks as whites. Bathrooms, waiting rooms, and drinking fountains acquired the labels "for whites only" or "colored." Jim Crow legislation partitioned every public space in the South. The South Carolina code of 1915 "prohibited textile factories from permitting laborers of different races from working together in the same room, or using the same entrances, pay windows, exits, doorways, stairways, or windows, at the same time, or the same 'lavatories, toilets, drinking water buckets, pails, cups, dippers or glasses' at any time."[15] Those spaces not governed by law were segregated by custom—which varied from region to region.[16] Arkansas Delta plantations provided separate drinking buckets or cups, while in Texas a white worker recalled sharing the same cup with his black co-worker. "At the end of the row, there would be a jug of water, and he'd drink first and I'd drink second right out of that jug and . . . that was not a problem at all." If the two men had gone into town, the worker explained, things would have been different. "I wouldn't be allowed to sit next to him or drink with him or eat under any circumstances."[17] Black men, women, or children who violated the norms of segregation met with swift retribution.

Violence against black people rose in tandem with the loss of civil liberties. Over four thousand African Americans were lynched in the South between 1877 and 1950.[18] In September 1889 black Baptist leaders experienced the terror of Jim Crow as they traveled from Georgia to Indianapolis for a Foreign Mission Convention. An agent of the East Tennessee, Virginia and Georgia Railroad contacted Emanuel Love, pastor of the historic First African Baptist Church of Savannah. The agent offered to sell Love and his colleagues tickets for their long journey, "assuring them of first class accommodations." When the convention delegates arrived at the train station, they discovered that the train had only one first-class car available. The other car was a smoking car. As the train approached Baxley, Georgia, Love noticed some of the "train men" behaving suspiciously and rushed to warn his companions. But he was too late. "Almost immediately as the train drew up at Baxley, fifty or seventy-five men armed with clubs, pieces of iron, pistols, etc., rushed into the car" and began beating the delegates. The mob did not ask them to move or give them any warning. Emanuel Love stated: "If the ruffians had ordered us out we should have gone without . . . protest, seeing the ghastly situation." After treating their injuries the delegates continued on to the meeting in Indianapolis. Love later expressed the hopelessness engendered by this climate of persecution. "We look to God and ask what are we to do? What is the use of appealing to the government? Our sufferings and inhuman outrages are known. . . . It does seem that the glory of American citizenship means no glory for us."[19] The escalating violence convinced many African Americans of the need for unity in the face of oppression.

A conflict over Sunday school publications cooled cooperative efforts between black and white Baptists and further highlighted the need for a unified black denominational voice. In 1889 the American Baptist Publication Society (north) published an announcement that articles by three influential black Baptists would be included in the 1890 issue of the *Baptist Teacher*. Walter Henderson Brooks, Emanuel Love, and William James Simmons were scheduled to submit articles titled "The Doctrine of God," "Regeneration," and the "Lord's Supper" respectively. At that point Southern Baptists had not been able to sustain a viable denominational press. Most churches in the South, black and white, still subscribed to ABPS literature. J. M. Frost and other SBC leaders quickly voiced their displeasure to the ABPS. The choice to publish Love, Brooks, and Simmons particularly offended Southern Baptists because these men had boldly voiced their opposition to racial violence and white supremacy. According to Frost these writers "outraged the people of the South in language that should be condemned in any court of common decency."[20] Under pressure the ABPS withdrew its offer to Brooks, Love, and Simmons, which did little to mollify anyone involved. Southern Baptists used the event to gain support for a distinctly "southern" religious press. Black Baptists viewed the decision as yet one more chapter in an endless tale of betrayal.[21] These disappointments, combined with the steady march of Jim Crow violence, fueled the growing consensus that black Baptists needed a unified denomination and an independent publishing house. In 1895 African American Baptists met in Atlanta where they voted to merge the three leading conventions (ANBC, BFMC, and NBEC) to form the National Baptist Convention with Elias Camp Morris as president. The following year entrepreneur and businessman Richard Henry Boyd chartered the National Baptist Publishing Board.[22] In 1906 the National Baptist Convention boasted a membership of 2,261,607 with 17,000 ministers, and by 1916 it ranked as the third largest denomination in America.[23]

WOMAN'S CONVENTION OF THE NBC AND ANNIE ARMSTRONG

African American Baptist women began their struggle to establish an independent women's missionary board in the 1880s. The leadership of an exceptional woman named Nannie Helen Burroughs helped bring their hopes to fruition.[24] Burroughs was born in Orange, Virginia, in 1879 to ex-slaves John and Jennie Burroughs. John Burroughs was a Baptist preacher and farmer. Jennie Burroughs worked as a cook. Nannie Burroughs moved with her mother to Washington, DC, at the age of five. After graduating with honors from M Street High School in 1896, Burroughs became a bookkeeper and stenographer at the Foreign Mission Board of the National Baptist Convention in Louisville, Kentucky. In 1900 at the tender age of twenty-one, she delivered a speech to the National Baptist Convention titled "How the Sisters Are Hindered from Helping." Burroughs proclaimed: "For a number of years there has been a righteous discontent, a burning zeal to go forward in His name among the Baptist women of our churches and it will be the dynamic force in the religious campaign at the opening of the 20th century."[25] Her speech marked the culmination of many years of struggle to establish a women's missionary society. At that convention Burroughs was named the first corresponding secretary of the Woman's Convention of the National Baptist Convention, a position she held for forty-seven years.

The path to this independent woman's missionary organization had not been smooth. Black Baptist men resisted the formation of an independent women's missionary society as vociferously as did their white counterparts. The women of Kentucky organized the first statewide convention in 1883 and were soon followed by the women of Alabama, Arkansas, South Carolina, Virginia, Louisiana, Mississippi, Tennessee, Texas, and West Virginia. Evelyn Brooks Higginbotham narrated the development of these state conventions and noted the opposition women faced from male ministers. Virginia Broughton, a missionary in Tennessee, wrote: "Ministers and laymen, who looked with disdain upon a criticism that came from a woman, and all those who were jealous of the growing popularity of the woman's work, . . . all rose up in their churches with all the influence and power of speech they could summon to oppose the woman's work and break it up if possible."[26] Yet the women persisted. According to Higginbotham, urban churches provided "fertile ground for the growth of the black women's convention movement."[27]

Women sought approval for a national women's organization in two of the early conventions in 1890. The leaders of the American National Baptist Convention refused outright. The National Baptist Foreign Mission Convention seemed amenable at first but eventually withdrew its permission as well. At the founding meeting of the National Baptist Convention in 1895 the women proposed a national women's missionary society and even chose leaders. Alice A. Bowie of Alabama, Virginia Broughton of Tennessee, and Mrs. C. J. Robinson of Arkansas were selected as officers. In spite of enthusiastic support from the women, the male leadership of the National Baptist Convention disbanded the fledgling organization.[28] Burroughs and her colleagues refused to accept this as a final word and redoubled their efforts.

While Burroughs worked to change opinions from Washington, DC, there were others making efforts to help black women organize. Lewis G. Jordan, secretary of the Foreign Mission Board of the NBC, proved to be a valuable friend and supporter of the women's cause. Jordan initiated the first meeting between Burroughs and Annie Armstrong. In January 1897 Armstrong wrote the following letter to R. J. Willingham, secretary of the SBC Foreign Mission Board: "Yesterday I received word that the Rev. L. G. Jordan, Secretary of the National Baptist Convention, will shortly come to Baltimore and will arrange to have the colored woman from Washington, whom he expects to take a prominent role in inaugurating mission work among the colored women, to meet him here so they can have some conference with me in regard to the organization which is about to be formed for the colored women." Armstrong asked Willingham's advice about having the black women's executive headquarters in Baltimore because she had a woman in mind as corresponding secretary. "There is a woman here who I think would make an efficient President, if not Corr. Sec. I have worked with her for fourteen years and consider her not only a very devoted Christian, but gifted with a great deal of good, common sense."[29] In a letter to James Marion Frost, corresponding secretary of the SBC Sunday School Board, Armstrong named the woman she hoped would be president and repeated her earlier praise. "This woman is a Mrs. Martha Clark whom I have known, and with whom I have worked for 14 years. She is, I consider, not only a very earnest Christian, but a person of remarkably good sense and of some executive ability."[30] In both letters Armstrong noted her fourteen years of cooperation with black women in Baltimore.

Apparently Lewis Jordan was aware of Armstrong's years of work with black women in Baltimore. Armstrong had formed an interracial home mission society at Eutaw Place Baptist Church (her home church) as early as 1880 to provide aid to Native Americans in the Southwest who had been forcibly removed from their homes. The plan began when Armstrong enlisted Baptist churches in Baltimore (eight white and six black) to provide suits of clothing for the children in a new school. After the 140 summer suits were made and shipped to Wetumka, Oklahoma, Armstrong encouraged the participating churches to form a permanent aid society. "[Armstrong] called for a meeting of the Baptist women of Baltimore churches, white and Negro, on the afternoon of May 16, 1882, at Eutaw Place Church. There they formed a central society with the name Woman's Baptist Home Mission Society of Maryland. Local societies were formed in white and Negro churches."[31] By 1887, black women's participation in the joint society began to wane, but Armstrong was determined not to allow the cooperation of the church women to dissolve. She once commented that ministry must not be "for" black women, but "with" black women.[32] She formed a committee of three white women to visit each of the black Baptist churches in Baltimore to encourage them to remain active in the mission society. Armstrong helped to establish two missions for African Americans in Baltimore and persuaded the Home Mission Board to employ black missionaries to staff them. These missions offered mothers' meetings, industrial schools, literacy education, and Bible studies. For a while, Armstrong personally conducted a mothers' meeting in one of the poorest missions. Later she helped establish three more missions and an orphanage for black children.[33] Armstrong's work with missions and her support for the work of black women made her an obvious choice to aid in the organization of a women's mission society for National Baptists.

In a letter dated January 26, 1897, Armstrong gave a report of her meeting with Jordan to James Marion Frost: "Last Tuesday morning we had quite a prolonged conference, lasting about four hours, with Rev. L. G. Jordan, secretary of the National Baptist Convention. He had arranged to have meet him here a colored woman from Washington, Nannie Helen Burroughs. I invited Rev. G. R. Waller (missionary of the Home Board and pastor of one of the Baltimore colored churches), Mrs. W. J. Brown and Mrs. W. J. E. Cox to be present at the interview, these ladies being members of the Standing Committee on Work among the Colored People."[34] She then reported six decisions that had been made at the meeting. First of all, the women would wait to officially organize until the annual meeting of the NBC scheduled to convene in Boston the following September. Second, the secretaries of the boards would work in the interim "to interest women in missions and get pastors in sympathy." Third, women would be encouraged to give to missions. Fourth, "a Constitution and By-laws for Woman's Mission Societies should be printed in the February edition of the *Afro-American Mission Herald*, with other articles calculated to interest women in the work." The *Herald* would, thereafter, incorporate a Woman's Department, and Armstrong explained that "I will for the present largely furnish the data for said department." Fifth, mite boxes would be sent out on request of the mission boards by Martha Clark of Baltimore. Finally, a mass meeting would be held in Washington, DC, in March "to interest colored women who may be there in missions. . . . The woman, Nannie H. Burroughs, whose letter I forwarded you, will between this and September try to interest the women of the churches in the District of Columbia."[35] Armstrong met with Jordan several more times that year. On July 2, 1897, she wrote: "Mr. Jordan has recently made several visits to Baltimore. During these, plans have been devised for getting the Woman's Work in shape. . . . While Mr. Jordan was in Baltimore, I saw him several times—he spent two mornings at the Mission Rooms, beside my attending two meetings that he addressed—and I really feel that he is an earnest good man."[36]

Because of her interest in interracial work, Armstrong sincerely hoped the executive committee of the black women's society would be located in Baltimore. She intended to provide supplies, advice, and financial aid to the women—although from behind the scenes. "Should the general organization for colored women be located in Baltimore," Armstrong explained, "we could quite materially aid those who have work in charge without it appearing publicly that we were doing so."[37] She was determined to keep her work in the background. Armstrong hastened to assure Frost that "the officers of the Woman's Missionary Union will not appear to have any part in this movement, we will be helping those who have this work in charge in every way in our power. I am sure, for many reasons, it is better for us to be working out of sight and trying to fit the colored people to do their own work."[38] Armstrong embodied one of the many "paradoxes" of southern progressivism in that her paternalistic desire to remain "out of sight" also represented a genuine respect for the autonomy of black leadership.[39] "I am looking and hoping for a great work to be done by the colored people themselves," she wrote to R. J. Willingham in 1902, "and I believe that they are our best agents."[40]

Armstrong did not elaborate on other of the "many reasons" for remaining behind the scenes, but it is possible to hazard a guess or two. First of all, Armstrong was clearly worried about how racial cooperation would be perceived by denominational leaders. She worked diligently to remain in the good graces of the male leadership of the SBC. Armstrong corresponded most frequently with J. M. Frost, corresponding secretary of the Sunday School Board. Frost's involvement in the 1889 conflict over the *Baptist Teacher* revealed his commitment to white supremacy. After voicing "outrage" that the ABPS would consider publishing articles by Simmons, Brooks, and Love, Frost stepped up his campaign to establish a Southern Baptist publishing concern. I. T. Tichenor encouraged Frost in his endeavor to establish a publishing house controlled by southerners. Frost noted: "My first article proposing the new Board was published the latter part of February, 1890, in the *Religious Herald* at Richmond."[41] Apparently Frost capitalized on the racially charged debate to push forward his plan for the Sunday School Board, which was founded in 1891 with Frost as corresponding secretary. In spite of his vocal opposition to the publication of articles by black ministers in *Baptist Teacher*, Frost himself developed a cordial working relationship with Richard Henry Boyd after Boyd founded the National Baptist Publication Board in Nashville, providing him with funding, advice, and printing machinery.[42]

Second, Armstrong was careful to remain "behind the scenes" not only because she did not want to anger male leadership but also because she shared their views on race relations. She defended the South in conversations with American Baptist women by insisting that northerners simply did not understand the culture of the South. Armstrong acknowledged that there had been instances of violence against black southerners, but she did not believe the problem to be systemic. Conflict between Northern and Southern Baptists would continue, she argued, "as long as the missionaries of the Northern Boards were encouraged before Northern audiences to so misrepresent the Southern people by giving exceptional cases of injustice, wrong doing, etc. and leading persons to believe that these were the custom."[43] Armstrong then expressed outrage that northern Baptists would hold Southern Baptists accountable for lynchings. "I insisted that they had no more right to hold the Christian people of the South accountable for lynchings than we had to reflect on the New York Baptists for what occurred in the slums of the city. There is a mob element everywhere and we must make distinctions."[44] Armstrong was tethered to her cultural context and simply could not comprehend the scope of racial violence; nor did she view segregation as unjust or its advocates as wrongdoers.

In 1900, following Nannie Helen Burroughs's impassioned speech, the National Baptist Convention affirmed the creation of the Woman's Convention, Auxiliary to the National Baptist Convention. S. Willie Layten of Philadelphia was elected president; Sylvia C. J. Bryant of Atlanta, vice president; Nannie Helen Burroughs of Washington, corresponding secretary; and Virginia Broughton of Tennessee, recording secretary. Burroughs remained in the role of corresponding secretary from 1900 until 1947. Armstrong's hope that the black women's executive committee be based in Baltimore did not materialize. Most of the work of the Woman's Convention (WC) was conducted from Washington, DC, under Burroughs's leadership. It is important to note that in spite of all her careful phrasing and sidestepping, Annie Armstrong eventually did promote interracial cooperation quite openly. After black Baptist women organized, Armstrong became a visible presence at their meetings and included black women on the programs of WMU meetings. Through the WMU Mission Rooms in Baltimore, Armstrong published tracts promoting ministry with black women, including one authored by Virginia Broughton.[45]

Armstrong maintained close ties with the Woman's Convention through her relationship with Nannie Helen Burroughs and other WC leaders. Armstrong's personal notes indicate she was present at a WC meeting in September 1901 in Nashville, Tennessee. "Mrs. Broughton presided . . . [and I] noted with much pleasure her manner of conducting the exercises," wrote Armstrong. "Later that same month, by invitation, we attended the first annual meeting of the Woman's Auxiliary which was held in Cincinnati."[46] Leaders of the WC asked Armstrong to address the delegates of that first meeting. WC minutes summarized her statements: "She congratulated our women upon the work they had begun. . . . She emphasized the great truth that God was the over ruling power that shaped the destinies of all his creatures, and bade us be courageous, trust God, and go forward."[47] Armstrong attended the sessions of the meeting and conferred with Woman's Convention president S. Willie Layten.

Layten celebrated Armstrong's visit in several of her presidential addresses to the WC: "One of the happy features of this year's work," she noted in 1902, "has been the encouragement given us by the white Baptist women of the South. You, no doubt, remember Miss Annie Armstrong . . . and her visit to our meeting last year in Cincinnati, Ohio, her words of good cheer and encouragement. As a result of her visit to us, she succeeded in awakening much interest in our work among her sisterhood and secured material help to the amount of $250.00, given by a Christian woman of Baltimore, Maryland."[48] In her presidential speech of 1905 Layten again referred to Armstrong's visit. "Our first Year's anniversary was encouraged and complimented by the presence of Miss Annie W. Armstrong, Corresponding Secretary of the Woman's Missionary Union of the S. B. C. Many remember that meeting in Cincinnati, how she sat quietly throughout each meeting, observing our doings. We were happy to have had her. We little dreamed then what her presence meant."[49] Layten also described her private conversation with Armstrong. "I remember it well. She called me aside for a conference and said, 'I am very much impressed with what you women are trying to do—go on, you far surpass our expectations. Do you want the cooperation of the southern white Baptist women and in what way can we help you?'"[50] Armstrong's paternalism should not negate the fact that she genuinely desired to be of assistance to the Woman's Convention. Layten clearly regarded Armstrong's words as supportive and encouraging.

A month or so after the Cincinnati meeting, Armstrong contacted Layten to see if she would set up a meeting between Armstrong, Layten, and Richard Henry Boyd. (Boyd, who had established the National Baptist Publishing Board in 1896, was also, at that time, head of the National Baptist Home Mission Board.) Layten reported that this meeting resulted in a plan to support black female missionaries: "first Mrs. Murchison and later Sisters Whitfield and Edwards."[51] Boyd elaborated on the agreement at the 1903 NBC Convention held in Philadelphia, Pennsylvania. According to this agreement, WMU would supply $250 a year, the National Baptist HMB would supply $150, and the WC would provide $150 in order to "pay the salaries and expenses of two women missionaries to do from house to house missionary work on home fields."[52] Boyd was quick to defend the agreement between the SBC and the NBC by insisting that the SBC "assumes no authority, no responsibility, gives no orders, receives no reports . . . but leaves the entire management and responsibility exclusively with our Board and Secretary."[53] During her 1903 address to the WC, Layten referenced the cooperative agreement with WMU. "We rejoice to say that the cooperation between our boards and the Southern Baptist white women yet continues, and in larger sphere of helpfulness than last year," declared Layten. "It seems that this is one of God's own ways of . . . helping to bring about a better understanding and brotherly feeling between the races of the South." She also suggests that Armstrong was present at the meeting. "We gratefully receive and acknowledge the Christian interest given us by these women and their representative, Miss Annie W. Armstrong."[54] Nannie Helen Burroughs added her thanks to the WMU at that same meeting. "It is our pleasure to again extend our thanks to the Woman's Missionary Union of the Southern Baptist Convention. . . . Dr. [R. H.] Boyd, Secretary of our Home Board, informed us early in the year that a contribution of $250.00 was in hand for our field work and during May we were agreeably surprised when a letter from Miss Annie W. Armstrong announced that $100.00 had been added to this sum. The women of the Southern Baptist Convention will never know the good they have done by the help thus rendered."[55]

In 1904, during the annual WMU meeting in Nashville, Armstrong invited WMU delegates to attend a meeting with African American women of Nashville. "Your president was invited to be present and present the work of the Woman's Convention, Auxiliary to National Baptist Convention before the Woman's Missionary Union from which a better understanding of our work and its need was given, and how our white sisters can help and cooperate in our work," explained Layten. "Following this was a meeting of the colored women of Nashville representing all the black churches of that city—at which was present the officers of W.M.U. and representatives of all the southern states." The minutes of the Woman's Convention reported that the women held a "heart to heart conference" at the Spruce Street Baptist Church. "Tears flowed freely from the eyes of many white and colored women," recalled Layten, "and many hearty amens were heard."[56] No discernable advances resulted from the meeting, but an integrated meeting in Nashville, Tennessee, in 1904 at the height of racial segregation in the South is worthy of note.

Why was Armstrong so committed to helping black women organize for missions? Part of the answer lies with her conviction that black women would be crucial to the work of world evangelism. Armstrong made no secret of her belief that black Baptists would be the key to evangelizing Africa—a belief common among southern progressives. The notion that African American Christians could be instrumental in the salvation of Africa dates back to a proposal made in the late eighteenth century by New England theologian Samuel Hopkins, who suggested commissioning black ministers as missionaries to Africa. The American Colonization Society, founded in 1816, "carried . . . a strong missionizing theme that was accepted by many Christians."[57] Social gospel historian Ralph Luker pointed out that "the idea that black Americans had a providential role in the redemption of Africa . . . appealed to southern white churchmen." Methodist Bishop Atticus G. Haygood opined, "Let the Christian Negroes in America get ready to carry the light of God to their brethren beyond the sea, who 'sit in darkness and the shadow of death.'"[58]

Black Baptist leaders shared this grand vision for the conversion of Africa, and some early leaders felt that missions provided some salve for the wound of slavery. "We have met to think, talk, pray and give in order that the gospel may be given to Africa, the land of our fathers," asserted Emanuel Love in 1889: "I am convinced that God's purpose is to redeem Africa through us. The evils of slavery were turned to gracious account conferring upon us the blessings of civilization and in return placing the negro Christian of this great country under lasting obligation to the work of African evangelization. This work is ours by appointment, by inheritance, and by choice."[59] Armstrong echoed this hope, but in decidedly paternalistic tones. "An immense amount of good can be done—not only in developing the colored women here at home, but in work in Africa," she explained to R. J. Willingham in 1897, "if we can get the colored women organized as missionary workers."[60] She made a similar statement to J. M. Frost a few weeks later. "You have no idea how glad and thankful I am that God is allowing us this opportunity to help to elevate the colored women as well as to assist the work in Africa."[61] Armstrong's personal notebooks posed the same idea: "Does not the future evangelization of Africa rest mainly in the hands of her sons and daughters here? . . . Perhaps the chief function of the white race in America in relation to the evangelization of Africa is one of help. . . . It is through Africa in America that the continent of Africa ought to be evangelized."[62]

In 1901, Armstrong quoted a missionary speech she heard Sarah Willie Layten give to black Baptist women. According to Armstrong, Layten "advocated Christian service which should begin in the home, extending in ever widening circles until, in Mission Work for their own in Africa, the negro women of America should become a power in answering the prayer 'Thy Kingdom Come.'" "Does it not seem probable," mused Armstrong, "that in the Providence of God, the evangelization of Africa is to be accomplished through the instrumentality of these who are now in our midst?" Interestingly, Armstrong allowed for the possibility that this might not be God's plan. "Whether this be true or not," she concluded, "there is no doubt that 'Duties are ours, events are God's.' In His hands we can fearlessly entrust the future of the negro race, but upon us lies the responsibility of the present."[63] In her typical, pragmatic fashion Armstrong preferred to focus on the work to be done now rather than overindulge in theological speculation.

Annie Armstrong addressed the WC for the last time at the Chicago meeting in 1905. She used the opportunity to promote her vision of home and foreign missions. According to WC minutes, "Miss Armstrong said that our great work is two-fold: The developing of our race in the United States and the redemption of Africa. She said the work of developing the race is to be done largely by colored people themselves and we could only do effectual work by coming in close contact with those needing help."[64] In that same year, Armstrong became embroiled in a conflict with the women in her own organization of WMU over plans to establish a missionary training school. The discord culminated with Armstrong's resignation from her position as corresponding secretary of WMU. This effectually ended a season of cooperation between WMU and the WC. Of course, it is tempting to wonder whether or not greater strides in racial accord would have been achieved if Armstrong had remained. We do know that it would be nearly a quarter of a century before the Woman's Missionary Union would produce another leader who shared Annie Armstrong's commitment to National Baptist women.[65]

THE WOMAN'S CONVENTION, EDUCATION, AND LABOR

In 1906 when Annie Armstrong was in the twilight of her national career, Nannie Helen Burroughs was at the dawn of her role as a leader of black Baptist women. Burroughs, Layten, and other leaders of the WC shared a vision that was progressive in every sense of the word. Burroughs had ambitions for both the general advancement of her race and for improving the status of women. Under her leadership the Woman's Convention called for educational opportunities, equal employment, and voting rights for women. Evelyn Brooks Higginbotham noted that "during the late nineteenth century they developed a distinct discourse of resistance, a feminist theology."[66] The WC's bold support for women's rights stands in sharp contrast to the position of their Southern

Baptist counterparts in WMU. Although WMU established a missionary training school for women, they carefully distanced themselves from the women's labor movement and never issued a single official word endorsing the right to vote.

Burroughs is probably most celebrated as the founder and president of a women's training school in Washington, DC. She led the Woman's Convention to form a committee to study the issue of education in 1906. Three years later Burroughs and two committee members "made a down payment on the $6,500 purchase price of a six-acre farm with an eight-room house" in Lincoln Heights.[67] Three years later, the National Training School for Women and Girls officially welcomed students. Like Booker T. Washington's Tuskegee Institute in Alabama, the Training School opted to provide industrial education rather than a traditional liberal arts program. This reflected "the convention's identification with the working poor and its concern for the employment options of black women."[68] Burroughs wanted to provide practical solutions for the myriad of women employed as domestic servants.[69] By 1929, 102 students studied in eight buildings on eight acres of land preparing women for service jobs, particularly housekeeping.[70] Burroughs believed that black women needed professional training in home economics in order to compete with the large numbers of European immigrants.

Burroughs also believed that the professionalization of domestic labor would uplift the entire race.[71] Her vision for professionalism included industrial training and organized labor. In 1919 the Woman's Convention pledged its support for a national organization of domestic workers. Burroughs then led her Baptist sisters in the campaign to create a labor union. Under Burroughs's leadership the National Association of Women Wage Earners was founded in 1921. With one exception, all of the organizers were Baptists.[72] By professionalizing domestic work, Burroughs and the WC dignified and validated black women's labor, which she believed contributed to the elevation of the race.

Burroughs and WC president Willie Layten understood racial uplift as religious work. It is no coincidence that the National Association of Colored Women (NACW) was founded in Burroughs's home church (Nineteenth Street Baptist Church, Washington, DC) in 1896. The motto of NACW was "Lifting as We Climb," which was often quoted by delegates at gatherings of the WC. Baptist women figured prominently in the state and national meetings of the NACW, and their political activism throughout the first half of the twentieth century revealed a well-developed vision of racial and gender justice.[73]

The Woman's Convention also promoted racial uplift through self-help. Layten said, "we believe the Negro has largely got to work out his own destiny. Among the aids now given him those will yield best results that help him to help himself."[74] Black Baptist women taught that racial uplift required conformity to white middle-class social mores. Evelyn Brooks Higginbotham refers to this as the "politics of respectability." "The Baptist women's adherence to temperance, cleanliness of person and property, thrift, polite manners and sexual purity," she explained, "served to refute the logic behind their social subordination."[75] The WC accepted middle-class definitions of respectability in order to reject prevailing racial stereotypes. Virginia Broughton extolled the virtues of domesticity in a 1901 pamphlet: *The Development of Christian Homes: The Hope of the Negro Race*. "The hope of our people, and indeed, of the world," she asserted, "is proper marriages, and the establishing and developing of Christian homes. Civilization advances in proportion as the family life advances." Like their white sisters, black Baptist women generally accepted the teachings of the "cult of domesticity." Virtuous women were the key to Christian homes and thus civilization. "The atmosphere of home in a large measure determines the destiny of the children; hence it is of greatest importance that our mothers and wives be encouraged to put all the powers of their beings into making their homes the happiest places on earth for their husbands and children."[76] The WC promoted an idealized version of home life in order to affirm social equality and reject racial stereotypes, but they also perceived domesticity as an expression of spiritual devotion. Women demonstrated their Christian faith by being both exemplary employees and ideal mothers. Burroughs believed that domestic workers could consider themselves home missionaries in the most practical sense. "Personal service offers an opportunity for the Domestic Servant to impress her employer with the genuineness of the Christian religion by her daily conduct and fine demeanor," wrote Burroughs. "Domestic Service offers a real adventure of home mission conquest."[77]

White southern progressives working for interracial cooperation often began discussions about race with household issues because they represented an intersection of the interests of both black and white women.[78] Fannie Heck raised the issue of domestic labor as the point of contact between black and white women before the turn of the century. Heck's speeches represent some of the more positive attitudes toward race but are still infused with paternalism. In an 1895 speech to the WMU of North Carolina, Heck said, "Bear with me while I call your attention to one other form of mission work . . . what I call household missions—the work among the colored women in and around our homes. Again and again the necessity of organized work by Christian women among these neighbors of ours has been emphasized in the recommendations of the Home Board to the WMU. For this vast field each of us is a qualified worker and I would urge you to lay before your societies the practicability of undertaking some organized religious work for colored women."[79] Fannie Heck reminded her audience of southern women that "God is no respecter of persons."[80] "We need again and again to remind ourselves that Christ died for souls," exhorted Heck, "not Chinese, Mexicans, or dwellers in Brazil—but, souls, in whatever body or clime." Then Heck spoke bluntly about the issue. "The neighbor we term worthless, is of immortal value in God's eyes, and the servant who so tries and vexes you is one of the great multitude for whom Christ died."[81] In spite of her biases, Heck endeavored to communicate a basic message of spiritual equality.

RACIAL ATTITUDES IN WMU MAGAZINES

In the first two decades of the twentieth century, writers in WMU magazines discussed African Americans and racial issues under titles such as "The Negroes," "The Negroes in the Cities," or "Brothers in Black."[82] Since WMU magazines solicited writers from different states, the attitudes expressed ran the gamut from blatant white supremacy to a "romantic racialism," which embraced spiritual equality while defending segregation.[83] No articles in WMU magazines openly endorsed racial or social equality. Most narrate a painfully conflicted story of Christian ethics distorted by racial prejudice.

A 1911 article in *Our Mission Fields* illustrates the convoluted and contradictory reasoning of a Christian struggling valiantly to come to terms with the race issue, but who was ultimately unable to transcend the assumptions of her racist culture. When considering the "negro problem," the writer described solutions that she had heard proposed. "One possible solution is that the lesser might be crushed by the greater: the negro starved out and driven out by the white people." Then she hastened to add that "no great number of southern white people even for a moment" entertained this thought.[84] In spite of her protests, some southerners had speculated that African Americans would suffer a fate similar to that of Native Americans. Rufus Spain noted that there were a number of Baptist writers in the latter part of the nineteenth century who discussed the "Vanishing Negro." One suggested that the black race would "melt away before the white race as did the Indians"—"melt away" being a euphemism for slaughter and starvation. One popular myth purported that the birth rate among African Americans was falling. A Virginia Baptist predicted that in a century, "the negro race, dying at the present rate, will cease to be a disturbing factor in politics and society."[85]

The writer of *Our Mission Fields* continued her discussion of the race problem with a reference to lynching: "Though drastic punishments have been meted out to individual black men, often with a lawlessness which made those who participated in the deed animals, even this lawless element, always condemned by the better class, stopped with the single offender. The way of wholesale oppression will never be taken."[86] This quote is fraught with racist assumptions. First, the use of the words "punishment" and "offender" connotes her acceptance of popular belief that lynching victims were guilty of the charges leveled against them by white mobs. Second, even though she condemned mob violence, the writer excused the murder of an individual here and there by reasoning that random execution was better than "wholesale oppression," by which we can assume she meant genocide. Clearly she did not view the Jim Crow system as "wholesale oppression." Third, she associated the "lawless" "animals" with poor whites, asserting that mobs were "always condemned by the better class." Regardless of the evidence to the contrary, she perpetuated the myth that vigilante mobs were solely populated by poor whites and eschewed by wealthy elites.

The writer finally arrived at her own solution for the "negro problem." "What . . . is the most potent factor for good in the life of the colored race?" she queried. "We do not hesitate to say the black church. . . . It is far from perfect. Some tolerate sins and practices which put them to shame, but as a whole, it is the chief force for righteousness, originated and maintained by colored people. The colored preacher is the moral teacher. He has an influence unequaled. He stands for the religious as well as the political hopes of his people. As he goes, so go his people. He is no character for the comic-corner of the daily press. He is a leader of men, and as such is to be reckoned with."[87] Although the compliment is horribly backhanded, the writer did manage to praise the African American church and defend the authority of black clergymen. She exhorted her readers to offer respect rather than ridicule. Unfortunately, her essay devolved into heavy-handed racism in the next paragraph urging white women to use the black minister as an instrument of social control. "Reach him, teach him, and help him to preach not only theology, but the highest standard of living. Show him . . . the moral dignity of work, the degradation of wilful poverty. . . . Do this and you have gone far to solve the problem."[88]

One of the most interesting aspects of the 1911 article was a comment the author made by way of illustration. "Some of us may remember that our nurses of pro-bellum [*sic*] days told us, when our mothers were well out of hearing, that they were 'dark-skinned white ladies.' Be that as it may, the colored minister is, three times out of five, a dark-skinned Baptist preacher."[89] The offhanded nature of this anecdote suggests that she believed her readers shared a common experience of black nurses teaching racial equality. It also reveals that both nurses and children understood the teaching to be subversive. Then she softens the illustration for white readers with the phrase, "be that as it may." Basically she meant: whatever you may think about the equality of your black nurse, three out of five black ministers are equal to any white preacher. It is ironic that the writer alludes to racial equality to defend African American pastors in the same paragraph that she indicates he needs the help of white women in teaching and preaching to his own congregation.

In an earlier issue of *Our Mission Fields* a writer lamented the problem of "Negroes in the Cities": "We cannot overlook the crowded negro quarters which form a black fringe to every town and city. . . . There is in every Southern town of any size a large element of the colored population who live either from necessity or idleness just above the starvation line, crowded in ill kept houses and disregardful of many of the fundamental laws of decency and morals." The article blamed the moral and social condition of black men and women in the cities on poor parenting. "The present generation are [*sic*] the grandchildren of the freed slaves. Many of these, especially of the house-servant class, were true Christians, but themselves children in the upbringing of their children," explained one WMU writer. "The splendid old mammy with the worthless or degraded son or daughter is so common a sight that we become almost hopeless."[90] Not all articles were so condescending. Many were simply benign. The January 1910 issue of *Our Mission Fields* contains this myopic statement: "Southern Baptists fully recognize the obligation to preach the gospel to the black race which lives in the South and to behave toward them with kindness and helpfulness."[91]

The majority of references to black domestic workers in WMU magazines were overtly racist. The Young Woman's Auxiliary Program for August 1924, prepared by Mrs. I. E. Enlow, proclaimed that "great progress of the negro race has been made in the south in the last fifty years." This was quickly followed by the statement: "The Negro girl inherits certain weaknesses, such as lack of restraint, lack of honesty, a love of show and parade, and lack of initiative."[92] When discussing the "negro maid," Mrs. G. Harvey Clarke asked a series of questions designed to challenge domestic servants to higher Christian principles. "Does the colored girl realize that it is not fair to expect full pay for services when she has not rendered full service?" "Does the colored girl understand she is obligated not to be wasteful or dishonest with the belongings placed in her care?"[93] The nature of these questions assumed moral deficiency in domestic servants, and the corresponding questions for the white women merely suggested that "mistresses" be good moral examples and friendly guides to their employees. Occasionally, a slightly more progressive voice would emerge. One pamphlet circulated by WMU during the last decade of the nineteenth century endorsed spiritual equality. "Our bodies are diverse in color, but our souls, if they have any color, are by nature equally dark, and by the blood of the lamb, may be made equally white."[94]

Some of the more positive comments about race came from other denominational publications that WMU leaders simply reprinted. In 1912 WMU president Fannie Heck wrote Lulie Wharton, chair of Personal Service, recommending the publications on race relations by Methodist women.[95] Heck wrote: "I wonder if Dr. Pollard has seen the publications of the Southern Methodist Women along these lines. I think since our organizations so nearly parallel one another in work theirs would be interesting to him. Their recent publication or report of Commissions on work among colored women (a most difficult subject) has interested me."[96] *Royal Service* later published a number of these Methodist recommendations.[97] The anonymous author indicated that the Woman's Missionary Council of the Methodist Episcopal Church, South, had prepared a leaflet called "Plan for Cooperating with Negro Women" that contained "valuable suggestions, some of which we quote." Of course, none of the suggestions challenged segregation, but they instructed women to police the "equal" ideology of *Plessy v. Ferguson*. One recommendation proposed "looking into the needs of the negro public schools, requiring of the public authorities that their premises be kept sanitary, helping to secure colored teachers of a high grade, and favoring the introduction of industrial training." Another promoted "looking after the recreation (or lack of it) of negro children and young people; endeavoring to interest the Christian women of all denominations in securing for them opportunities for clean play in playgrounds." Still another urged school boards to allow the use of black schools as community centers. White women were admonished to visit jails and courts to ascertain "the measure of justice accorded negroes in the local courts, and by creating a sentiment for justice to youthful criminals whom wise treatment may reform." Mission-minded women should "study negro housing conditions and their bearing on sickness, inefficiency, and crime . . . insisting that local authorities enforce in the negro district the sanitary regulations of the community." The final recommendation encouraged the women to create: "in the local white community higher ideals in regard to the relation between the two races; by standing for full and equal justice in all departments of life; by endeavoring to secure for the backward race not only the full measure of development of which they are capable but the unmolested possession and enjoyment of all legitimate rewards of honest work; by standing, in short for the full application to the negroes and to ourselves of the Mosaic law of justice, 'Thou shalt love thy neighbor as thyself.'"[98] These statements, published in *Royal Service* in 1915, represent the most advanced thinking on the issue of race produced by white southern progressives. It is telling that the most progressive article in a Baptist publication was borrowed from southern Methodist women.

COMMISSION ON INTERRACIAL COOPERATION

A subtle shift in attitudes about race occurred in 1921 when WMU voted to participate with the Woman's Committee of the Commission on Interracial Cooperation (CIC). Founded in 1919 by Methodist minister Will W. Alexander, the CIC "emphasized approaching the volatile Southern race issue in a manner that combined social gospel Christianity with social science analyses of the problem."[99] The commission operated from 1919 until 1944 and made its most important contribution in the publication of a 1933 study on lynching. This study, *The Tragedy of Lynching*, documented that the majority of victims put to death were not guilty or even accused of violence against white women. The circulation of the study reduced the number of southern lynchings and exposed the popular justification for lynching to be false. The CIC did not, however, address segregation or disenfranchisement, which led critics to accuse the CIC of endorsing these practices.

In 1920, leading Methodist women, with financial support from the CIC, invited southern women to attend an interracial meeting in Memphis, Tennessee, to discuss race relations. Three of the one hundred women attending the first meeting were Baptist: Mrs. J. G. Jackson of Arkansas, Ella Broadus Robertson of Kentucky, and Mrs. Ashby Jones of Atlanta.[100] The Federal Council of Churches lauded the Memphis meeting as the "strongest force yet organized in the nation in behalf of the colored race."[101] Because of its success, the Woman's Committee became a formal part of the CIC. This ecumenical committee included women from the Presbyterian, Baptist, Disciples, Congregationalist, Methodist, and Episcopalian denominations as well as representatives from women's clubs. The meetings of the CIC and the Woman's Committee were integrated during a period of "growing racial antagonism."[102]

One year after the Memphis meeting, WMU named the Personal Service chair as their permanent representative on the Woman's Committee of the CIC and began featuring race relations more prominently in their publications. It was natural to classify race relations with the Personal Service division of WMU because the Personal Service Committee had earlier demonstrated an interest in the subject. The committee encouraged "work with the negro" in their Personal Service reports beginning in 1910, and "Work for the Negroes" appeared as a heading in the first statistical Personal Service report of 1915. Promotions of "inter-racial work" typically appeared in the Personal Service column of *Royal Service*, though it was mentioned in the mission study program on some occasions. Still the relationship with the CIC set the Personal Service department on a new path "to help change race prejudice into Christian sisterliness."[103] "The study of the plans of the Inter-Racial Commission will give us excellent ideas for helping the negro woman in her home life," reported the October 1922 issue of *Royal Service*, "and for enlisting her into community service for her people."[104]

Ella Broadus Robertson made suggestions for local WMU women in the January 1923 issue of *Royal Service*. "[Our] inter-racial work, our newest form of personal service, calls for every talent that we possess," said Robertson. She suggested that local women use their talents to form interracial committees to learn more about African American leaders in their communities. "We know scarcely anything about the educated negroes among us," admitted Robertson. "Yet they have now many excellent speakers and writers and trained men and women in various professions. We need to inform ourselves, to balance ourselves, to exert ourselves on behalf of the present-day negro."[105] Robertson recommended the writings of Methodist leader Lily Hammond for further reading. Robertson stated she preferred Hammond's book called *In the Vanguard of a Race* over Booker T. Washington's *Up from Slavery*. "Mrs. Hammond's recent pamphlet, 'Southern Women and Racial Adjustment' is so practical that every woman's missionary society should own a copy," insisted Robertson. Hammond stated in the pamphlet that white women in the South have come to a place "where we are willing to work in broader ways for common justice to the negroes." Robertson insisted that greater work for African Americans was necessary and concluded, "For though we have often been kind to them, we have seldom been just."[106]

In 1923 and 1924 the Personal Service column featured a report from the third meeting of the CIC. Emma M. Whitefield of Virginia related the spirit of "vibrant" good feeling, "hope and determination" that characterized the meeting. She summarized the message of speakers such as Dr. John Hope, president of Morehouse College, and Dr. George E. Haynes, who represented the Federal Council of Churches. Whitefield provided the most details on the speech of Haynes regarding domestic workers. Haynes spoke of an informal survey of households that his wife had taken. "The peace and happiness of the home," said Haynes, "is involved in the question of domestic service." Both "mistress and maid" are interested in better relations, and "hours and wages" cause the most strife between the two.[107] Haynes then reminded women that most domestic workers possessed less than a fourth grade education. If the "mistress" remembers this, "she will realize the need for education and training for colored girls."[108] WMU leaders were interested in the issue of domestic service and returned to the subject in a later column in *Royal Service* titled "The Negro Maid in the Home." The Virginia Commission for Inter-Racial Cooperation sent this article to WMU in an effort to encourage something "practical and fundamental in race relationship[s]." Predictably, the article recommended no direct action. It only encouraged women to "search their own hearts and ask themselves some timely questions."[109] After discussing the speakers, Whitefield recounted the reports of field workers for the CIC. Their achievements included the establishment of parks, libraries, playgrounds, vocational schools, orphanages, and a hospital for African Americans in the South.

The programs for black women recommended by the Personal Service Committee paralleled WMU's social service programs for other women and children in the South. WMU urged local women to establish Good Will Centers, Vacation Bible Schools, day nurseries, and missionary societies among "negroes" of the South. The committee asked local societies to report their work among African Americans. These were included with the other Personal Service statistics. Unfortunately, WMU grouped the efforts on behalf of the black population under one general title of "work for the negroes," and it is impossible to tell from the national statistics exactly how many of the various kinds of programs were conducted on the local level. From 1915 until 1925, an average of 9.7 percent of the local WMU societies reported "work for the negroes." The number seems large compared to the 5 percent of societies involved in settlement work. The definition of "work with negroes" varied from state to state and society to society. The December 1922 issue of *Royal Service* reported five states offering courses in mission study for black women. Oklahoma women appointed two members to their state Interracial Commission. South Carolina supported a "domestic science" teacher at Morris College. Texas invited "negro leaders" to attend the state convention and made contributions to the "negro Training School and Orphan's Home." In that same year Virginia merely communicated with their societies to "promote good feeling" between the races.[110] The chair of the Louisiana Personal Service Committee reported in 1923 that "very few [Louisiana] societies reach out to help the negro and foreigner." After reminding WMU members that "all races are equally dear to the Father in Heaven," she urged state societies to study the "negro and foreign communities in regard to housing, sanitation, education, morality and religion."[111]

In August 1924, *Royal Service* magazine dedicated the monthly mission study to interracial work under the title "The Negro in Our Midst." In this study the author urged readers to "think black." "If we could get on the other side of the picture and see ourselves as the colored people see us," she explained, "perhaps we would not talk so much about our negro problem and would understand a little better the white problem of the negro."[112] Six of the fifteen prayer calendar topics that month suggest prayer for cooperative efforts such as: "schools for Negroes in Chattanooga, Tenn."; "Negro mission schools in Illinois"; and "Committee on Program and Field Activities, negro work in Virginia."[113] The mission study that month was divided into sections beginning with "A Study in Black and White," which provided biblical support for segregation. "God 'made of one every nation of men to dwell on all the face of the earth, having determined . . . the bounds of their habitation.' These habitation bounds required physical differences which God in His wisdom has provided to each race. These differences must be respected."[114] Surprisingly, the author denied that "difference" necessitated white supremacy. "Although God so placed and so safeguarded the races of men He 'is no respecter of persons,'" she explained. Quoting from 1 Samuel 16:7, the writer continued, "'He seeth not as man seeth, for man looketh upon the outward appearance, but the Lord looketh on the heart.' If the black and white races view each other from God's standpoint they must be no respecter of *persons* and must act with perfect justice; if from man's standpoint they will see the *outward differences* and should have every respect for them." Then, with a typical Progressive Era appeal to science, the writer continued, "How then can we say that one race is inferior to another? Scientists are rejecting race as a basis of inherent worth and deny that any one group of human beings is either superior or inferior to any other."[115] The only reason that one race might appear superior to another is because of "environment, opportunity and education." The formidable voice of science, however, could not penetrate the walls of segregation. "Having been brought together by circumstances these two races can live in peace and harmony if God's righteousness worketh in them. Segregation cannot affect this harmony but fairness and justice to both races must be observed."[116]

WMU literature uniformly endorsed segregation, but explicit references to segregation laws were rare. The author of one article described a black man who left the South because there was "too much Jim Crowin' down here."[117] The WMU narrator of the story did not elaborate on the man's trouble with segregation. Later the writer placed a pro-segregation speech on the lips of a "middle-aged black woman." "The trouble with our two races is that we do not understand one another. You think we want social equality. We don't. We only want a fair chance to better our own people. You think we want to ride with you on the trains. We don't. We only want decent cars to ride in."[118] In this clear support for segregation WMU differed little from other members of the CIC. The CIC and other southern progressives understood justice in terms of securing "equal" institutions for blacks.

At first African American women worked for equal accommodations and did not immediately reject institutional segregation. Evelyn Brooks Higginbotham noted that the earliest protests by black Baptist women "attempted to hold white America accountable for 'equal' though separate, accommodations." In 1902 Nannie Helen Burroughs issued a public plea for white women of the South to speak out on their behalf. WMU historian Catherine Allen commented: "Surely she was asking, in an indirect but pleading way, for the help of the white women she knew best, Woman's Missionary Union. She got no answer. In fact, the next year's response from WMU was almost dead silence."[119] Three delegates from the Woman's Convention of the National Baptist Convention submitted a petition to the Interstate Commerce Commission demanding separate toilet facilities for black women in 1908. "We want a separate toilet for colored women, just as they have a separate toilet for white women. We want basins, soap and towel," Burroughs insisted in a speech to the Woman's Convention. "We pay the same fare and are entitled to the same treatment."[120] Their demands were ignored. In 1913 the Woman's Convention published a clear, concise statement of their demands titled "What We Want and What We Must Have," which called for equitable administration of segregation. According to the WC, black Americans needed:

1. Well built, sanitary dwellings . . . and streets that are paved and kept just as clean as others in the town are kept.
2. Equal accommodation on common carriers.
3. Franchise for every negro—North, South, East, and West—who is an intelligent and industrious citizen.
4. Equal treatment in the courts.
5. Equal division of school funds.
6. Lynching stopped.
7. Convict lease system broken up and better prisons and humane treatment of Negro prisoners.[121]

By 1918 leaders of the WC had abandoned appeals to "separate but equal," recognizing segregation as an instrument of white supremacy. "Nothing short of a repeal of the separate laws is going to bring permanent and satisfactory change in travel in those states where the law is in operation. . . . The very purpose of the 'Jim Crow' car law is to make such striking differences in accommodation and treatment as will suggest the inferiority of one race to the other and humiliate the race thus discriminated against."[122] WMU literature reveals no similar progression.

The consistent support of segregation in WMU literature is not remarkable. What is surprising about the August 1924 mission study is that it did introduce, however obliquely, themes of human rights and social justice. Having appealed to the Christian scriptures, the WMU author turned to the "civic scriptures."[123] "Through the thirteenth amendment to the constitution of the United States," declared the article, "the negro race in our country has a right to his place as a citizen." The mission study references the impressive war record of the "American negro." "Not one negro was found guilty of disloyalty. Hundreds of them received individual and regimental citations for bravery." The implication is that African Americans had earned their place as citizens. Then, using a time-worn tactic of Baptist women, the writer quotes an anonymous source. "Says one writer: 'The great feature which distinguishes a Christian nation from pagan nations is that the latter believed and acted on the principle that some men are born to be "always up" while others were destined to be "always down." In a Christian nation there are no impassable gulfs fixed by the accident of race. If America is a Christian nation the negro, if he meets the requirements of American citizenship, has his place in American life and there is not an intelligent American living who does not know what that place ought to be.'" Likely this was a speech made during the proceedings of the CIC. This anonymous quote is the nearest any WMU writer came to acknowledging civil rights for African Americans.

This writer rested her case for racial justice with the one warning designed to strike fear into the hearts of devout Christians: judgment day. "In God's plan for the races it would seem that He is calling upon the white man to guard the rights of the black race. . . . The cause of the negro is not up for a hearing. It is the white man who will come to judgment. . . . The principles of the Golden Rule and the Sermon on the Mount apply alike to the black and white man everywhere."[124] This statement marks a sharp departure from the earlier southern attitudes about race. Baptist pastor Richard Furman's famous 1822 defense of slavery, lauded by Southern Baptists for over a century, explicitly denied any application of the golden rule that would undermine slavery. Now in 1924 the writer included "black and white men everywhere" in the biblical category of "neighbor" and warned southerners that they would be judged if they failed to champion the cause of the black race.

The mission study also addressed one of the most egregious violations of human rights: lynching. "The [CIC] report was especially encouraging," stated Whitefield, "which noted the reduction of the number of lynchings and the efforts of officials to enforce laws protecting life and prevention of mob violence between the races."[125] The August 1924 mission study on race commended the work of the Woman's Committee of the CIC for working to "enact laws to prevent lynching and for the punishment of lynchers," also that the laws already existing be enforced.[126] The 1927 Week of Prayer for Home Missions included a prayer about the "disgrace of lynching." In that same year WMU published a pamphlet called *Racial Revelations* by T. B. Maston.[127] In the following years Maston would become the conscience of Southern Baptists on the issue of race. At Southwestern Baptist Theological Seminary, where he served as professor of ethics, he persistently worked for desegregation.

The work of the Personal Service Department with the Commission for Interracial Cooperation placed WMU leadership squarely in line with the more liberal white voices of the South. The commission maintained close ties with both the Federal Council of Churches and the Southern Sociological Congress.[128] WMU leadership maintained its affiliation with the CIC until it was dissolved in 1943. "Long before the Southern Baptist Convention took notice," argued Catherine Allen, "most state WMUs officially endorsed the commission and participated in forming state affiliates of the Woman's Committee."[129] Although Southern Baptist women constituted the most conservative element on the Woman's Committee, their presence in the commission was a liberal move for Southern Baptists. The racial attitudes of the CIC are reflected in the pages of WMU magazines read by thousands of Southern Baptist women. Allen notes that of the twenty-three founders of the Association of Southern Women for the Prevention of Lynching formed in 1930, four were Southern Baptist women.[130]

CONCLUSION

Nannie Helen Burroughs and Annie Armstrong forged a professional relationship that produced meaningful cooperation between black and white women in the south. Burroughs's dynamic personality shaped the Woman's Convention of the NBC from its founding in 1900 until her death in 1961. Throughout her tenure as a leader in WMU, Armstrong maintained close ties with National Baptist women and worked diligently to aid them in founding an independent women's missionary society. She provided moral and financial support for their missionary endeavors. When Armstrong left WMU in 1906 the impulse for racial cooperation waned. Fifteen years later Southern Baptist women joined the Woman's Committee of the Commission for Interracial Cooperation, bringing a renewed emphasis on race relations.

From 1888 to 1930 the missionary literature of Southern Baptist women expressed a wide range of attitudes toward African Americans—from blatant white supremacy to romantic racism. After 1921 writers issued condemnations of lynching and urged readers to behave more justly toward black citizens. Southern Baptist women understood justice to mean ensuring "equal" accommodations within the system of segregation. Like other southern progressives, Baptist women firmly believed that segregation provided the best answer for race relations in the South. Not once did a WMU publication challenge the system of Jim Crow.

Burroughs once stated that "the southern white woman . . . holds the key to the solution of the race problem in Dixie. Her word is law and gospel to southern white men."[131] Burroughs was not unaware of the issues of power and gender faced by white women; still she remained convinced that if white women exerted themselves for their black sisters, if gender could trump race, then huge strides could be made in race relations in the South. The Association of Southern Women for the Prevention of Lynching formed in 1930 demonstrated the possibilities of her conviction. Sadly, Southern Baptist women did not share Burroughs's vision of gender solidarity and very few, if any, successfully mastered the ability to "think black." Race divided them more profoundly than gender could ever unite them. Charlotte Hawkins Brown, an African American educator and activist in North Carolina, lamented the divisions between black and white women in 1922: "What a chasm there is between us, deep, fathomless! The Negro woman wonders if there is a place on earth where she can stand and breathe freely and think in terms of a woman."[132] This deep, fathomless chasm defined race relations throughout the period. Although Burroughs and the women of the National Baptist Convention worked diligently to build bridges, ultimately Southern Baptist women proved to be unreliable allies.

CHAPTER FIVE

Saving Society

The Personal Service Department and the Social Gospel

IN 1909 WMU PRESIDENT FANNIE HECK established a department within WMU called Personal Service. The department's stated purpose was to apply the "religion of Jesus Christ" to the "social problems of the day," essentially introducing a new emphasis on social action into the formal programming of WMU.[1] The WMU Annual Report of 1913 explained the view of their Department of Personal Service. "When a man loves God he is saved; when he loves his neighbor society is saved." The author of the report further explained: "These two great needs—the need for personal salvation and the need for personal service in the interests of society—are embodied in the intention and design of religion."[2] By couching social action in biblical language, WMU leaders hoped to commend not only social reform but also social salvation to their conservative southern membership. Individual leaders of the WMU such as Fannie E. S. Heck, Maud Reynolds McLure, and Lulie Pollard Wharton endeavored to introduce the values of progressivism and the ideas of the social gospel to their constituents. These women introduced progressive ideas to Southern Baptist women through training manuals, educational programs, and publications.

The following pages offer evidence that WMU leaders, particularly those engaged with Personal Service, embraced progressivism and at times openly endorsed the social gospel. It is important to note one key caveat: while it is certain that progressivism shaped key WMU leaders, this did not mean that progressivism penetrated to all the rank and file members of WMU. As a denomination Southern Baptists were, essentially, socially and theologically conservative. WMU leaders had to proceed with caution. The Progressive Era assumption that Christians should be engaged in reform hinged on the more liberal social gospel belief in social sin. This focus on social problems introduced a theological conundrum. Personal Service leaders insisted that social reform and social work fit within the historic mission of WMU. Yet, Baptist women had organized WMU specifically to support the work of Southern Baptist mission boards whose singular goal was *individual* salvation—not the salvation of society. WMU expanded their doctrine of salvation beyond individual conversion when they challenged southern women to view social reform as religious work. While Personal Service leaders consistently argued that their goals were consistent with the conversion model of salvation, the fact remained that Personal Service objectives potentially undermined conservative theology. Like most social gospel writers, WMU leaders believed they were recovering a broader application of the gospel, not departing from Southern Baptist orthodoxy. In spite of these theological tensions, WMU succeeded in creating programs, institutions, and systems to support social reform. Changing minds proved to be a little more difficult.

This chapter explores the social gospel and Personal Service in three major sections. It begins with a description of the social gospel, its key leaders, and the central tenets of social gospel theology. Second, the chapter discusses points of contact between Southern Baptist women and the social gospel. There were some social gospel sources (albeit limited) within their own denominational circles. Baptist women exchanged ideas with other Protestant women and encountered both progressivism and the social gospel through their participation with such organizations as the Woman's Christian Temperance Union and the Southern Sociological Congress. The third and largest section of this chapter narrates the history of the Personal Service Department, including its organization on the national and local level, its methodologies, and program training. Personal Service leaders closely identified their programs with the field of professional social work and promoted social reform as an integral component of their missionary enterprise. The department urged women on the state and local levels to develop social reform goals and to adopt social work practices. A regular column in the missionary magazine, *Our Mission Fields* (later *Royal Service*), touted the work of Personal Service, celebrated social work, and quoted social gospel theologians. WMU leaders produced neighborhood surveys, reading lists, and Bible studies designed to promote social reform. Occasionally these publications explicitly endorsed the social gospel.

THE SOCIAL GOSPEL

In the summer of 1886, a young minister named Walter Rauschenbusch accepted a call to pastor a German Baptist congregation in New York City. It was an inauspicious beginning to his ministerial career. In a letter to an old friend he bluntly described the situation: "The church is not large, about 125 members; . . . The building is old-fashioned, inconvenient and rather ugly, situated in a tough West Side neighborhood."[3] Second German Baptist Church of New York City stood on West Forty-Fifth Street in the neighborhood known as Hell's Kitchen. This appointment brought him face to face with some of the most devastating social problems of the Progressive Era—from child labor to the overcrowded tenements that were "breeding grounds for numerous contagious and fatal diseases, including Typhoid fever and Cholera."[4] On Sundays Rauschenbusch endeavored to preach a message of God's love to men, women, and children living in desperate circumstances. A biographer noted that "the stark poverty that he observed in his church and in his New York neighborhood had an indelible effect on both his theology and his personality."[5] As a pastor, Rauschenbusch aided the elderly, sat with the sick and dying, and frequently officiated funerals. Troubled by the abject poverty and host of other social problems his parishioners faced, Rauschenbusch soon came to believe that the church needed to address these devastating conditions. He believed the Gospel applied to the present life as well as the life to come. Soon Rauschenbusch cultivated close relationships with other ministers in his community. They read books together, discussed theology, and began to publish articles proposing ways the church could address current problems. In 1907 Rauschenbusch's published his mature views in *Christianity and the Social Crisis.* This book was "one of the best selling non-fiction" works of the era and marked "the beginning of a new chapter in the history of American Protestantism."[6] *Christianity and the Social Crisis* focused the attention of American churches and the American press on a growing theological movement known as the social gospel. Eleven years later, Rauschenbusch provided the movement with a systematic theology in *A Theology for the Social Gospel.*

Rauschenbusch was not the first minister to apply the Gospel to social problems. Over a decade before Rauschenbusch accepted his first pastorate, the Congregationalist minister Washington Gladden became the religious editor of the *New York Independent.* In his news column Gladden exposed the corrupt political practices of New York's infamous Boss Tweed. He continued to challenge social injustice as a pastor and writer in Massachusetts where, to the consternation of mill owners, he encouraged local workers to unionize. Without collective bargaining, Gladden maintained that the work force would be "steadily forced down toward starvation and misery."[7] Gladden published hundreds of poems, articles, books, and essays. Historians have extolled Washington Gladden as the "father of the American social gospel," while Walter Rauschenbusch ranks as the leading theologian for the movement.[8]

Protestant theologians across denominational lines added their voices to that of Gladden and Rauschenbusch. Josiah Strong and Graham Taylor gave voice to the social gospel among the Congregationalists. Unitarians were identified with the movement in the person of Francis Greenwood Peabody. Samuel Zane Batten and Shailer Mathews endorsed the social gospel from the ranks of Northern Baptists. Frank Mason North, Harry F. Ward, and Francis J. McConnell preached the new theology among Northern Methodists. Presbyterians were represented by Charles Stelzle and Episcopalians by Richard Ely. Such works as Francis Greenwood Peabody's *Jesus Christ and the Social Question* (1900), Lyman Abbott's *The Ethical Teachings of Jesus* (1910), and Rauschenbusch's *The Social Principles of Jesus* (1916) reflect the growing emphasis on Christ's teachings as the basis of social theory. "The new civilization, with its social problems, has led us to search for the social teachings of Jesus, which had been long neglected," explained Josiah Strong, "and we find that those teachings fit modern conditions as a key fits its lock."[9] Much of the early scholarship on the social gospel focused on these men. More recent scholarship on the social gospel illuminates the diversity of social gospel voices and points out the blind spots of the movement—particularly regarding race and gender.[10]

Social gospel theologians emphasized the social teachings of Jesus, social sin and salvation, the immanence of God and His Kingdom, and faith in human progress. They insisted that the church needed to broaden its theology to encompass social as well as individual concepts of sin and salvation. Shailer Mathews defined the social gospel as the "application of the teaching of Jesus and the total message of Christian salvation to society, the economic life, and social institutions, . . . as well as individuals."[11] For Mathews, this was "not a new gospel, but the message of the saving power of God as applied to society as well as individuals."[12] Rauschenbusch also insisted that this was not a new innovation. "The social gospel is the old message of salvation," he explained, "but enlarged and intensified." While the individualistic gospel had "taught us to see the sinfulness of every human heart" and "inspired us with faith in the willingness and power of God to save every soul that comes to him," this individualistic faith was insufficient.[13] "It has not given us an adequate understanding of the sinfulness of the social order and its share in the sins of all individuals within it. It has not evoked faith in the will and power of God to redeem the permanent institutions of human society from their inherited guilt of oppression and extortion. Both our sense of sin and our faith in salvation have fallen short of the realities under its teaching."[14] As an alternative to strictly individualistic theology, Rauschenbusch proposed the social gospel. "The social gospel seeks to bring men under repentance for their collective sins," he said, "and to create a more sensitive and more modern conscience. It calls on us for the faith of the old prophets who believed in the salvation of nations."[15] "Sin is a social force. It runs from man to man along the lines of social contact. Its impact on the individual becomes most overwhelming when sin is most completely socialized. Salvation, too, is a social force. It is exerted by groups that are charged with divine will and love. . . . A full salvation demands a Christian social order which will serve as the spiritual environment of the individual."[16] One of the foundational principles of the social gospel was the "explicit and consistent recognition of the social nature of personal existence," a theme borrowed from Horace Bushnell.[17]

Rauschenbusch lamented that despite tremendous political changes in the world—the collapse of monarchical systems, the rise of democracy—the "church has not broadened its ethical teaching. . . . It still confines its ethics to the personal and family life."[18] Rauschenbusch cited the church's obsession with private concerns such as "drunkenness, sexual impurity, profanity, Sabbath-breaking, dancing, card-playing, and theater going."[19] He and his fellow theologians believed the church needed to press beyond these private issues. "The redemption of the social order is, then, the problem now before us," insisted Gladden.[20] Solving the problem required a theological perception of the social order, a soteriology capable of addressing corporate as well as individual sin. As Gladden stated, "The conviction of social sin is the beginning of social righteousness."[21] Although they firmly embraced the need for individual conversion, these ministers believed that the church must also preach the need for institutional and social redemption.

Social gospel writers also emphasized the immanence of God and God's concern for the human condition. Washington Gladden explained God's immanence in terms of natural revelation. "Nature, as we have seen, is instinct with Reason, and the Reason which is revealed in Nature is only another name for God. It is the immanent God, the Eternal Reason, who has been patiently disclosing himself to us in the world round about us, and thus cleansing our minds from the crude and superstitious conceptions with which in our ignorance and fear we had invested him."[22] By emphasizing God's nearness, social gospel theologians simultaneously embraced the growth and progress of human intellect. People were being freed from "crude and superstitious conceptions," from "ignorance and fear" by the process of natural revelation. God's nearness signaled the dawning of a new day for humanity to understand and participate in the will of God.

Rauschenbusch pointed to Jesus's teaching as evidence of God's nearness. "When Jesus spoke of God as our Father, he democratized God himself. . . . By raising the value of the human soul and its life on the one side, and by bringing God down close to us as our Father, he [Jesus] laid the religious foundation for modern democracy and anticipated the craving of the modern spirit."[23] Rauschenbusch creatively linked the incarnation to American democracy, effectively marrying liberal theology to broader themes in the Progressive Era. Many social gospel advocates perceived their work with the poor and the reshaping of society as an attempt to apply not only the gospel but also democracy to every level of society. Jane Addams described her settlement work as an attempt to "interpret democracy in social terms."[24]

Another aspect of the social gospel was its emphasis on human progress, the "latent perfectibility in human nature."[25] The idea of human progress, absorbed from evolutionary theory, featured most visibly in the emphasis on the coming Kingdom of God on earth. Rauschenbusch believed the Kingdom of God was the "first and the most essential dogma of the Christian faith" and the "lost social ideal of Christendom."[26] For Rauschenbusch, the notion of the Kingdom of God was an earthly ethical system instituted and empowered by Christ to bring social redemption to the entire human race. "The kingdom of God, my friend, is a social conception. It is a conception of this life here of ours, because Jesus says: 'Thy kingdom come, thy will be done' here. It is something that is here on this earth; that quietly pervades all humanity; that is always working toward the perfect life of God. . . . It is a matter of community life. The perfect community of men—that would be the kingdom of God."[27] This perfect community constituted the reign of God on earth that would change the world, "making it righteous, making it habitable, making it merciful, making it brotherly."[28] Beneath the banners of righteousness, mercy, and brotherhood, social gospel proponents crusaded for economic justice, the regulation of industry, humane working conditions, and to abolish child labor. They believed that social justice would usher in the Kingdom of God on earth.

The social gospel was not limited to theological abstractions. Its ideas were adopted into the programs of major American denominations and institutions. By 1908 the Congregational, Episcopal, Presbyterian (North), and Northern Baptist churches had all taken steps to incorporate the social gospel.[29] In that year the Methodist Church boldly affirmed the social gospel by designating the Federation of Social Service an official agency of the church and by adopting a very progressive "Social Creed." Also in 1908, the chief institutional expression of the northern ecumenical movement—the Federal Council of the Churches of Christ in America (FCC)—organized in Philadelphia. The stated purpose of the FCC was "to secure a larger combined influence for the Churches of Christ in all matters affecting the moral and social condition of the people, so as to promote the application of the law of Christ in every relation of human life."[30] When the council met officially in December 1908, delegates were present from more than thirty denominations, making the FCC the "most representative body in American Protestant history."[31] From its infancy the Federal Council distinguished itself as an advocate for social justice and a liberal voice in Protestantism.

The Chautauqua Assembly also provided a platform for the social gospel. Chautauqua began as a Sunday school training institute and grew to showcase a broad spectrum of cultural and educational issues during the Progressive Era. Although social topics featured prominently on the Chautauqua schedule during most seasons, attention to the social gospel began during the season of 1889 when Richard T. Ely, Washington Gladden, Lyman Abbott, and H. H. Boyesen all lectured on social issues.[32] A tradition of preaching, called daily devotionals, was established at Chautauqua. These devotions drew social gospel orators from across the country. A visiting minister would serve as chaplain for the week, preaching on Sunday morning and for the five days following. Shailer Mathews conducted daily devotionals on many occasions and directed the Department of Religious Work for the Assembly. Washington Gladden and Charles Stelzle also filled the pulpit at Chautauqua along with Francis G. Peabody, Josiah Strong, Graham Taylor, and Francis McConnell.[33]

The social gospel provided a theological framework for social reform that intersected with other intellectual developments of the period. Scholars began applying scientific methodologies to the study of people in community, giving rise to new fields of learning such as sociology, anthropology, and political science. Lewis Gould noted that one of the themes of the Progressive Era was "the application of scientific ideas to social problems."[34] During the last half of the nineteenth century, a close relationship existed between social scientists, philanthropists, and social reformers. For example, Jane Addams's social settlement, Hull House, served as a social laboratory of sorts, providing facts for social scientists to study. Social gospel advocates Richard Ely and Josiah Strong can be numbered among the social scientists. Charles Hopkins asserted that "social science, social work, and social reform became the mutual partners of the social gospel. All were the fruits of an age of scientific advance, moral striving, social confusion, and optimism."[35] Social work was one of the direct results of the confluence of social gospel theology and social science methodology. Rauschenbusch celebrated the emergence of social work programs in 1912. "Social workers are in the direct line of apostolic succession," he wrote. "Like the Son of Man they seek and save the lost."[36] Southern Baptist women embraced social work with both arms, and a school of social work would become one of their most enduring legacies.

SOURCES OF THE SOCIAL GOSPEL FOR SOUTHERN BAPTIST WOMEN

Where did Southern Baptist women encounter the social gospel? First, some sympathy for the social gospel did exist in the SBC. In Southern Baptist circles the most likely sources for social gospel ideas were the state Baptist social service committees. Southern Baptist progressives created these committees to address social problems at the state and south-wide levels. Most of the committees were initially formed to fight "demon rum." The SBC and state temperance committees gradually expanded to address a broader range of social problems under the title "social service" or "social action." Studies reveal that "every state [social service] committee gave allegiance to the social gospel at some time or other."[37] For example, the 1912 minutes of the Baptist General Association of Virginia include a report on social service that begins with an extensive quote from Rauschenbusch's *Christianity and the Social Crisis*. After citing the problems of political corruption, labor conflicts, poverty, oppression, and immigration, the committee recommended that the churches play a role in eradicating these problems. "The church stands for the consummation of the work that Christ came to inaugurate on earth. The fundamental purpose of Christ's coming was the establishment of the kingdom of God, by which is meant 'the regenerating of human relations and reconstituting them in accordance with the will of God—the transforming of the life on earth in harmony with the life in heaven.'"[38] The social service committee in Alabama encouraged Baptists to "take the social gospel seriously and enter upon a crusade to achieve its meaning in human society."[39]

Conversely, most state committees also rejected the social gospel at some point. The Texas Baptist Social Service Commission insisted: "Social service is temporal and material; the work of the church is eternal and spiritual. Social service seeks to improve the housing problem in the slums, the church points to mansions in the skies."[40] In 1920, Virginia Baptists concluded, "The Baptist attitude towards all social reform work and services is that the unadulterated gospel preached and accepted solves all social problems."[41] Whether for or against the social gospel, no state committee conducted an active social service program.

A proposal by the Baptist World Alliance in 1913 prompted the first convention-wide commission on social service called the Southern Baptist Social Service Commission. It consisted of seven members with W. Louis Poteat as chairman. Poteat's first report expressed a full endorsement of the social gospel. Under his leadership, the commission possessed great potential as a social gospel agency, but it suffered from lack of funds and an obscure assignment. Its duties were unspecified beyond the annual convention report. A year later, the Social Service Commission was combined with the Southern Convention's Temperance Committee under new leadership, and the influence of the social gospel diminished.

Sociology courses in the two Southern Baptist seminaries introduced another stream of social gospel influence to Southern Baptist life. Charles S. Gardner was the first professor of sociology at Southern Seminary in Louisville, Kentucky. Historian Paul Harvey claims that Gardner was "the most articulate exponent of Southern Baptist social consciousness." He was "a prototypical social gospeler rather than . . . a minister with a rhetorical recognition of and vague concern for social problems."[42] Gardner's work, *The Ethics of Jesus and Social Progress*, is the only full-length treatment of the social gospel by a Southern Baptist. Gardner believed that the Christian social ideal required more than basic services of protection and order from the state. He insisted the government should "regulate wealth, provide welfare services, and abolish conditions that produce crime and poverty."[43] Gardner attributed many of society's problems to unregulated capitalism and felt that the ethic of competition ran counter to Christian principles of love, service, and cooperation. J. M. Price taught sociology at Southwestern Baptist Theological Seminary in Fort Worth, Texas, for ten years. Price addressed aspects of the social gospel in his book, *Christianity and Social Problems* (1928). Although more conservative than Gardner, Price endorsed government regulation of business, legislation for improving labor conditions, and public ownership of utilities and natural resources.[44] Southern Baptist women attended classes at both Southern Seminary and Southwestern Seminary. They had access to these sociology courses and the books written by Price and Gardner.

Nearly all of the theologians associated with Southern Baptist Theological Seminary in Louisville, Kentucky, attended academic conferences with Rauschenbusch, Mathews, and other Northern Baptist advocates of liberal theology. From 1881 until 1913 Baptist theologians, North and South, met together annually at a Baptist Congress where they presented academic papers on a given theme.[45] These Southern Baptist scholars often participated in panel discussions with the Northern Baptist liberals and debated a broad range of issues including immigration (1888), the ethics of competition in business (1906), criminal justice systems (1910), poverty (1911), and the implications of democracy on religious life (1912). Most Southern Baptist academics were aware of the social gospel, but few of them publicly identified themselves with this movement. Among those Southern Baptists who can be counted as progressives, some still rejected the social gospel because they disagreed with the theology, plain and simple—even though they supported social reform. They represented the more conservative wing of southern progressivism. Other Southern Baptist progressives embraced and promoted the social gospel. They sought to reform southern society because they believed social institutions could be sinful and counted social reform as a legitimate work of the church. These more liberal Baptists remained in the minority of their conservative denomination. As I mentioned already, a small group of Southern Baptist women attended classes at Southern Baptist Theological Seminary. Other women discovered the social gospel through family connections to faculty or through relationships with the seminary community in Louisville.

WMU leaders also encountered the social gospel through relationships with other Protestant women. Southern Baptist women established close working relationships with evangelical women through women's clubs, charity work, and interdenominational missionary societies. One of the most powerful women in the life of WMU, Annie Armstrong, participated in charity work in Baltimore and stayed abreast of the missionary activities of other denominations. For example, Armstrong kept scrapbooks that she used for preparing her own talks and studies on missions. In those books are clippings from such groups as the Presbyterian Missionary Society; the Woman's Club at Chautauqua; Episcopal Theological School, Cambridge; and the Woman's Christian Temperance Union (WCTU). Edith Campbell Crane, who followed Armstrong as corresponding secretary of WMU, served as a delegate to the 1910 World Missionary Conference in Edinburgh. She brought back a "new vision of the powers and possibilities of the Union" from the trip to Scotland and shared "the purpose and ideals of this great meeting" with local women.[46]

Fannie Heck participated consistently in interdenominational endeavors. In 1900 she attended the Ecumenical Missionary Conference held in New York City and was impressed with the broad plans for ecumenical cooperation discussed at the meeting. In a letter to her mother she reported: "It is proposed to have a great 'International, Interdenominational Confederation of Women's Mission Boards.' This Confederation through its national committee to propose a uniform and broad course of mission study covering seven years—International mission lessons; besides this to recommend and superintend missionary-book publications, gather libraries, etc." Heck was frustrated when she realized that other Southern Baptist women, who would be gathering for the WMU national meeting in Hot Springs later that same year, would not be exposed to these themes. "When I heard all this, so much what I have felt the women needed," she explained, "my heart grew heavy to think no member of that union who could take active steps was here, who would keep this, or any of the other great world movements before them—that not one single echo of this meeting will be heard at Hot Springs in the woman's meeting."[47] As a result, Heck wrote a circular pamphlet titled "A Great Event," which summarized the important points of the Ecumenical Conference. In her concluding remarks, Heck endorsed an ecumenical spirit. "How shall we advance now? One universal answer, which ran through every session . . . was, by the closer union of the churches at home and abroad. This did not imply that we should be less true Baptists, or less loyal Episcopalians, Methodists, or Presbyterians, but as different branches of the one great army of the Lord, we should with solid front march on to victory."[48] Baptist papers celebrated the ecumenical meetings by publishing speeches and articles. The Baptist paper of North Carolina, *Biblical Recorder*, printed Fannie Heck's 1911 address to the WMU of North Carolina describing the Missionary Conference in Edinburgh and the Jubilee Year of Women's Missionary Organizations in the United States.[49] The jubilee was particularly significant because WMU actively encouraged Southern Baptist women to participate in this celebration on the local level. Edith Campbell Crane, corresponding secretary of WMU from 1907 to 1911, begged the central committee of the ecumenical jubilee celebration for a "Southern Extension Jubilee Tour" featuring speakers from the Episcopal Board of Missions, Congregational Church, Christian Woman's Board of Missions, Missionary Union, Northern and Southern Presbyterian Churches, and the Congregational Church. Crane's pleas were heard. The resulting tour was described in the Foreign Mission Board's *Foreign Mission Journal*.[50] Although the subject matter of these lecture tours was missions, the interaction among the women provided a foundation for a broader exchange of ideas.

In the 1917 annual meeting WMU adopted a resolution concerning Personal Service, "that we study the policies and methods of kindred missionary and social service organizations, adapting those best suited to our aim of preventing and eradicating community evils."[51] Southern Baptist female leadership exchanged ideas with Southern Methodist women more than with any other group outside their own denomination. John Patrick McDowell's monograph, *The Social Gospel in the South: The Woman's Home Mission Movement in the Methodist Episcopal Church, South, 1886–1939*, demonstrates that Southern Methodist women embraced the social gospel in its entirety.[52] Lucinda Helm, the force behind the Methodist Woman's Home Mission Society, insisted: "A perfect religious hope must include not only eternal life for the individual, but the establishment of the Kingdom of God for humanity."[53]

When WMU formally organized in 1888, they met at the Broad Street Methodist Church in Richmond while the men met at the First Baptist Church of Richmond a block away. Since national WMU meetings were held simultaneously with the Southern Baptist Convention, the women often met in Methodist or Presbyterian churches.[54] This was the practice during state denominational meetings as well. For example, the WMU of North Carolina alternated between Methodist and Presbyterian churches from its founding until 1905 when they decided to meet separately from the state convention.[55] Baptist women read and studied the work of Methodist women on both the local level and the national level of leadership. In 1894, Annie Armstrong wrote a note to the secretary of the Sunday School Board, T. B. Bell, confirming an order for "5000 cuts" from the Methodist Episcopal Church, South. Armstrong noted, "I would be glad to have as large . . . a selection of their missionary and other first class cuts as either you or the Publishing House shall be willing to furnish and I can send them on ahead to our contributors as a basis of information for their stories, etc."[56] Evidently Baptist and Methodist women were sharing information in their magazines.

WMU leadership also benefited from the experience of the Methodist women in applied ministry. Methodist women began social ministries in southern cities around the turn of the twentieth century.[57] They were the first denomination in the South to establish social settlements, a program designed to accomplish urban reform by establishing a permanent presence in underprivileged neighborhoods. Prior to the establishment of the Baptist settlement work at the WMU Training School, students learned methods of city missions at the Wesley House in Louisville.[58] When the Personal Service Committee began preparing a manual to help local women establish Baptist settlement houses in cities across the South, they turned to *The City Mission Manual of the Methodist Episcopal Church, South*. WMU adapted this manual for their needs and wrote an acknowledgment to the Methodists in the bibliography.[59] Local Baptist women studied the work of their Methodist sisters as well. The superintendent of missions for the WMU of the Birmingham Baptist Association lamented in 1913 that she had not accomplished all she wished because "to attend the meetings of our Executive Board, visit three societies, and take one visit to investigate the work which the Methodist women are doing at Avondale is the best I could do."[60]

WMU leaders genuinely respected the contributions Methodist women made to ministry and considered them fellow workers in the Kingdom of God. One of the last stories Fannie Heck wrote in the year before she died was titled "The Pageant of the Golden Rule." The story was later turned into a pamphlet and advertised as a "Christmas Story" to be recited at local society meetings.[61] The setting is a futuristic, Christian America in which the Golden Rule had been applied throughout society. The tone is postmillennial and utopian. Heck's narrator explains what brought about the change in society. "That is the great lesson we learned from the awful European War. We found that we could not just label money Christian and send it out to make Christians; we had to show what kind of men and women, countries and states Christianity made. . . . Soon we demonstrated . . . that 'right dealings pay,' that 'godliness is profitable.' . . . The merchants began to take up our methods." Heck's narrator continues by naming two specific institutions that had set the example for all of society: Good Will Centers and Wesley Houses. These are the settlement programs of the Baptist and Methodist women. Thus, in Heck's dream, the Baptist and Methodist women worked side by side to usher in the Kingdom of God, to forge a Christian nation.

Some WMU leaders encountered progressivism and the social gospel directly through social reformers and social reform organizations. The work of Jane Addams at Hull House was of particular interest to WMU leadership, although the leaders were consistently critical of her lack of emphasis on religion. In notes for a speech, Fannie Heck praised Jane Addams, the "first citizen of Chicago," not because she was a "suffragists" or "society" woman but because Addams and her colleagues were "putting their hearts and lives below the lowest and lifting."[62] In 1912 Fannie Heck wrote to Lulie Wharton of her initial impressions of Hull House. "I have read this summer, *Seventy Years at Hull House*. The point of view is interesting but I can but believe that Miss Addams has left religion far too much out of her plans."[63] Three years later Maud Reynolds McClure, principal of the WMU Training School, wrote to Fannie Heck regarding her research in social service methods. "We spent much time at Hull House but came away feeling that without the love of Christ as the dynamic . . . such work as that of Hull House is a failure," she reported. McClure and Emma Leachman also investigated both Baptist and Presbyterian church work in Chicago and insisted: "these were much more to our liking."[64] In spite of McClure and Leachman's disappointment with Hull House's approach, they borrowed Addams's ideas for their social ministry. "In one of the clubs at Hull House we heard them planning for gardens in the outskirts of the city where small plots were to be rented at $1.50 a season," they confided to Fannie Heck. "Later we may be able to get the city to let us use some ground in this way." The physical facilities of the settlements in Chicago also made an impression on the women. "The thing that has taken definite shape as the result of our Chicago trip is our resolve to have a large room suitable for play parties, entertainment of various kinds, etc."[65]

Most WMU members were enthusiastic about the Woman's Christian Temperance Union. Texas state WMU leaders resolved: "We must heartily endorse the W.C.T.U. and Anti-Saloon League, the two organizations whose nonpartisan and nonfactional work commends them to every anti-saloon Texan."[66] Annie Armstrong actively promoted the WCTU. Armstrong kept a notebook on temperance with clippings concerning the WCTU and copies of their pamphlets. Of particular interest were the pamphlets she kept from the WCTU's Department of Social Purity. This was one of the more progressive plans of the WCTU aimed at eliminating prostitution.[67] The WCTU department presented prostitution as a problem affecting evangelical women because of the danger of sexually transmitted diseases. At first, the department sponsored programs to rescue individual women. In the 1890s, the Department of Social Purity began lobbying to raise the legal age of consent that remained in some states as low as ten years old.[68] This WCTU emphasis on "social purity" may explain the questions that appeared in a WMU social survey: Is there any sex immorality? What is being done to teach purity and the dangers of disease from an immoral life?[69]

Speakers for the WCTU often appeared on the programs of both national and state WMU meetings. National WMU commended the work of the WCTU and recommended its pamphlets for their membership.[70] WMU historian Catherine Allen contends that the Baptist members of the WCTU were typically members of the WMU.[71] The WMU of Woodlawn Baptist Church of Birmingham, Alabama, for example, advertised WCTU meetings in their own gatherings. Often the organization met in the same room of the church as the WMU and listed its meetings on the church calendar. The relationship between WCTU and the WMU of the Woodlawn Baptist Church was repeated in other states. Ruth Provence, a historian of the South Carolina WMU, discovered that many state and local WMU leaders also accepted leadership roles in the WCTU.[72] The first secretary of the Tennessee WMU traveled across the South with Frances Willard.[73] The founder of the Mississippi WMU was one of the founders of the Mississippi chapter of the WCTU.[74] Texas WMU matriarch Fannie Breedlove Davis commented in an unpublished memoir that she had been "President of the local WCTU work" in San Antonio "for five years."[75] In 1925, Lulie Wharton listed WCTU as an example of the "awakening" of social service in the nineteenth century.[76] Frances Willard, wrote Wharton, "rallied women to fight the forces of King Alcohol. . . . This delicate, womanly woman of clear brain, loving heart and powers devoted to the cause of uplift and the eradication of evils that slay manhood and womanhood is proudly claimed by us all as a compatriot."[77]

Although Southern Baptist women never occupied any of the prominent leadership roles in national WCTU, they did serve on the state and local levels and were visible members of the southern WCTU.

The WCTU was not the only reform movement in which WMU participated. In March 1913, Fannie Heck was commissioned by the governor of North Carolina to attend the Southern Sociological Congress (SSC). Organized by southern progressives to address social problems, the SSC held annual meetings in various southern cities from 1912 until 1920. Governor Ben Hooper of Tennessee invited southern governors from fifteen states "to study and improve social, civic, and economic conditions in the South."[78] Their stated purposes included abolishing the convict lease system, abolishing child labor, the suppression of prostitution, enforcing school attendance, and "solving the race question in a spirit of helpfulness to the Negro and of equal justice to both races."[79] SSC meetings featured lectures from prominent southern progressives and church leaders who advocated the social gospel.

In 1914, Heck was elected second vice president of the SSC. Maud Reynolds McClure, director of the WMU Training School, also attended the congress as a delegate from the state of Kentucky and served on the Race Relations Committee in 1915. During these meetings, the women were exposed to the leaders of the social gospel and to some of the most progressive ideas of their day. For example, at the 1914 meeting in Memphis, the women witnessed an unusual approach to race relations taken by members of the SSC. Willis D. Weatherford was chairman of the Congress's committee on organization. The first night, the meeting was not racially segregated. This drew protest from a group of Memphis businessmen. The next night the organization committee gave in to pressure and imposed strict segregation. The black representatives walked out in protest. Then, Willis Weatherford moved the location of the meeting to the Methodist Church in Memphis and did away with the segregation. His bold move to affirm the black members of the SSC did not hurt the cause of the gathering. In fact, the 1914 meeting was one of the best attended.[80]

In affirmation of the Southern Sociological Congress, *Royal Service* printed reports from the meetings and quoted their resolutions concerning such issues as child labor, poverty, inner city slums, health, literacy, and recreation.[81] The editors of *Royal Service* did not hesitate to endorse a clear social gospel agenda with their choices of information from the Southern Sociological Congress. For example, four long paragraphs on the responsibility of the church to conserve public health quoted in a March 1916 issue of *Royal Service* were drawn from a speech made at the 1915 congress by Samuel Zane Batten, a Northern Baptist minister and strident social gospel advocate. Batten's words are resplendent with the social gospel message.[82] "First," says Batten, "the churches must teach people the wide scope of redemption and must make them know that health is a Christian duty."[83]

He continues with an admonition for the churches to go beyond the "results and deal with causes." "Thus far we have been content to feed the hungry, to nurse the sick, to rescue the perishing, to lift up the fallen. It is all very well to rescue the outcast, but it is better to abolish the white slave traffic. It is well enough to take the sickly child out of the slums; but it is more sensible to abolish the slums. It is well enough to feed the hungry family; but it is more Christian to create an industrial order where every man can earn and eat his daily bread without scantiness and anxiety."[84] Batten's words, endorsed by WMU leaders, strike at the heart of a conservative Christianity. Batten dared to suggest that the "industrial order" was to blame for poverty and want. A 1910 Home Mission Board pamphlet analyzed the problems of a southern mill town and pointed to different sources for hunger and poverty: "This glimpse at the situation will make one ready to believe that these cotton mill companies should not be too quickly criticized for the many undesirable things to be found in the life of the ordinary cotton mill operative. . . . The basal trouble with the average mill operative seems to be that he has lost initiative and enterprise."[85] According to the Home Mission Board periodical, it was the worker's own fault that he could not make ends meet. These phrases reveal the conflict between laborer and mill owner, between the conservative view that lays blame on the worker and the liberal that blames the industrial system. Batten's position is clear. "It is well enough to build an orphanage," Batten implored, "but it is more religious to protect machinery and keep the fathers alive. The time has come for us to find the causes of poverty and sickness and deal with these. . . . There is something as foolish as it is un-Christian in nursing sick people and running a hospital when you can keep people well by abolishing bad housing and providing pure water."[86] Editors of *Royal Service* boldly printed Batten's final point: "We must realize that this work of preventing social evils is religious and spiritual work."[87]

Batten's words stand in contrast to the writings of Victor I. Masters of the Home Mission Board, who warned against equating social service with redemption, righteousness, or individual conversion. Masters was careful to keep the "gospel" strictly separate from the "good works" of social service. "The Home Mission Board and its missionaries," reported Masters, "have done and are doing a work of social service which is of immense value. But they have shrunk from featuring this work as a chief thing, lest the weak and unwary should stumble and become entangled in the net of the false belief that man is justified by the works of the flesh rather than by faith in Christ."[88] This literal rendering of *sola fides* prevented Masters and other Southern Baptists from embracing an integrated concept of social service *as* faith and is one of the theological distinctions between a conservative social Christianity and the social gospel.

Fannie Heck was a prominent member of the Southern Sociological Congress and made every effort to bring its message of social reform to her home state. In

North Carolina, Heck founded the North Carolina Conference for Social Service, a corollary to the south-wide congress with basically the same objectives. Her involvement with these organizations enabled Baptist women across the South to have access to the agenda of progressivism. In the pages of *Royal Service*, particularly in the years 1915 and 1916, Southern Baptist women found a solid endorsement of the work of the Southern Sociological Congress and approval of the social gospel.

INSTITUTIONALIZING THE SOCIAL GOSPEL: PERSONAL SERVICE

In 1909 the leadership of the Woman's Missionary Union established a department called Personal Service that endeavored to enlist the entire membership in "united efforts to meet the community needs for uplift."[89] The Personal Service Department served as the main thoroughfare for the delivery of progressive impulses to WMU members. The committee that directed the program used social science methodology, promoted professional social work, affirmed social gospel theology, and introduced WMU to the progressive reform agenda. The publications of the Personal Service Department favored a holistic concept of salvation that included both souls and society. Personal Service columns in WMU magazines, study manuals, annual reports, and pamphlets provide the best illustrations of the influence of progressivism and the social gospel on WMU.

Fannie Heck was one of the more prominent progressives in the leadership of WMU.[90] She was the primary force behind the founding of the Personal Service Department. Heck not only served as national WMU president but also served as the president of North Carolina WMU. She made a career of volunteer service to her denomination and her local community. Her résumé serves as a veritable "who's who" of the social reform programs of the day. It also represents a wide variety of theological perspectives. In addition to her role in the Southern Sociological Congress, Heck founded the Associated Charities of Raleigh and served as vice president of the Wake County Betterment Association. With four like-minded women Heck founded the Woman's Club of Raleigh and served as its first president.[91] She presided over a joint meeting of Northern and Southern Baptist women at the Jamestown Exposition and delivered an address to Baptist women of the world at the Philadelphia gathering of the Baptist World Alliance.[92]

Fannie Heck profoundly shaped the course of WMU. She was influential for several reasons. The first is sheer longevity. Heck held the office of president, off and on, for a total of fifteen years, longer than any WMU president to date. Because she was unmarried and financially independent, Heck enjoyed greater freedom than most women of her generation. These privileges were compounded by her beauty, engaging personality, and oratory skills. Heck's hair was prematurely gray, lending an ethereal quality to her features. Women described Heck as a fashion plate and often requested copies of her dress patterns. As president Fannie Heck accepted speaking engagements across the South leaving audiences enthralled. After one of her speeches, a college student recorded her impressions of Heck: "Her beautiful dark eyes reflected joy in the discussions. She was dressed in pastel pink or blue (as she usually was). God painted her cheeks. Her voice was full, strong, forceful, rich. . . . As one listened one felt as if one could lay down her life for the cause she presented."[93] The effusive response was typical.

Fannie Heck proved to be a prolific writer with a keen intellect and a strong work ethic. She founded and edited the first official WMU publication, *Our Mission Fields*, in 1906. By the time the publication was replaced by *Royal Service* in 1914, circulation had reached nine thousand. She wrote numerous plays, pamphlets, and short stories. Heck authored the first history of WMU, *In Royal Service*, published in 1913. Fifteen thousand copies of the book were in circulation by 1915. Local WMU classes studied Heck's history in their meetings for over twenty years.[94] Because of the popularity of *Our Mission Fields* and *In Royal Service*, every member of WMU in the South had access to the persuasive words of Fannie Exile Scudder Heck.

In the summer of 1914, at age fifty-two, Heck became ill with what most observers deemed to be cancer. She checked into Hygeia Hospital in Richmond where she lingered in extreme pain until her death fourteen months later. During this suffering, she continued to be involved in the work of WMU. In the hospital Heck contributed to *Royal Service* with such volume that the editor wondered how she could think of so much to write.[95] One of her letters to the editor of *Royal Service* proved to be so detailed that it had to be taken "by subject" and answered in "installments."[96] The words of her final address as president of WMU, written from her deathbed, and read by proxy at the 1915 annual meeting, reverberated across the South. Heck's closing remarks to the women of WMU are phrased like proverbs. "Be prayerful in your planning," she advised.

> Endeavor to see the needs of the world from God's standpoint.
> Plan not for the year but for the years.
> Think long thoughts.
> Strive for the conversion of those around you as faithfully as for the heathen.
> Train the children for world-wide service.[97]

The powerful charge of the dying president stirred the minds and hearts of WMU members, launching Fannie Heck to a status nearing sainthood among Southern Baptist women. Her obituaries claim that she "expressed the richness of God's revelation through her writings," and that the influence of her "consecrated life and personality" would never die.[98]

The Seeds of an Idea

One of the earliest uses of the term "personal service" in WMU material occurred around 1905 in notes for a speech Fannie Heck made while chair of the Associated Charities of Raleigh. A piece of a pamphlet from the Charity Organization Society of London was pasted in the middle of Heck's handwritten notes. The reference read: "There can be no real charity without personal service. In order that this personal service may be something worth giving and worth receiving, the Charity Organization Society believes strongly in the power of education."[99] Heck probably co-opted this phrase for WMU.

In the final version of the speech Heck presented to the Associated Charities of Raleigh, she noted her detailed study of the issue of poverty in both England and at home in Raleigh. Heck discussed the creed of the Charity Organization Society of London as a model for charity work in Raleigh and provided statistical analysis of the work that had been accomplished in Raleigh in the twenty months since the founding of the ACR. Heck laid out a plan of social work for the Raleigh organization based on the work of the London society and pledged to study the work in London "in more detail."[100] In the speech she referenced the "poor laws of England," which authorized a general "dole" to the poor during the first years of the twentieth century. She says the results were disastrous to the working classes and threatened the "integrity of the nation." To remedy the situation, the tax on bread items was removed and "wages increased by law." Heck endorsed the use of a minimum wage and lowering prices on staples to enable the poor to make their own living.[101] Interestingly, Heck's interpretation of the problem reveals her belief that poverty must be addressed by legislation.

In her early years of service on the state WMU level, Heck's speeches and writings referred to social work variously as "personal missions," "neighborhood missions," "household missions," or "personal service." As these terms indicate, Fannie Heck understood social work and missions to be virtually interchangeable terms. Social ministry and individual salvation were not mutually exclusive ideas. This attitude harmonizes with that of social gospelers.[102] Unlike many Southern Baptists who considered social work to be a secondary task of ministry, Heck consistently emphasized social service as an intrinsic element of the missionary enterprise. Her commitment to social work is evidenced by her early projects with the North Carolina WMU. In 1896, she added a "Department of Neighborhood Missions" to the work of North Carolina women to encourage societies toward "a larger, fuller consecration of self to mission work within the radius of their own neighborhoods."[103]

Heck's experience with the Associated Charities of Raleigh informed her approach to social service within WMU. During her third tenure as national WMU president, Fannie Heck established a Personal Service Department and named Lulie Wharton chair, a position Wharton held for fifteen years. Wharton was married to Henry M. Wharton, a Baltimore pastor and editor of the *Baltimore Baptist*.[104] Wharton and Heck guided the work of Personal Service through its fledgling years with the help of a Personal Service committee. The publications and training manuals published by the department of Personal Service during their tenure were designed to engage Baptist women in social work. Heck and Wharton encouraged local WMUs to establish their own Personal Service committees and to send detailed reports of their activities to national headquarters.[105] State organizations began to form Personal Service committees in 1911. In 1912, WMU added Personal Service to the Standard of Excellence, requiring societies to participate in Personal Service in order to meet a rating of "excellence" in WMU work.[106] The national office soon prepared training pamphlets and a *Handbook of Personal Service* for local societies to follow. In 1913, WMU highlighted Personal Service as part of the twenty-fifth anniversary celebration of WMU.

Lulie Wharton and the Personal Service Committee took great pains to articulate the purpose for their department. "In laying the foundation for this department," they explained, "the aim has been to make it broad and comprehensive, to line up with the most progressive thought and movements of the day and to seek those methods most conducive to the carrying out of our purpose—'to fight for prohibition, for observance of the Sabbath, for the sanctity of the home and the fight against crime, disease and poverty.'"[107] The "progressive thought of the day" meant social science methods and themes drawn from the social gospel. Under the banner of the "fight against crime, disease, and poverty," Personal Service leaders included investigations of housing, sanitation, health, education, recreation, child labor, family conditions, industrial conditions, church and Sunday school membership and attendance, conduct of jail, orphanage, county home, and other local institutions. Lulie Wharton stated that Personal Service was meant to apply the "religion of Jesus Christ" to the "social problems of the day" and also to be "in line" with the "new phase of modern thought," namely, social service.[108]

Personal Service and Social Science Methodology

Leaders of Personal Service deliberately identified their Personal Service Department with the broader movement for social reform. Social scientists trace the rise of urban sociology to the last half of the nineteenth century. The social gospel, applied sociology, and the settlement house movement shaped the new discipline of sociology. Scholars argue that these movements "were not only overlapping, but often indistinguishable."[109] Baptist women were particularly enthusiastic about applied sociology—called social service or social work. "Christ enjoined social service," pronounced the November 1913 WMU mission study program, "and plainly taught that His treatment of men in the last day would depend on their treatment of each other here."[110] WMU writers celebrated the history of social service organizations and wanted local women to know that "all such agencies draw their inspiration and their strength from the example of Christ."[111] In 1925 Wharton devoted four months of Personal Service columns to the "Bible Principles of Social Service." After her biblical exposition, Wharton traced the history of social service in the nineteenth century from Lord Shaftesbury's philanthropic work in England to the founding of the Red Cross Society, the Salvation Army, the WCTU, the YMCA, and social settlements.[112] Wharton and others WMU leaders urged Baptist women to study social service and adopt its methods.

WMU leaders acknowledged attitudes toward poverty were shifting. The older Charity Organization Society (COS) view often blamed the poor while social settlement workers; they believed that the causes of poverty, though complicated, had more to do with the forces of industrial capitalism than with an individual's moral convictions.[113] They promoted the "new studies" designed to help change perceptions of poverty. As early as 1912, writers were explaining the change: "A generation ago it was considered that poverty was a disgrace. Now we are forced to recognize that social conditions are such that a man through no fault of his own may be brought with his family to destitution. When so many thousands exist on the bare margin of a living wage it takes very little in the way of sickness or loss of work to plunge whole families into the abyss. From investigations made by Robert Hunter, one-third of the people of New York go hungry."[114] Here the editors deliberately endorsed the social gospel view of poverty by separating the issue from personal sin. People could end up destitute "through no fault" of their own. Baptist women began to emphasize social and institutional sources of poverty. The *Handbook of Personal Service* encouraged societies to keep detailed records of families, their ages, and their general condition as well as their church affiliation. One of the five points on the "star of personal service" was "study." The diagram pointed to the study of the "community," of "up-to-date methods," and of "financial resources."[115] The 1913 annual report on Personal Service insisted that "lack of information is a hindrance to the eradication of evils and to the prosecution of any plan for the good of all. In all work for uplift, investigation is an important factor."[116]

The Personal Service Department encouraged formal, systematic neighborhood studies with the publication of *The Survey*. The survey was a broad-based analysis of local communities on issues ranging from sexual immorality to economics. The process of asking the questions was intended to raise the conscience of women on local labor, health, education, or housing conditions and was skewed toward social reform. For example, regarding labor the survey asked: "What is the chief industry? Any factories or mills? Is the work regular? Any seven day work? Any women or children employed? What is the lowest wage paid to men? to women? Is it a living wage? What proportion of wages has to go for rent? How many own homes? Is the safety of the factory or mill workers properly protected?"[117] *The Survey*, published by Baptist women, was part of a larger "survey movement" in American history that emerged during the Progressive Era.[118] Advocates of the new surveys believed that if ordinary citizens had the correct information, they would be able to solve social problems.

Following the publication of *The Survey*, the Personal Service column in *Royal Service* urged societies to take advantage of the pamphlet and other local resources to study their communities. They pointed to the network of social service organizations available for information and aid to the local WMU societies. "The Russell Sage Foundation and the American Red Cross . . . will give information on social services," explained a Personal Service column, "so will your State Board of Charities or Welfare, your state university and all the great denominational publishing houses; so also does the splendid paper *The Survey*."[119] The same column offered veiled criticism of local WMUs for their lack of "study of fundamental principles of social work" or "thorough knowledge of the conditions and needs of our own communities."[120]

What should local societies do with the information they gathered from a survey? Personal Service writers urged local women to solve the problems they discovered. Baptist women were not alone in the naive belief that information alone would provide clear solutions. It was a typical assumption of the survey movement that "whatever facts were collected by a survey would be put to good use."[121] "When you have learned the actual facts as to housing, sanitation, health, education, recreation, child labor, family conditions, industrial conditions, church and Sunday school membership and attendance, conduct of jail, orphanage, county home and other local institutions in your community, you will then find what is the greatest need and where your society can best put its time and effort."[122] The energy of the local WMU members should be directed toward removing the causes of social problems, not toward salving the effects. Poor families need more than "haphazard donations of food and clothing," sermonized the Personal Service writer. "Soup and jelly to the sick are not solving the health problems that kill the babies in your town."[123]

The pages of Personal Service literature were strewn with admonitions to deal with "causes" of social problems. "Too long God's people have endeavored with self-sacrificing but short sighted charity to help the victims of crime and want by dealing with the effects always more apparent than the deep seated and often unrecognized causes," declared the 1913 annual report of Personal Service. The Personal Service address at the twenty-fifth anniversary celebration of WMU maintained: "More important than all other effort is to find the causes of sin, destitution, ignorance and indifference to religion and remove these causes."[124] Lulie Wharton charged in 1914 that "the time for indifference and palliation is past. Causes must be found and dealt with."[125] In a rare, succinct statement the *Handbook of Personal Service* placed the responsibility for removing "causes" on the government: "The state which punishes vice should remove the causes which make men vicious."[126] The implication of this last statement was that social forces shape human behavior. Sinful institutions produce sinful people.

This emphasis on the scientific study of social problems demonstrates WMU's use of the methods of Progressive Era reformers. Furthermore, the attention to "causes" of societal problems indicates that Personal Service leaders embraced a progressive social philosophy, if not a more a liberal theological framework. Whereas many Baptist leaders followed E. Y. Mullins in the conclusion that social problems were caused by individuals who lacked "moral discipline," these WMU leaders pointed to industry, housing conditions, poor sanitation, child labor, and poor working conditions as sources of community ills.[127] Baptist women had organizational structures, programs, and methodologies for social reform. Next, they needed to educate and inform the rank and file.

Organizing Personal Service on the Local Level

Personal Service leaders worked diligently to help women in local churches implement their recommended social service programs. They created guidelines, pamphlets, study guides, and Bible studies to give women across the South the tools for social action. Personal Service leaders wanted local women to do essentially three things. First, they encouraged members to create committees in each church, association, and state. In order to promote their program among local women, the national Personal Service Committee of WMU needed to establish a base of support with coordinators on every level. Societies and associations from Corpus Christi, Texas, to Norfolk, Virginia, began to organize for Personal Service.[128] By 1912, ten out of sixteen states affiliated with WMU had Personal Service Committees including Arkansas, Alabama, Louisiana, Mississippi, North Carolina, South Carolina, Tennessee, Texas, and Virginia.[129] The committee commended Florida that year for its useful state organization "composed of a general social service committee with sub-committees for legislation, education, religion, philanthropy and hospitals."[130] The national Personal Service Committee led by Lulie Wharton urged states to continue strengthening their organizations, to conduct state surveys of needs, and to devote a tenth of their "waking hours" to some form of Christian service.[131] They urged societies to be consistent, to adopt a standard pattern of organization consisting of a state chair, an associational chair, and a society chair of Personal Service.[132] In spite of Wharton's admonitions, states were slow to establish parallel organizations. WMU practiced the Southern Baptist policy of cooperation instead of coercion and depended on gentle persuasion and encouragement to accomplish their organizational goals.

Second, after the women formed an organizational structure, national Personal Service leaders wanted Baptist women to actually engage in social service. Local women usually dedicated the majority of their time and resources to home and foreign missions; as a result, Personal Service chairs often struggled to interest women in their programs.[133] For example, eleven years after the introduction of the Union's Personal Service Department, the Personal Service chair of the Louisiana WMU reported that interest in Personal Service was "growing."[134] In 1921 she reported that the work was moving "forward slowly," but "gaining ground."[135] Although she expressed gratitude in 1922 that "the women are realizing the possibilities of this work," she lamented in 1923 that the women were "merely 'marking time' instead of marching forward."[136] Louisiana's troubles proved to be the norm rather than the exception.

Finally, the national Personal Service Committee wanted data. In order to evaluate how much personal service was actually being done on the local level, the national office needed local WMU's to record and report their work. They urged local societies to use a form provided in the Woman's Missionary Union Yearbook to submit quarterly Personal Service reports to their associations.[137] Associations were to report to the state Personal Service chair, and the chair to the national committee. In spite of repeated encouragement, local societies were reluctant to report their activities to WMU. It is likely that most local churchwomen were simply not participating in community service. Those who did carry out social service programs, however, still hesitated to explain their work. Many local women were slow to send records because they believed documenting their good deeds contradicted scripture. They were keenly aware of the passage in Matthew 6:1, which warned, "Beware of practicing your righteousness before men to be noticed by them; otherwise you have no reward with your father who is in heaven." It was not until 1916 that the first statistical records were published, documenting the activities of the previous year. The chair of the Louisiana Personal Service Committee still struggled with the problem of reporting as late as 1921. "Realizing that we shall never reach the full measure of our helpfulness until the prejudice against reporting is broken down, we beg that our women prayerfully study God's word in regard to this matter, seeking to know His will and submitting ourselves to His guidance."[138] The prejudice against reporting began to wane by the 1920s.

The earliest reports submitted by local societies for Personal Service were vague and difficult to assess. One of the early reports states that North Carolina participated in "ministry to sick, poor, destitute and prisoners," Arkansas women made visits to "sick and poor," and "Georgia started a new work for the negro."[139] The national committee pushed for more details. Societies who did report often submitted incomplete figures or responded randomly. The national committee complained about these inconsistencies. In 1915, 57 percent of local WMU societies reported participation in Personal Service programs. The average number of societies reporting from 1915 to 1921 was 38 percent—partially due to a drop in participation during the war years. During the 1920s, the percentages rose steadily, reaching 92 percent by 1929.[140] These numbers do not suggest, however, that the majority of WMU societies were involved in social service. Those reports they eventually submitted often failed to reflect the plans the national WMU outlined. The information collected in Personal Service reports ranged from "Good Will Centers" to "Bibles distributed." Thus, local societies who gave baskets at Christmas and Bibles in Sunday school could fall into the category of personal service. Basically, the data from "societies participating in personal service" reveals that by 1930 the majority of local WMU societies were filling out a report and sending it to the Personal Service Department.

The inconsistent nature of the reports suggests that many Southern Baptist women often failed to grasp the aims of Personal Service. Why was it such a challenge for local women to understand and implement the goals of Personal Service? Part of the problem was that Personal Service represented a new way of understanding the Gospel, even though WMU leaders often insisted it was not. WMU had been organized to support and serve the Southern Baptist Foreign Mission Board and Home Mission Board. This original agenda was crystal clear: Southern Baptists aimed to save souls at home and overseas. They formed the Personal Service Department to study and eradicate social problems. When it was established in 1909, the new department of Personal Service faced an important challenge: how could it find its niche within the clearly defined goals of WMU? Personal Service leaders studiously avoided placing the new department into competition with missions but struggled to help women understand exactly how Personal Service fit into their organizational structure. Personal Service literature proclaimed that the "Gospel was its motive and conversion was its aim." Still it was neither fish nor fowl because it was not a typical program of evangelism designed for individual salvation. Although the name presented the work as "Personal" it was only personal in that individual "persons" carried it out. The broad program of Personal Service was designed to alleviate the social problems that affected individual sinners.

While promoting Personal Service, the WMU committee endeavored to reassure local women that their focus on missions had not changed. Even though personal service was a "local work," Fannie Heck emphatically insisted that home and state missions were a priority for WMU. "It must be distinctly understood that [these personal services] in no way interfere with or overlap the work the societies are now doing and the far larger things they expect to do for home and State missions," explained Heck. "To these two agencies the Union as a whole, and the State Central Committees as parts of the Union, have shown and will ever maintain the deepest allegiance."[141] Heck expressed her absolute allegiance to mission work, but she also admitted that Personal Service did not "overlap."

Personal Service was not synonymous with mission work and was indeed a different way of understanding the Gospel and the work of the church. I do not think Fannie Heck was being coy. She sincerely believed that the church should be saving souls at home, saving souls overseas, *and also* saving society. But this message was complicated and difficult to communicate to a very conservative Southern Baptist audience.

The *Manual of Personal Service* plainly stated that the "end and object" of Personal Service was "full salvation" for individuals that included "the betterment of the physical conditions, the development of the mental powers, the culture of the moral sense, in a word, making men better citizens because they are conscious citizens of the Kingdom of Heaven, whose laws are justice, peace and righteousness for all the world in all relations of life."[142] The revised *Handbook for Personal Service* explained that personal service had two facets: individual and social. Individual personal service was simply "Christ-like living with regard to those around us." The second level was social service, an organized service in which "some definite phase of this kind of work is adopted and a committee placed in charge."[143] The missionary society of the Wichita Baptist Association in Texas followed national standards and divided "organized Personal Service" such as mission Sunday schools, day nurseries, literacy classes, and rescue work from "other personal service results" such as "talks to the unsaved" and "Bible distribution."[144] They differentiated between general missionary activity and social service. Other local societies did not display the same discernment.

Personal Service leadership hoped to clarify their goals by redesigning the reporting form in the WMU Yearbook. The form asked societies to identify their work with specific programs such as Good Will Centers, Mission Sunday schools, Homemakers' Clubs, Cottage Prayer Meetings, Cheer-All Clubs, Boys' Clubs, Industrial Schools, Rescue Work, Sewing for Poor, Work for Negroes, Work for Foreigners, and Work for Prisoners. Any society that conducted or helped with such programs could be counted in that category. For example, if one society hosted a Homemakers' Club and three societies helped with it, the count in the national report for Homemakers' Clubs would be four. For this reason, it is difficult to determine exactly how many programs were in operation. In addition to programs, there were categories for Visits, Services, Conversions, Bibles Distributed, Good Literature, Garments Made and Distributed, and Baskets Sent. In 1918, the categories expanded to include such programs as Americanization, Kindergartens, Day Nurseries, and Daily Vacation Bible Schools. Also in that year a category for Red Cross and War Relief efforts appeared that was later simply called Nursing. Star Classes, focused on adult education, were added in 1921. These later additions more closely follow the work of secular settlements. Thus, there was a mixture of standard missionary activity and potentially progressive programs listed under the umbrella of Personal Service.

WMU's press consistently presented personal service information to local women to help them define the work. Beginning in 1913, *Our Mission Fields* conveyed the personal service message directly into the homes of thousands of Southern Baptist women through articles and weekly columns. *Royal Service* continued the emphases of Personal Service until 1962.[145] The leading resource for Personal Service work was a *Manual of Personal Service* later revised as the *Handbook for Personal Service*.[146] The initial pamphlet not only provided local societies with information on forming Personal Service committees but also offered detailed instructions for organizing mothers' clubs, hospital work, prison work, work with "shop and factory girls," forming industrial schools, cooking schools, boys clubs, night schools, day nurseries, establishing playgrounds, and even organizing neighborhood entertainment. Fannie Heck and Emma Leachman prepared the first manual. In the revision, the committee lengthened the foreword and asked Maud McLure to reorganize Heck's material under the rubric of settlement work.[147] The result was a detailed manual for implementing Baptist settlement work. Few societies adopted such a complete program of Personal Service.

The older and more urban the WMU society, the greater the likelihood it would embrace the full agenda of Personal Service. Occasionally rural societies exposed to urban issues such as industry or immigration also embraced Personal Service. For many rural societies, personal service consisted of no more than talks given at associational meetings. The minutes of the Texarkana Missionary Baptist Association in 1916 report a typical first exposure to Personal Service work: "Mrs. McCall, by invitation, told us eloquently and forcibly of personal and social service work being done by their Union of 'the Cheer up Club,' of their classes in the Industrial Arts, showing the crying needs of these things in the cities."[148] The writer of the minutes was obviously unfamiliar with the new Cheer-All Club designed for young women working in industrial conditions.

Most societies gravitated toward simple missionary service and were uncertain about the meaning of personal service. The women of the Lauderdale County Baptist Association in Mississippi included "sending four girls to our college" as a phase of their personal service for the year 1920.[149] The Birmingham Baptist Association included contributions to a ministerial relief fund in their organized Personal Service report. Societies tended to include almost any Christian act, such as "a smile," or "a word of encouragement," under the department of Personal Service.[150] Local WMU chapters largely failed to understand the importance of social service. The national committee bemoaned the fact that "in many places the women have no very clear conception of what is meant by Personal Service."[151] WMU writers reminded women that individual personal service was certainly "Christ-like living with regard to those around us," but organized personal service should be defined as work that is "local, for the uplift of the community of which the society is a part, carried on by its own members, and reported to the society."[152] The national committee persistently urged women to undertake more challenging programs and pointed them toward their ideal for service: the social settlement. A few societies attempted to implement more formal programs of social reform. (The story of these Baptist settlements or "Good Will Centers" will be explored in a later chapter.) Personal Service leaders worked tirelessly to educate societies about personal service and to introduce local women to the tenets of the social gospel. The next chapter takes a closer look at the informal and formal educational programs developed by Personal Service.

CONCLUSION

The leadership of Personal Service imbibed reform ideas, social gospel theology, and social work methods through their ties with women of other denominations, through reform organizations, and through the literature of social gospel writers. WMU leaders learned about the social gospel and social work from Methodist women, the WCTU, the Southern Sociological Congress, Jane Addams, and other ecumenical missionary programs. They lifted whole passages from the proceedings of the Southern Sociological Congress and printed them along with reports from the Congress in 1915 and in 1916 publications of *Royal Service*. Baptist women studied and respected the work of the Social Gospel Movement.

Fannie E. S. Heck was the most important leader in the founding of this department of WMU and the most progressive. Heck encouraged the members of WMU to participate in ecumenical endeavors and was enthusiastic about the ecumenical missionary movement. From the beginning of service with North Carolina WMU and as president of the south-wide organization, Heck promoted social uplift as a legitimate and necessary element of WMU work. She worked with the Southern Sociological Congress and founded the North Carolina Commission on Social Service. In 1907, she called on her background in charity work and women's club work to implement a social service arm of WMU called Personal Service. Local women were slow to embrace these programs of personal service. Women active in state, associational, and church WMU organizations committed the majority of their time to the support of home and foreign missions. They were slow to organize Personal Service committees, reluctant to report the work they conducted, and remained largely deaf to the broad social agenda advocated by Personal Service.

In spite of the fact that local women did not fully comprehend or implement the vision, the Personal Service Department provides the clearest evidence for progressivism within WMU. The goals of Personal Service, its programs, and methodologies mirror the emphases of the broader movement. Virtually every impulse to reform society originated with the Personal Service leadership. Personal Service programs also bear the imprint of the social gospel. The leaders of the department sincerely believed that the church must reform individuals *and society*. The Gospel according to Personal Service required more than simply saving souls from hell. It urged Christians to free people from hell on earth and challenged Baptist women to create a society committed to peace, justice, and righteousness.

CHAPTER SIX

"A Gospel for All of Life"

Teaching and Proclaiming the Social Gospel

W. O. CARVER, A SOCIOLOGY professor at Southern Baptist Theological Seminary in Louisville, Kentucky, allowed Baptist women in his classrooms well before the founding of the WMU Training School. He was a towering influence at the WMU Training School, and his name would eventually become synonymous with Baptist social work. Carver embraced the social gospel and spent his career reminding Southern Baptist students of their social responsibilities. In his memoirs, Carver reported a conflict over the social gospel that occurred as late as 1936 when he invited Toyohiko Kagawa to Southern Seminary for a series of lectures. Kagawa was a Japanese Christian socialist noted for his passionate advocacy of the poor in Japan. Largely through his efforts, the Japanese government passed legislation to abolish the slums and to allow the organization of labor unions. Kagawa was known as the "St. Francis of Japan." Southern Baptist conservatives sharply criticized Carver for bringing Kagawa to Southern Seminary. V. I. Masters, editor of the Kentucky Baptist paper, the *Western Recorder*, publicly attacked Kagawa's views. Carver defended Kagawa vigorously. He personally confronted Masters and informed him he would have to answer to God for the sin of misrepresenting Kagawa, whom Carver called "one of the world's foremost Christians."[1] Carver described an incident when someone questioned Kagawa about the social gospel: "Kagawa replied emphatically, 'I know but one gospel,' explaining that personal salvation by Jesus Christ involves accepting the ethics of Jesus and applying them in human relations. No one will undertake to live the ethics of Jesus unless and until he is renewed in the spirit of his mind, nor can he achieve even an approximation to the ideal of Jesus save in the power of the Holy Spirit."[2] Teachers like W. O. Carver trained generations of Southern Baptist men and women. He represents the formal training in social work available to Baptist women at the WMU Training School, but this was not the only avenue available for study. The Personal Service Department worked to provide training tools for any Baptist woman who wished to understand and practice social reform.

This chapter begins with an explanation of the types of training in social service available to Southern Baptist women. Personal Service promoted informal education through lecture tours, study guides, manuals, and handbooks to train local women in their programs. The department published a detailed handbook for Personal Service that borrowed heavily from a social work manual produced by Southern Methodist women. In order to provide formal education for Baptist women in missions and social work, WMU established a missionary training school in Louisville, Kentucky, in 1907. This WMU Training School developed a curriculum emphasizing social work and founded a model Baptist settlement house to provide women with practical experience in social work methods. Baptist women from across the south traveled to Louisville for missionary training; there they could participate in programs for the poor in the neighborhood surrounding the settlement house. Largely these programs reflected the conservative attitudes of Southern Baptists, but they did raise awareness of the plight of the poor and the needs of immigrants. They highlighted unsafe industrial conditions—particularly for women and children—and provided practical training in social work for generations of Baptist students.

The second section of this chapter describes specific references to the social gospel in WMU publications. WMU promoted the new Personal Service Department in a dedicated column in *Royal Service*. These articles provide the clearest statements endorsing social reform and the social gospel. Occasionally, they quoted social gospel writers like Charles Stelzle, Graham Taylor, Josiah Strong, and Shailer Mathews. The Personal Service column also published proclamations and proceedings from the foremost institution of progressivism in the south: the Southern Sociological Congress. Some of the articles in the Personal Service column suggest a corporate understanding of sin and salvation and emphasize the immanence of the Kingdom of God. Not every Personal Service column endorsed the social gospel. The tone of the column depended on the writer for that particular issue. In spite of some of the mixed messages, the sources indicate that WMU leaders were conversant with the social gospel and that many of them adopted social gospel theology.

PERSONAL SERVICE TRAINING AND EDUCATION

Personal Service training was available in both informal and formal educational settings. In 1915 the Personal Service Committee published a pamphlet series designed to teach local women about personal service.[3] The outline course of six studies called Our Duty to the Community was full of social gospel citations. Dr. Edward Bagby Pollard prepared four of the six studies. Pollard was professor of English at Richmond College for fifteen years and then a professor of homiletics at Crozer Seminary in Pennsylvania. Lulie Pollard Wharton, chair of the Personal Service Committee, prepared the other two studies.[4] Pollard's study titles were: "The Social Teachings of the Scriptures," "The Place of Social Service in the Christian Life," "Our Social Relationships," and "Studying a Town—Essential Facts."[5] Pollard's studies were presented in outline form in the brochure, and his subject headings reflect social gospel emphases. He began with general social teachings, addressed the "Social Teachings of the Prophets," and concluded with the "Social Teachings of Jesus—The Kingdom of Heaven." This approach was a favorite of social gospel writers.[6] Pollard provided biblical references to support each subcategory in the outline.[7]

Pollard's first study further highlighted Progressive Era reform issues such as the regulation of industry, good government, public health, labor rights, and prison reform. Under the social teachings on "Trade and Industry," Pollard listed "Honesty" and "Fair Wages." Regarding community life, Pollard addressed "health and sanitation," "community responsibility for crime," "criminal carelessness," "charity," "protection of the poor," and "protection of dumb creatures."[8] Under the teachings of the prophets, Pollard included such topics as "Against Oppression of the Poor," "National Punishment for National Sins," "Against Cruel Monopoly," "Against Social Injustice," and "For Good Government, Prosperity, and Peace."[9] In the final section, on the social teachings of Jesus, Pollard examined the Kingdom's "Citizens," the Kingdom's "Laws," "Its Righteousness," and "Its Realization on Earth."[10]

Pollard's study became boldly social gospel in the second lesson, "The Place of Social Service in the Christian Life." He defined social service as "the principals of Christianity applied to our total life and environment." The aim of social service was, "Complete manhood and womanhood in a perfected society. Realizing the Kingdom of God."[11] Pollard listed six reasons for social service:

1. Christianity is a religion of personal service as well as of personal faith. Luke 4:17ff., John 13:3–17, Acts 10–38, Matthew 25:34.
2. The Gospel is a message of social redemption as well as of personal rescue. Matthew 6:10, II Pet. 3:13, Rev. 11:15.
3. There are social vices and virtues as well as individual sins and graces. Matthew 11:21–24, Rev. 2, 3.
4. God in saving society, works through service of saved persons.
5. God in saving individuals, works through social forces.
6. The individual life is made up of relationships, social contacts.[12]

At the end of this lesson, Pollard listed five books for further study. He mentioned two books by Shailer Mathews, *The Social Gospel* and *The Individual and the Social Gospel*, one by Samuel Zane Batten, *The Social Task of Christianity*, another by Charles Gardner, *The Ethics of Jesus and Social Progress*, and one titled *The Kingdom of God*. Pollard continued these social gospel themes in the third study on social relationships. The fifth study provides information on conducting a social survey. Lesson V concluded with a quote from Shailer Mathews: "And this is the social Gospel! the joyful message that the power of Jesus Christ, the Son of God, is sufficient to regenerate the social order which tends to express itself in individuals; that the Gospel is the power of God unto salvation not to the individual or society, but to the individual *in* society. And thus the individual gospel and the social gospel are seen to be the same glad news of the saving power of God in Christ.—Mathews."[13] Fannie Heck approved of these studies and apparently shaped their content. Lulie Wharton sent Heck a draft of the pamphlet in March 1915. "I enclose you the outlines Dr. Pollard sent. He wishes that you would suggest just what you think it needs. He says 'merely a first attempt' at getting what you have in mind."[14]

Lulie Wharton's lesson outlines were not as obviously progressive as Pollard's, but there were some social elements evident in her work. She wrote lessons four and six on "Woman's Organizations in Social Service" and "Applying the Remedy" respectively. In the lesson on women's organizations, Wharton offered examples of associations of women that were doing good work in social service.[15] She hailed the National Congress of Mothers as the "Largest Child Welfare Organization in the World." It promoted parent-teacher organizations, infant hygiene, pensions for widowed mothers, and general programs for children's education.[16] Next, Wharton discussed the "Five Great Divisions" of the Woman's Christian Temperance Union and outlined the development of the Young Women's Christian Association. In the last section of lesson four, Wharton referenced the roles of Methodist and Baptist women in social service. "Women's Clubs, Civic Leagues, College Settlements, Camp Fire Girls, Red Cross Nursing and kindred organizations of women," concluded Wharton, "are doing a great deal for social improvement."[17]

The sixth study listed recommendations for addressing the social problems women discovered after they surveyed their communities. The lesson was divided into four main subject headings including "Use Agencies Already Established," "Establish Good Will Centers,"[18] "Promote the Welfare of Infancy, Childhood, Youth, and Maturity," and last, "Benefit All Classes" by work in "sanitation," "good housing," and "conservation of health."[19] In the section promoting the welfare of all age groups, Wharton lists programs and issues Baptist women could support such as baby clinics, day nurseries, milk funds, visiting nurses, kindergartens, industrial schools, children's clubs, the abolition of child labor, good schools, libraries and reading rooms, concerts and orchestras, a living wage, Sabbath observance, ten-hour work days for women, and English classes for immigrants. Wharton concluded her lesson with a quote by Graham Taylor: "We must build the community up out of the church and school and not the church and school up out of the community."[20] In other words, the impetus of community reform should come from religion and education. While not an overtly social gospel statement, the quote comes from Taylor who was known for his social gospel commitments and his work at the Chicago Commons settlement. Taken in total the six courses of recommended study are firmly social gospel in their position.

In 1918, the Personal Service Committee suggested a slate of speakers on personal service for the Woman's Missionary Union.[21] *Royal Service* published the list in the January edition. Lecturers were recommended for each state along with the speaker's preferred topics. Many on the list were sympathetic to the social gospel. For the state of Pennsylvania the list suggested Dr. E. B. Pollard of Crozer Seminary, Upland. Dr. J. H. Strong, a Congregationalist and social gospel author, appeared on the list for Maryland. For North Carolina, the women submitted the name of Dr. William Louis Poteat, president of Wake Forest College.[22] As chairman of the denomination's Social Service Commission, Poteat advocated a "liberal social philosophy" and presented a report to the 1914 Southern Baptist Convention that fully affirmed the social gospel.[23] William Poteat's nephew, Dr. E. M. Poteat of Furman University, appeared on the list for South Carolina speakers. The list also included sociology professor Dr. W. O. Carver for Kentucky and Drs. Powhatan W. James and J. B. Weatherspoon for Texas. Dr. James listed "The New Social Gospel" as his topic for discussion. Dr. Weatherspoon submitted the topic "Social Ills and the Christian Cure." Other speakers listed such topics as "The Social Task of the Local Church," "The Significance of Social Service," "Civic Righteousness or the Christian and the Community," "Some Present Day Calls to Social Service," and "The Church and Social Service." These speakers and topics demonstrate Personal Service leadership's connection to the network of progressives within the denomination as well as social gospel advocates from other Protestant groups.

At the turn of the twentieth century, Baptist women began to explore a permanent solution for higher education in missions and social service. As early as 1883 unmarried young women had been slipping into classrooms at the Southern Baptist Theological Seminary in Louisville, Kentucky, to attend lectures. They could not, however, formally enroll or earn a degree. Southern Baptist women who wished to earn a degree could attend the Northern Baptist missionary training school in Philadelphia or the Methodist Training School in Chicago. Responding to this desire for theological education, the Woman's Missionary Union (WMU) proposed a women's missionary training school. The idea of training women for a profession—even a missionary profession—was still a hot topic in Southern Baptist circles. Surprisingly, Annie Armstrong proved to be one of the most vocal opponents of the training school. Armstrong believed, first of all, that the northern schools sufficiently met the needs of Southern Baptist women. Second, she resented the jokes in Baptist papers about a WMU school that could provide marriage partners for Southern Seminary students.[24] Her final point of opposition stemmed from a personal conflict between Armstrong and several key WMU leaders. Texas women initially promoted the idea for a Woman's Missionary Union Training School because they felt the northern schools were located too far outside the South. The Texas group, led by Mina Everett, attempted to place the issue of the school on the agenda for the 1895 WMU meeting. Annie Armstrong blocked this effort, stating, "It is not time yet to discuss the subject."[25] In Armstrong's defense, there was at least one powerful Louisville woman who also opposed the Training School—Eliza Broadus, the daughter of one of the seminary's founders. When Texas women encountered this resistance they took their campaign directly to the WMU Executive Committee who again, under Armstrong's leadership, refused to consider the plan. The matter seemed closed until E. Z. Simmons, a missionary home on furlough from China, traveled around the South promoting the idea. He persuaded the key leaders of the SBC that women missionaries desperately needed formal training. The executives of the mission boards were thrilled with Simmons's well-developed plan and presented it to Armstrong assuming that WMU would simply make it happen. Armstrong was outraged and refused to participate.

In 1903 W. O. Carver, a missiology professor at Southern Baptist Theological Seminary, established a missions methodology class for women at Southern Seminary. Twenty-five women enrolled in the first term. By this time, Eliza Broadus had apparently experienced a change of heart. She spearheaded a plan to provide lodging for all the single women who were flocking to Louisville to study missions. Soon the Louisville women needed more money and hoped to enlist the support of the national WMU. They knew that Armstrong would block their efforts, so they bypassed her altogether and wrote letters to state WMU presidents. This slight wounded Armstrong deeply. Armstrong dug in her heels and drew a line in the sand. If they continued in the efforts to bring the matter to a vote without her permission, she threatened to resign. Her threats fell on deaf ears. The idea for the school had already captured the imagination of Southern Baptist women, and not even Annie Armstrong could hold them back. In 1906, when it became apparent that her cause was lost, Armstrong resigned from her post as corresponding secretary of WMU. WMU established a school to prepare Baptist women for missionary service the following year.[26]

WMU TRAINING SCHOOL AND THE SOCIAL GOSPEL

W. O. Carver's class on mission's methods charted the course for the WMU Training School. Carver affirmed the social gospel and invited social gospel teachers to Southern Seminary. After the WMU Training School formally opened in 1907, Carver served on the advisory council. He maintained this position as advisor and supporter until his death in 1954. During the years that Carver taught and advised the women of the Training School, he was accused of sympathy with the social gospel. Carver answered his critics in a chapter of his memoirs titled "My 'Heresies' and Controversies." "If we stress the ethical content of the gospel and advocate its serious application to the relations and obligations of living society and expression in contemporary institutional life, we are 'social gospel heretics.' I have shared such charges. In a general way, I have rightly been regarded as one of those who believe in the sincerity of Jesus in the Sermon on the Mount and so have been suspected of the heresy of substituting social ethics for personal regeneration. For there are those who cannot endure the pragmatic test of the new birth as applied by Jesus: 'By their fruits ye shall know them.'"[27] In subsequent years Carver's sympathies with the social gospel would become more pronounced.

Carver defended the social gospel and highlighted the deficiencies of fundamentalist theology. One of Carver's strongest criticisms of millennial dispensationalism was its "denaturing of the gospel of its ethical content and passion."[28] Carver traced the hatred of the social gospel to dispensational theology. "It's delusive dividing of the Christian gospel into a gospel of personal salvation and a social gospel and its utter detestation of the social gospel," claimed Carver, "contribute to the sinful tendency of man to seek personal security for the future world while evading the demand for righteousness in the present world."[29] For nearly fifty years W. O. Carver shared his bold vision of faith with the faculty and administration of the WMU Training School. Carver's influence was profound. The year before he died the trustees of the school chose to honor his service by renaming the WMU Training School as the Carver School of Missions and Social Work.

Another influential figure at the WMUTS was Maud Reynolds McLure, who served as principal from 1907 until 1923. In this role McLure served as a bridge between national and local leadership within WMU. Although her education exposed her to social work and the social gospel, she largely adapted her studies to fit the Southern Baptist tradition. McLure pioneered a model settlement house at the Training School and along with W. O. Carver shaped the social work curriculum. She took over Carver's course in personal mission work when the Training School was established in 1907. WMUTS curriculum indicates that "the training school's course called 'Personal Work' taught soul-winning as well as social work methods. The first year students studied 'Christ's methods in winning souls,' while the second year they focused on 'Relief Problems, Settlement and Welfare work.'"[30]

Maud McLure's life experience brought her into contact with the social gospel. In the summer of 1909, McLure began spending her vacations at Chautauqua, New York.[31] As mentioned earlier, Chautauqua began as a Sunday school training institute and grew to showcase a broad spectrum of cultural and educational issues during the Progressive Era. We do not have the exact dates of her visits, but McLure most likely would have heard discussions of current events and social issues, including the social gospel. Shailer Mathews conducted daily devotionals on many occasions and directed the Department of Religious Work for the assembly. Washington Gladden and Charles Stelzle also filled the pulpit at Chautauqua, along with Francis G. Peabody, Josiah Strong, Graham Taylor, and Francis McConnell.[32] McLure also participated in the Southern Sociological Congress along with Fannie E. S. Heck and used the reports of the Congress to help prepare the instructions for Baptist settlement work in the *Handbook of Personal Service*.[33] Thus, the principle of the WMU Training School was shaped by leading Progressive Era reformers. The model social settlement that McLure helped establish (discussed in greater detail in the next chapter) served as the laboratory for WMU social workers.

THE SOCIAL GOSPEL IN PERSONAL SERVICE LITERATURE

The Personal Service Department made its case for social reform directly to local women through columns in WMU magazines. The primary writers for Personal Service for most of the years from 1907 to 1930 were Fannie Heck, Lulie Wharton, Emma Leachman, and Maud Reynolds McLure. These women were also the leading contributors to the *Handbook for Personal Service* and for the training courses. But they were not the only voices represented. Many other WMU workers contributed to the Personal Service column in *Royal Service* during these years. Unfortunately, the columns and monthly studies rarely included a signature. It is difficult, therefore, to determine precisely how many women agreed with the more progressive policies of the department.[34] The theology varied in *Royal Service* depending on the column and the issue. Some articles endorsed the social gospel and some did not. Those columnists who espoused social gospel ideas often qualified their statements or masked them in Southern Baptist terminology. In defining salvation, the writers alternated between individual and corporate notions of redemption. Writers described personal service as work to usher in the kingdom, insisted that social justice and Christianity were inextricably linked, and they occasionally suggested concern over capitalism. Their literature represents a fascinating intersection of social gospel liberalism, Southern Baptist conservatism, and Progressive Era reform terminology.

This theological dissonance in the writings of the Personal Service Department and other WMU literature is comparable to the struggle, noted by John Lee Eighmy, of other progressives within the Southern Baptist Convention to appropriate the social gospel. Eighmy discovered conflicting messages in the reports of the Southern Baptist Social Service Commissions that were organized in response to a 1911 resolution from the Baptist World Alliance (BWA).[35] The

Southern Baptist Convention formed a south-wide Social Service Commission, and five southern states followed suit. These included Georgia, North Carolina, South Carolina, Virginia, and Texas. Eighmy argued that these commissions struggled most with determining the practical role churches should play in bringing about reform. The Texas commission, for example, "simultaneously backed social-reform movements while claiming that evangelism alone could cure social evils."[36] In Virginia, the commission was more progressive, but it hesitated to endorse direct political activity for fear it violated the separation of church and state.[37] Eighmy concluded from his research on state social service committees that there existed a "divided mind" among Southern Baptists between the conservative evangelical and social gospel traditions.[38] WMU leaders also demonstrated this "divided mind" with passages supporting both the social gospel and the gospel of individual salvation. While the theology may have been ambiguous at times, WMU's commitment to social work never wavered.

Often social gospel ideas appeared in WMU magazines in a single declarative sentence with no explanation. Sometimes the editors placed these sentences in the header of a handbook. A writer in the earliest WMU periodical, *Our Mission Fields*, insisted that "the city needs salvation from the un-Christlike spirit of selfish commercialism."[39] One *Royal Service* column argued that the creation of a just industrial order was within the purview of Christian responsibility.[40] The *Handbook for Personal Service* denounced unjust practices of big business with this comment: "The resources of the earth being the heritage of the people, should not be monopolized by the few to the disadvantage of the many."[41] The handbook also printed pro-labor sentiments. "Every worker should have a day's rest in seven and reasonable time for recreation and family life."[42] The handbook also recommended that "suitable provision should be made for the old age of workers and for those incapacitated by injury or sickness."[43] Personal Service writers even addressed the rights of women workers. "Women who toil," said the handbook, "should receive equal pay with men for equal work."[44] Again, these more radical statements appeared without clarification or explanation.

It was not uncommon for WMU literature to reference the social gospel obliquely. One very basic allusion, that would have been familiar to the contemporary reader, was Charles Sheldon's 1897 social gospel novel, *In His Steps*. The novel described the influence of a small congregation who begin to order their lives around the question, "What would Jesus do?" That question, and the notion of walking "in his steps" became slogans for Christian-based social justice efforts and watchwords for the Social Gospel Movement. The leadership of WMU indicated their familiarity with the novel in several instances. Transcripts of speeches and articles in *Royal Service* had direct quotes from Sheldon, demonstrating the significance of the social gospel writer's influence. In a speech by Fannie Heck to the North Carolina WMU one year after the publication of the novel, her written manuscript climaxes with a direct quote of Sheldon's famous refrain: "if in your place, 'what would Jesus do?'" As late as 1923, years after the publication of the novel, a writer in *Royal Service* points again to Sheldon's work with a direct quote: "As personal service is a sacred trust committed into our hands by One who fed the multitude, prepared breakfast for weary, hungry disciples, healed the sick, changed home life by His presence and gave the peace of God in the forgiveness of sins, we can but follow with humility 'in his steps.'"[45] The quotes belong to the writer. She is clearly alluding to Sheldon's phrase. It is interesting to point out the very feminine image of Christ in this passage as well. Christ is the one who prepared meals for hungry people, nursed the sick, and changed "home life" by his presence. The author drew parallels between the roles of Christ and the roles women were expected to play. The writer not only used Christ imagery to support social service but also those elements from Christ's ministry that would be uniquely appealing to her audience.

Another interesting allusion concerned Horace Bushnell's 1847 publication *Christian Nurture*. Although Bushnell's work predates the social gospel, Sydney Ahlstrom contends that his "romantic notions of process and development facilitated an accommodation of evolutionary thought and opened into the Social Gospel of Washington Gladden."[46] *Christian Nurture* addressed the issue of original sin and basically asserted that children could be nurtured to salvation without ever experiencing being "lost in sin." This theological position would be in direct opposition to the Southern Baptist's emphasis on revivalism and conversion. Nevertheless, a reference to Christian nurture can be found in the pages of *Royal Service*. In a lengthy explanation of social service ministries in the 1915 issue of *Royal Service*, the writer explains the chart of Personal Service. In the diagram, the church is located centrally and connected to all the leading institutions of society by large sidewalks. The writer indicated that these were sidewalks of service that could bring children to a settlement house where there were boys' and girls' clubs and libraries that would release them from "the brambles of child labor." From there, the child could be led to the church "where its opportunities for development manifold." The writer concluded her section on caring for children with the observation: "Today we interpret the gospel in 'terms of nurture' instead of 'terms of rescue.'" She did not indicate the source for her quotes, but the language echoes that of Bushnell.[47]

In other instances, WMU leaders bluntly quoted social gospel theologians. The 1915 Personal Service report to the annual meeting of the WMU opened with a quote from Graham Taylor, first chair of Christian Sociology in the United States, and founder of the Chicago Commons Settlement.[48] The bibliography and recommended reading section of the February 1914 *Royal Service* listed Graham Taylor's book *Religion in Social Action* in addition to recommending the reports of the 1913 and 1914 Southern Sociological Congresses. The mission program for August 1917 in *Royal Service* contained a two-page section taken directly from Josiah Strong's book *The Challenge of the City*. Mary Faison Dixon, who prepared the program, said that Strong was "a careful student of city problems and knows whereof he speaks."[49] Even when the first WMU report on Personal Service sought to assure readers that the new department would not stumble into an "overemphasis on social service," a social gospel theologian was referenced to make the point. The author of the report used the words of Shailer Mathews to voice her caution: "Dean Shailer Mathews, president of the Federal Council of Churches in America, issues a warning against the substitution of social service for spirituality in the church. He says: 'picnics are not the equivalents of prayer-meetings and Sunday-school baseball leagues have not yet developed into revivals.'"[50] The writer voiced caution about social service while legitimizing the teachings of Shailer Mathews and the Federal Council of Churches. This would immediately take critics off guard. She could have chosen any number of Southern Baptist leaders to issue a word of warning about social service, but she chose a social gospel leader.[51] Perhaps the author of this column was unaware of the irony of her quotation. Regardless, her choice of references demonstrated her familiarity with social gospel writers.

Leaders of Personal Service often defended social work and its methods by quoting the Bible and by stressing its benefits for individual salvation. *Royal Service* stated that Personal Service was "social service with the gospel as its motive and conversion as its aim."[52] In an annual report the committee asserted, "We cannot express the aim of this new department in better terms than to say it is social service upheld by grace."[53] WMU publications continued to use the phrase "social service" to describe their missionary methods even though there were strong sentiments against it among some Baptists. As late as 1920 a committee of Virginia Baptists pronounced that "right Gospel preaching will send nine-tenths of these special social service organizations to the scrap heap."[54] In contrast, the *Personal Service Handbook* stated, "The Founder of Christianity was the greatest social worker the world has ever known."[55]

Personal Service writers used biblical terms and passages in keeping with social gospel theology. For example, some employed the phrase "Kingdom of God" like Rauschenbusch did, as something that "is here on earth; that quietly pervades all humanity; that is always working toward the perfect life of God."[56] The *Handbook of Personal Service* states, "until the whole church is thus enlisted for the whole world, the kingdom of God cannot wholly come in any part of the earth."[57] Mary Livermore of Tennessee encouraged Southern Baptist women to cooperate with the secular movements for reform so that "their splendid humanitarian service" might help to "bring in the Kingdom of God in our midst."[58] In 1915, the Personal Service page of *Royal Service* featured a picture of a church with arrows connecting it to community institutions. The writer of the article comments: "What greater force in the coming of the Kingdom of God can there be than the church which he has established?"[59] These statements expressed WMU's acceptance of the social gospel premise that human participation could usher in the kingdom. Rauschenbusch believed that Christ could, through the church, transform the entire world, "making it righteous, making it habitable, making it merciful, making it brotherly."[60] Shailer Mathews defined the social gospel as the "application of the teaching of Jesus and the total message of Christian salvation to society, the economic life, and social institutions, . . . as well as individuals."[61] Fannie Heck's pamphlet *Pageant of the Golden Rule* depicted a dream of a perfected society in which the "Golden Rule" had been applied to institutions as well as individuals.[62] Her vision, and these references to the kingdom, assumed two principles: human progress and the perfectibility of society through application of the social ethics of Jesus.

The holistic perspective of salvation appears throughout Personal Service materials of the era. In fact, discussion of salvation became the doctrinal focus through which WMU leaders made their strongest social gospel statements. It was not unusual for a writer to quote a social gospel theologian (or an anonymous "social thinker" of the day who advocated the social gospel) then add a disclaimer for individual salvation. In 1913 the Personal Service Committee presented their answer to the basic question: What is the Personal Service work of Woman's Missionary Union? The committee responded: "It [Personal Service] is social service whose high ideal is not alone the lifting of mankind to better living conditions, to Christian business standards, especially regarding women and children employees, to proper and adequate opportunities for play, to social and cultural advantages, to educational privileges, but salvation for the life beyond through faith in Jesus Christ."[63] The phrase "not alone" suggests that human needs in the present life and spiritual well-being in the afterlife are both included in the goal of personal service. The *Handbook of Personal Service* began with an emphasis on individual salvation: "The end and object of the Personal Service Department is to bring men and women to a personal acknowledgment of Christ as their savior." The writers continued, however, with an explanation of precisely what they meant by salvation that moves nearer to the holistic emphasis of social gospel theologians:[64] "A full salvation includes the betterment of the physical conditions, the development of the mental powers, the culture of the moral sense."[65] The effort to bring people to "salvation" meant more than a personal confession. Full salvation, to this Personal Service writer, included both a changed spiritual condition and a changed physical condition.

A 1913 Personal Service report (mentioned in an earlier chapter) sanctioned social salvation with a quote by Josiah Strong. "'When a man loves God he is saved; when he loves his neighbor society is saved,' says one of the leading social teachers of the day. These two great needs—the need for personal salvation and the need for personal service in the interests of society are embodied in the intention and design of religion."[66] Strong's quote appeared in a 1912 issue of *Harper's Bazar*.[67] The emphasis on social salvation was typical of social gospel writers. "The redemption of the social order," wrote Washington Gladden, "is the problem now before us," and "the conviction of social sin [is] the beginning of social redemption."[68] In *Our Mission Fields*, one writer discussed salvation in the context of urban problems. "We are told," wrote the WMU columnist, "by that deep student of our country's conditions, Dr. Josiah Strong, that 'already one-fourth of the people of the United States live in the cities, and three-fourths of the wealth is there.'"[69] Something had to be done to bring salvation to the multitudes in the cities. In typical Southern Baptist fashion, the writer first affirmed individual salvation: "The saved city would be just a community of people in right relation to God through faith in the Savior; and nothing else, we know, can ever take the place of that truth." But to this truth, she insisted, must be added an awareness of the social dimensions of sin. "But in seeking the salvation of the individual we need to take account of some of the forces that draw him away from the influence of righteousness, and to see how our own Christian life may help negatively by removing these forces as well as by supplying the positive force of a saving knowledge of Christ."[70] In other words, social forces can inhibit or support individual salvation. Furthermore, the writer explained that there were two ways to view those forces: "Whether we look upon these facts as diseases of our national life that must be cured, or as symptoms of a deeper seated disease which is called sin, we shall all agree that extreme poverty, hard industrial conditions, the ever present saloon, increasing crime and other features of city life, are things to be reckoned with."[71] Either poverty and industrial conditions were national diseases, or they were the result of sin. Her wording is diplomatic and persuasive. Regardless of your conception of social problems, she is saying, "we shall all agree" that they must be "reckoned with." Her argument implies that individual salvation is very important, but social forces require a different sort of reckoning, a different sort of redemption. An article in *Royal Service* in 1921 offered a rather murky definition of "winning souls" that conflates solving "social problems" with "personal saving of human beings." "The [WMU] society that is not winning souls and that considers money gifts, perfunctory prayer and programs on distant fields as their whole duty, omitting personal service to the needy and neglected around them and cooperative effort to solve the social problems that wreck lives and ruin souls in every community, may have a large budget and much self-centered and complacent activity, but it will be like the fruitless vineyard so well tended and so disappointing to the Master. 'Cut it down; why cumbereth it to the ground?' Nothing but personal saving of human beings is going to satisfy Him."[72] Members of missionary societies could not be content with prayer meetings and missionary offerings. Unless women were personally involved in social uplift, argued this writer, they were useless to God. These writers challenged notions that the church's responsibility to society ended with individual, spiritual regeneration.

Fannie Heck was convinced that the gospel demanded personal involvement in social service. Rather than viewing social ministry as an optional, derivative element of religious conversion, Heck believed a social ethic was inherent in genuine Christian spirituality. She argued that one of the dangers of missionary organizations was that in their success, the work of ministry became second hand. She feared women would be content to "have someone else do our work while we languish and die for want of spiritual exercise."[73] By "spiritual exercise" Heck was certainly referring to the work of spiritual conversion, but Heck included social ministry in her definition of "saving the lost." In an April 1911 speech to the WMU of North Carolina, Heck commented that the North Carolina WMU was at "the beginning of a long march on a higher plane" that included improving the conditions of farm tenants, the isolated poor, and factory boys and girls.[74] Heck's conviction hinged on the notion that the gospel is not something one "believes," but rather it is something one does—a practical rather than exclusively propositional theological position. Her choice of titles for her history of WMU, *In Royal Service*, suggests the idea of personal work for the "kingdom." Her establishment of a Personal Service Department institutionalized her conviction that the Gospel had both social and individual implications.

One of the clearest presentations of the social gospel in the Personal Service material occurred in Lulie Wharton's 1915 annual report to WMU. Wharton placed the social gospel statement on the lips of an anonymous missionary: "Says a missionary: 'With every year of missionary experience the conviction has grown that the Gospel of Christ is a Gospel for all life—here not less than hereafter—and for all departments of life.'" This is the theme of holistic salvation. The missionary continued with an even more specific claim for the regeneration of the social conditions. He or she insisted that "for missionary workers to make [the Gospel] relate solely to salvation after death is a mistake, and to a great extent a defeat of its own ends; that godliness, in its ever-to-be-sought perfection, disallows crudities, unloveliness, barbarities, and cruelties in conditions of every-day life and relationship; that the Gospel of Christ aims quite as much at removing these as it points to the 'golden streets' and 'mansions' made ready." Finally, Wharton's anonymous missionary made a direct attack on the conservative primary emphasis on conversion: "The reformation of earthly life is indeed the preparation for the heavenly citizenship, and should be not the selfish saving of individual souls alive, but a work as broad and inclusive as is the Love that 'so loved the world'; so that no physical, social, governmental or intellectual obstacle to man's trust and highest development is too secular for the spirit of Christ and His Gospel to strike at through its missionaries."[75] In addition to defending social service against attacks that it is more "secular" than spiritual, the missionary undermines the notion that salvation consisted only of a verbal assent to propositional truths. It is more than the "selfish saving of individual souls alive." Wharton could not have been mistaken about the missionary's intent. The "anonymous missionary" was a woman named Dr. Grace N. Kimball, an American Baptist missionary serving in Van, Turkey. Her words were published in a work called *Christian Missions and Social Progress: A Sociological Study*, written by Rev. James Shepard Dennis in 1897. Immediately after Wharton's quote, Kimball's comments continued: "It seems to me that the somewhat tardy progress of missions in the past has been largely due to a hyperspirituality—a separation of the soul from its God-given earthly conditions. . . . I believe . . . we are waking up to feel that both the individual and society are equal objects of Christ's saving power."[76]

Wharton understood the theological implications of the quote. Even without the direct criticism of "hyper-spirituality" the missionary's words would have been startling to conservative Christians. Furthermore, the message of the missionary would have been abundantly clear to WMU ladies in the local church. The report made it clear: social work is God's work. The Gospel includes everything that helps human beings in this world and the next. Salvation applies to every aspect of human existence. Taken together, these ideas express the heart of the social gospel.

CONCLUSION

WMU offered training in personal service for both the laity and professional ministers. The Personal Service training studies, designed by the national Personal Service Committee, overtly taught the social gospel. The social gospel emphasis on the present world and its implicit concern for society manifested itself in WMU social work programs. Baptist women trained their leadership in professional social work and encouraged laywomen to use the methods of the new social sciences in their Personal Service programs. Southern Baptist women boldly advocated social work and the numerous organizations for social service that developed during the Progressive Era.

There is little doubt that key leaders of WMU were familiar with and sympathetic to the social gospel as it was articulated by theologians such as Gladden, Strong, and Rauschenbusch. At times they endorsed Rauschenbusch's concept of an earthly Kingdom, emphasized the social teachings of Jesus, and entertained perfectionist notions of human progress. Personal Service writers also articulated a vision for social salvation. At least one article stated bluntly that the Gospel must be more than the "selfish saving of individual souls." Most often WMU publications framed their social work goals in terms of individual salvation and insisted that "conversion" was the single aim of their social service ministries. But this does not undermine their concern for the social gospel. Walter Rauschenbusch was a German Baptist pietist who stated plainly: "We must not neglect the personal religious life and the tremendous problems of individual destiny. There are two objects of salvation, the race and the individual."[77] However oblique the references to the social gospel may have been at times, the message of the social gospel is present in WMU literature. Moreover, WMU leaders acted on the message of the social gospel and created an entire network of social reform programs that left an indelible mark on Southern Baptist life.

CHAPTER SEVEN

The Kingdom at Hand

Social Work Training and Social Settlements

In 1912, Southern Baptist women entered a new phase of social ministry when they established what they described as a "model settlement house" at the WMU Training School. The earliest reports on the school called it the "Baptist Training School Settlement."[1] From its inception in 1907 the WMU Training School offered theoretical and practical courses in social work.[2] The founders of the settlement hoped to train young women in social work methods for work in social settlements and institutional churches. While young women received training, WMU worked to provide places of service. In so doing, WMU addressed the problem faced by educated, qualified women who could not find jobs.[3] The WMU Personal Service office urged state WMU leaders to establish social settlement programs (called Good Will Centers) in their areas. A few societies answered the call of the national WMU and established formal Good Will Centers. These programs and centers needed trained directors, and the WMU Training School provided them. The WMU Training School, the Personal Service Department, and their supporters, opened new doors for Baptist women in vocational service, beyond the traditional field of foreign missions.

Social work historians have pointed out that WMU Good Will Centers functioned more as city missions than social settlements. This is undoubtedly true. If you compare the Baptist Good Will Centers to Jane Addams's Hull House, the differences are glaring.[4] The fact remains that WMU leadership studied social settlements such as Hull House and decided to adapt their structure for Baptist life. Baptist women *called* their programs social settlements knowing full well that they were associated with the social gospel, social reform, and more liberal theological assumptions. In so doing, members of the WMU leadership aligned themselves with social settlement workers, celebrated social work, and demonstrated their awareness of the social gospel.

ORIGINS OF CHRISTIAN SOCIAL MINISTRIES

Social settlements, social work, and the social gospel emerged in response to the constellation of social problems that plagued the nineteenth century in Europe and America. The first social settlement, Toynbee Hall, was established in the slums of East London in 1884. Two Oxford University students, Frederick Denison Maurice and Charles Kingsley, "set as their goals the replacement of competition by cooperation, and the establishment of the Kingdom of God on earth."[5] Influenced by social gospel theology, urban reformers in England launched a movement to improve the inner cities through social settlements. Social workers, usually young adults, moved into houses in poor neighborhoods in order to offer social services to the community. The settlement idea soon found its way to the United States. Jane Addams established the famous settlement, Chicago Hull House, in 1888—the same year that WMU was founded. Addams and the other founders of Hull House believed they were "establishing an instrument for social, educational, humanitarian, and civic reform."[6] Addams chose to place her settlement in Chicago's nineteenth ward, "a desperately poor neighborhood of immigrants, tenements, and sweatshops."[7]

By 1900 there were more than one hundred social settlements in the United States, ten years later there were more than four hundred.[8] During the Progressive Era the majority of the social settlements were concentrated in Chicago, Boston, and New York.[9] Women founded and/or staffed many of these endeavors. Mary McDowell founded the University of Chicago Settlement House; Mary Simkhovitch established the Greenwich House of New York; and Lillian Wald was responsible for the Henry Street Settlement in New York. The College Settlement Association (formed by Vida Scudder, Emily Balch, Kathryn Coman, and others) established houses in New York, Boston, and Philadelphia.[10] These settlement houses became avenues through which college educated women could "simultaneously launch careers" and "shape the civic development of industrial cities."[11] In her study, social settlement historian Mina Carson argued that college educated women dominated the movement.[12] Many social settlements were carved out feminine space, providing not only housing but also community, vocation, and purpose for the women involved. This may explain, in part, why WMU leaders felt a kinship with the settlement house movement.

A large number of Protestant ministers were attracted to the settlement idea because of the influence of the social gospel.[13] These men also gave the movement leadership and energy. Graham Taylor's work at Chicago Commons, George Hodges's at Kingsley House, and Clarence Gordon's residency at East Side House are examples of social settlements based in social gospel theology. While there was an attempt among most settlements to avoid the appearance of proselytizing, religion factored more prominently in the programs of the male-directed centers. For example, at Chicago Commons, "according to Taylor, religious observation was part of the routine through the years."[14] Jane Addams, although she did not believe evangelism to be the central purpose of a settlement, once commented that the "necessity for social settlements is . . . identical with that necessity which urges us on toward social and individual salvation."[15] The goal of social settlements, whether or not they held religious services, was to save society.

Most social settlements stressed three basic concepts: residency in a poor neighborhood, a nonsectarian program, and reform of the environment of poverty rather than the individual. Residency was intended to address the class divisions created by industrial capitalism. Reformers desired to "bridge the gulf that industrialism had created between rich and poor, to reduce the mutual suspicion and ignorance of one class for the other."[16] By living in the slums, university students believed they could bring education and culture to the poor, thus diminishing class division. Although many outsiders looked on the social settlements with suspicion, fearing they promoted socialism or even "revolution, the vast majority of settlement workers saw themselves as striving to make real the promises of democracy."[17] Their programs were designed to "ameliorate slum conditions and reconstruct neighborhood ties" by teaching English, sponsoring cultural events, or providing child care for families in the neighborhoods.[18] "The settlement is pledged to insist upon the unity of life," noted Jane Addams, "to work toward the betterment not of one kind of people or class of people, but for the common good."[19] Settlement workers hoped to resolve social tensions, in part, by helping the social classes become good neighbors.

Urban reform also factored prominently in the goals of social settlements. Programs from vocational training to urban gardens sought to transform the urban landscape. Jane Addams noted that "the Settlement, then, is an experimental effort to aid in the solution of the social and industrial problems which are engendered by modern conditions of life in a great city."[20] Settlement workers hoped to be good neighbors by addressing issues that threatened the lives or livelihoods of urban dwellers. Reformers collected data, secured government oversight positions, and lobbied legislators to press government to change public policy and regulate capitalism. For example, Florence Kelley, a resident of Hull House, studied the "sweating system" in Chicago. She led guided tours of the tenements for legislators and the press. Eventually the governor of Illinois appointed her as chief inspector of factories.[21]

Settlements also addressed the plight of immigrants. English-language programs and housekeeping courses, for example, attempted to help immigrants adjust to life in America. Progressive Era reformers called these efforts "Americanization." Social settlement historians Joyce Williams and Vicky MacLean asserted that "the Americanization of immigrant groups was an explicit goal in all of the settlements. Democracy, social science, and the social gospel were often indistinguishable."[22] Some differences existed among workers about how

Americanization should take place. Should immigrants abandon their native cultures and assimilate fully into American practices? Or should neighbors learn one another's customs and celebrate their differences? Graham Taylor promoted the latter approach of cultural pluralism. "We are all children of immigrants," he wrote. "Our country wants what you bring from the land of your birth. Do not lose it on your way. . . . It will enrich our lives and make America better for us all."[23] Although not all settlement workers shared Taylor's positive view of immigrant cultures, in general, they were leaders in affirming immigrant contributions to American life.

Social settlement workers blamed industrial conditions and unregulated capitalism for much of the poverty in urban America. But not everyone involved in social reform shared this view. Social work also has roots in a movement shaped by more conservative ideology. Modern social work methods can also be traced to the Charity Organization Society movement (COS). The counselors of the society, called "friendly visitors," visited people's homes and performed many of the tasks of present-day social workers. One historian of social work insists the COS "fostered and helped to develop the family service agencies of today, the practice of family casework, family counseling, councils of social agencies, schools of social work, employment services, legal aid, and many other programs."[24] Protestant reformers capitalized on the new social science methodologies in their ministry at the turn of the century. "Like the secular social workers Protestant sisters gathered information on social conditions during their visits of mercy," observed one Methodist scholar. "In these activities they were guided by the prevailing belief that the scientific study of society was essential to the . . . establishment of a just order."[25]

The Charity Organization Society and the social settlement movement were two of the approaches aimed at eradicating poverty during the Progressive Era. In the early 1890s, these two movements were clearly ideologically opposed. Settlement workers, influenced by ideas of the social gospel, perceived the poor as victims of social upheaval and corrupt institutions. "Rather than concern themselves with the moral fiber of their clients," contended social scientist Elizabeth Ferguson, "settlement workers concentrated their efforts on education and on reforms in the living and working conditions of their clients."[26] The charity movement, being more conservative, focused on individuals as the source of poverty. They were not alone. As one social work historian noted, "Most nineteenth century Americans believed that poverty was the result of sinfulness or laziness."[27] If sin caused poverty, then poverty could be eradicated by the promotion of personal virtue. Charity organization societies were heavily influenced by the Protestant work ethic that equated poverty with moral laxity. In the last decades of the nineteenth century, the COS and settlement workers moved toward a pattern of closer cooperation. The COS slowly began to turn its attention from charity to reform. One reason for the shift was that the two groups shared workers.

For example, one founder of the London COS, Canon Samuel Barnett, was also a founder of the first settlement, Toynbee Hall. In 1909, the cooperation in the United States was marked by the election of Jane Addams of Hull House to the presidency of the National Conference of Charities and Corrections.[28] Although the views of the workers were by no means monolithic, they joined together, liberal and conservative, for the common purpose of social reform.

SOCIAL SETTLEMENTS IN THE SOUTH

Methodist women pioneered social settlements in the American South.[29] Methodists began establishing settlement houses in southern cities as early as 1901. In these social settlements young women from middle-class families would move into poorer neighborhoods to set up model households. A worker described the first Methodist settlement house established in Nashville, Tennessee: "A house, which had formerly been a pool room, was rented and made habitable. Below there was a large hall in which the work was conducted, while above were clean and attractive living rooms for the workers."[30] A similar pattern emerged in other southern cities. Mrs. L. H. Potts created the Dallas City Board of Missions in 1902 to coordinate mission work there for the North Texas Conference. Mrs. Sara Estelle Haskins—missionary of the Dallas City Board of Missions—founded a Methodist settlement house in Dallas in 1902. Her purpose was "to minister to some three thousand people of seventeen nationalities surrounded by poverty, sin and degradation of the lowest type."[31] Haskins, with two other girls, moved into a "neighborhood where there were twenty-five saloons within a radius of six blocks of the settlement house, and where the houses of ill fame were blighting the lives of young men and women as well as little children."[32] When neighborhoods improved, Methodist settlement houses moved to another blighted neighborhood and turned the former facility into a local church. The Methodist settlement in Louisville, Kentucky, renamed Wesley House in 1906, served as a model for Baptist women at the WMU Training School.

In May 1912, Maud Reynolds McLure helped establish the model settlement house at the WMU Training School. She believed it would be beneficial for students to have more involvement in settlement work. Even before the settlement house was founded, McLure emphasized "practical mission work in the city" and required students to work with established social ministries in Louisville.[33] "Among the many places where the students did their practical work was the Wesley House, the Methodist expression of the settlement house idea. Gradually," explained Carrie Littlejohn, "McLure began to think in terms of a Baptist settlement house."[34] Social work historian Laine Scales suggests that a nondenominational settlement called Neighborhood House, founded in 1896, was equally influential in McLure's thinking.[35] Neighborhood House in Louisville was one of the two most important reform settlements in the South during the

Progressive Era.[36] After working with Neighborhood House and Methodist settlement, McLure began making plans for a model settlement run by the Training School and subsequently made her journey to New York to study settlement house methods. McLure took courses at the New York School of Philanthropy, the first school founded to prepare students for work with social agencies. The New York School of Philanthropy, founded in 1898 by the New York Charity Organization Society, originated as a six-week training course.[37] McLure spent the summer of 1912 studying social work methods and boarding at a social settlement on the East Side.[38] In Philadelphia McLure learned the rudimentary methods of social work: friendly visiting, record keeping, and cooperating with other charity organizations.

The director of the New York School of Philanthropy, Edward T. Devine, drew on the more conservative approaches of the COS but was equally influenced by the social settlement movement. McLure assigned Devine's writings in her training school classes. His writings guided McLure as she set up the model social settlement in Louisville. Although McLure and other teachers at the WMUTS were exposed to the more liberal theological assumptions of the settlement movement, they taught the Protestant ethic of the COS and concentrated their efforts on changing individuals.[39] McLure borrowed methods from both organizations and translated them into the Southern Baptist context. This amalgamation of progressive social activities and conservative Southern Baptist sensibilities is typical of the Woman's Missionary Union during this period. McLure brought settlement work concepts into the life of WMU, and her education in social settlements enhanced the social work emphasis at the Training School. In 1912, the doors of the Southern Baptist settlement house were opened in connection with the Woman's Missionary Union Training School in Louisville, Kentucky. The 1914 report of the Baptist Training School Settlement stated the purpose of the new venture was "to give Training School students experience in social service and to train directors of Settlements or helpers in Institutional churches."[40]

Emma Leachman directed the WMU settlement's daily activities. Leachman taught "applied methods in city missions" at the training school from 1907 until 1921.[41] One of the training school students explained her casework experience with the settlement in the March 1921 issue of *Royal Service*: "Each family constitutes a 'case' which we visit to find out as much about as possible and primarily to win for Christ. Eight short months is not sufficient time to complete the records but our filing system enables the new workers to begin where others left off."[42] In November of that same year, an article in *Royal Service* urged readers to use the same casework methods of the training school. "Case histories should be written of the families with whom you deal in order that intelligent, constructive work can be done from year to year," she instructed. Further, the writer urged societies to employ a trained social worker, if possible. "We should not be content to do in a blundering way what touches so many for good or ill," commented the writer. "Charity as it is usually administered by the untrained worker does more harm than good."[43]

The WMU Training School in Louisville produced the workforce to support local personal service programs. Graduates of the WMUTS took positions as mission workers across the South, bringing the lessons of social work with them. Graduates were awarded a bachelor of missionary training and were considered qualified professionals in the field of social work. Baptist settlement work was one new field of service becoming available for new graduates. As directors of Baptist settlements young women could receive salaries of up to $50 a month, with room and board.[44] The annual report of 1914 revealed that all four settlement houses in operation at that time (Meridian, Norfolk, Atlanta, and Richmond) were managed by WMUTS graduates.[45] The women of the Birmingham Baptist Association reported in 1919 the arrival of a missionary to head their settlement work at Pratt City. "Our new missionary, Miss Campbell, comes to us from the Training school well equipped for this work."[46] In May 1923, *Royal Service* reported that graduates of the WMU Training School were "working in the homeland as missionaries among foreigners at Tampa, St. Louis, Birmingham, Norfolk, and Baltimore; as settlement workers and missionaries in the cities; as missionaries among the women and children in the cotton mill villages in the south; as missionaries and teachers in the mountains and mountain schools; as Bible teachers in girls' colleges; as missionaries and leaders of young people's work in the churches; as state and associational leaders in Woman's Missionary Union, Sunday School and B.Y.P.U [Baptist Young People's Union] work."[47] A veritable army of well-trained social workers poured through the doors of the WMU Training School and entered the southern fields of service.

The graduates of the training school received mission training that equipped them to serve in a variety of contexts. For example, of the twenty-three training school graduates in 1915, ten applied their degrees to vocations in the South that required social work skills. Such work included starting kindergartens for immigrants, teaching in orphanages and mountain schools, settlement work, and work with "mill people."[48] Local church and association programs related to immigrants, cotton mill workers, and urban problems were classified under the heading of WMU personal service. As a result, personal service work frequently overlapped with home mission efforts. The overlapping interests of social work and home missions meant that salaries were often cobbled together. For example, a portion might come from a local WMU, some from a local Baptist association, and another portion from the Southern Baptist Home Mission Board.

In spite of all the positive results of their work, WMU writers acknowledged that many Southern Baptists remained suspicious of social work. "Some confuse a social worker with a socialist," reported a Personal Service columnist, "and even the well-informed of our church leaders do not always understand the ideals and methods of social agencies such as the Associated Charities, Public Health Service, American Red Cross and Community Service."[49] Baptist women struggled to educate the "well informed" church leaders regarding the benefits of secular organizations for social service. *Our Mission Fields* claimed that it was the "failure of the church to minister to the submerged masses that led to the formation of other organizations for community uplift." Furthermore, all social service agencies, according to WMU leaders, owed their impulse to Christianity.[50] The Personal Service column cautioned against the "narrow, jealous attitude assumed by our churches toward this movement" and warned societies not to "displease the greatest social Reformer who ever lived, He who said, 'I have come that they might have life and that they might have it more abundantly.'"[51]

To celebrate the twenty-fifth anniversary of WMU, leadership decided to emphasize the establishment of more permanent Personal Service ministries.[52] Five additional settlement houses, called Baptist Good Will Centers, were founded as a result of the anniversary—in Richmond, Virginia; Meridian, Mississippi; Charlotte, North Carolina; Newport News, Virginia; and in Atlanta, Georgia.[53] Local women organized many of the new Baptist settlement houses around existing ministries. For example, the settlement at Pratt City near Birmingham, Alabama, founded in 1916, developed from a sewing school for Italian children that had been established seven years previously.[54] As early as 1910 women's missionary societies in Norfolk began work among immigrants and collected funds to bring a full-time missionary to their area.[55] In Richmond, Virginia, Baptist women began working together as early as 1903 to hire a "female city missionary" to direct the work of their Baptist Neighborhood House.[56] After the house opened in the fall of that year, the women formed a "Big Sister Committee" that "found homes for orphans or unwanted children, and jobs for teenagers. They acted as intermediaries in courts, worked with police and juvenile officers, supplied food, money and clothing for the desperate."[57] After the Personal Service Committee recommended settlement work, Richmond women resolved to develop a complete Good Will Center.[58]

In 1915 Marie Buhlmaier, a city missionary supported by WMU, established a Good Will Center in Baltimore, Maryland. Nettie Anthon was the first director, hired in 1916. Mary Webb and Minnie Ebaugh took over as directors of this center in 1917. The Baltimore Good Will Center hosted such programs as sewing classes, Sunday schools, mothers' clubs, Bible classes, boys' and girls' clubs. A new building was erected in 1951 and dedicated as the Kathleen Mallory Center. It did not have a male director until 1966.[59] In 1918, WMU reported thirty-two Good Will Centers across the South.[60]

Although the settlement idea was most often implemented after national WMU recommended it, some Baptist women were involved in formal settlement work prior to the establishment of the model settlement in Louisville. In Waco, Texas, for example, Baptist women gathered in 1911 and formed an organization called "the Waco Baptist Settlement Association for Work among Mexicans."[61] Their settlement had a kindergarten, a sewing class, manual training classes, and a music class.[62] While they did not establish an official WMU Good Will Center, Waco women considered their support of the Mexican settlement to be personal service work.[63] By 1916 there were three formal Texas Good Will Centers established, in Abilene, Fort Worth, and Austin.

A *Handbook of Personal Service* provided detailed guidelines for establishing a Good Will Center. The model offered for Baptist settlement houses drew heavily from the "City Mission Manual, Woman's Board of Home Missions, M. E. Church South." The bibliography for the handbook listed the reports of the Southern Sociological Congress and the National Conference of Charities and Correction.[64] The yearbooks for Hull House and Chicago Commons settlements were cited, as well as a book called *Social Settlements* by C. R. Henderson. The bibliography includes a work of Charles Stelzle's along with pamphlets by the Federal Council of Churches and the American Baptist Home Mission Society. The handbook cites various children's advocacy groups such as the Bulletins on Child Welfare by the Federal Children's Bureau and the pamphlets of the National Child Labor Committee.[65]

In spite of the progressive bibliography, and some specific social gospel pamphlets, most Baptist Good Will Centers did not develop a progressive reform agenda. Laine Scales insists that the Good Will Center at Louisville would have been classified by leaders of the settlement movement as a mission rather than a settlement.[66] WMU leadership made no secret that the Gospel was the motive, and "conversion" was the aim of personal service.[67] A report of the Louisville settlement clarifies that goal: "the management has not believed that in this case, the social settlement idea, great and noble as it is, should be used without the specific teaching of Christianity, therefore every effort is being made to bring souls to Christ."[68] McLure's listed aims for settlement work maintain the missionary focus. Settlement work was designed:

1. To reach the little children that their tiny feet may be started in the upward path.
2. To inspire the older boys and girls with ideals that shall help them to improve their environment and shall give them strength against the awful temptations that sweep over them.
3. To interest the young people in sane and wholesome pleasures that their energies may be rightly directed.
4. To help the women to be better home makers, more careful wives and mothers, better Christians.
5. To give Christ to the neighborhood.[69]

These goals reveal McLure's more conservative emphasis on the individual as the key to social betterment. She hoped to help "boys and girls" resist "temptations" and aid mothers in becoming better "home makers." Most Baptist Good Will Centers followed her pattern and emphasized reform of individuals rather than environment. Local women believed that children, boys and girls, needed good morals—not changed institutions—in order to "be started in the upward path." Baptist women were not attempting to break down class barriers. Baptist Good Will Centers did not employ resident workers for the purpose of overcoming social divisions. They did not share Jane Addams's desire to "interpret democracy in social terms."[70] McLure indicates that the model settlement house in Louisville did not house resident workers.[71] Emma Leachman, the Louisville city missionary, kept offices at the Good Will Center, but it was not her residence.[72] The Training School students walked over from a better neighborhood to direct the clubs, kindergartens, and nurseries.

Good Will Centers did, however, share some things in common with their settlement counterparts. First of all, Baptist Good Will Centers used the same programs as the larger settlement movement. WMU Good Will Centers sponsored day nurseries to help women who worked in factories.[73] Day nurseries provided children with health care and free meals. Centers also staffed public playgrounds and provided circulating libraries for the children who came to play.[74] Good Will Centers often conducted night schools to educate factory workers. Industrial schools provided practical training for children from ages six to fifteen.[75] Blue Bird Clubs, affiliated with Camp Fire Girls, taught home economics to little girls.[76] Younger boys could learn lessons in heroism, patriotism, and woodworking in the Good Will Heroes Clubs.[77] Mothers' clubs or Homemakers' Clubs provided women with information on parenting, health, gardening, sewing, cooking, and other household tasks. These clubs were often tailored particularly for immigrant women. In addition, many settlements offered independent cooking classes, music lessons, story hours for children, and social events for young working women. All of these activities closely mirrored the work of other social settlements. Of course, in addition to these, Baptist centers added Sunday schools, Vacation Bible Schools, and Bible classes to their programming.

Another similarity between Good Will Centers and settlements were the practical methods they used to learn about families in the neighborhood. Baptist women emphasized casework methods of social work in their centers, including statistical surveys, detailed records, and professional workers. The handbook recommended that local societies gain a statistical survey of neighborhood conditions before establishing a settlement. Workers should acquire information from public records, from "experts," and from "personal investigation."[78] Personal investigation meant visits to families in poor neighborhoods.[79] The handbook advised WMU workers to keep careful records of each family who visited on 3 x 5 index cards. Workers made a file and added to it over the years. In keeping with the professionalization of social work in the early decades of the twentieth century, WMU encouraged the use of "trained workers" in their settlements. Most Good Will Centers were directed by Training School graduates. In the spirit of the Charity Organization Society movement, the Personal Service leadership encouraged directors of Good Will Centers to cooperate with organizations that provided aid to the needy such as Associated Charities, Babies' Milk Fund Association, Public Hospitals, Fresh Air and Rescue Homes, and the Juvenile Court. The handbook admonished directors to "cooperate earnestly with all the welfare agencies of the city, striving to avoid overlap of her work with theirs."[80]

One of the basic things that connected Good Will Centers to places like Hull House is that Baptist women believed they were organizing Christian settlements. In the handbook, in McLure's article, and in *Royal Service* the women deliberately identified their work with the settlement movement.[81] The Louisville Good Will Center was first called the Baptist Training School Settlement.[82] In the December 1922 mission study program, the unnamed writer linked WMU Personal Service work directly to social settlements. "The earliest organized personal service work was inspired by one individual, Arnold Toynbee, an Oxford (England) student." The writer continued with a brief explanation of the history of social settlements. She concludes her historical sketch with a reference to Jane Addams. "About this time [1887–88] also there was opened in Chicago what was destined to become probably the most famous social settlement in America, the 'Hull House,' established by Miss Jane Addams."[83] All the major cities in the United States, pronounced the writer, "are now conducting houses for social service."[84] WMU's work simply added a message of spiritual salvation to these "great and worthy benevolences." WMU leaders believed that social settlements could only reach their full potential if they preached "the gospel of salvation as well as the gospel of soap and sanitation."[85]

Because of their belief in the validity and necessity of social settlements, WMU leaders studied American settlement houses at length. Fannie Heck, Lulie Wharton, and Maud McLure visited settlements in New York and Chicago. Training School graduates Nannie West and Louise Ellyson traveled to New York to study settlements before erecting a permanent building for the Good Will Center at Richmond.[86] Even though the resulting Baptist centers functioned more like city missions than social settlements, Baptist women learned from social gospel institutions and adopted their methods to accomplish their missionary goals.[87] On the local level, women worked with social agencies and learned social work methods within a denomination that frowned on ecumenical cooperation and social service. And while the liberal social gospel lessons they learned only whispered from the pages of the Personal Service material—from the recommendations of the handbook, from the bibliographies, and from questions of the *Survey*—the practical lessons of the social work were manifest in their settlement work.

By 1924, attendance at Good Will Centers numbered over 103,000. More and more women seized opportunities for professional ministry. Centers continued to grow throughout the next two decades, resulting in thousands of conversions and several new churches. Baptist women were proud of their accomplishments. At the twenty-fifth annual WMU meeting in Saint Louis they stated candidly, "Today women's organizations are a most potent power in aiding reforms, perfecting plans, raising money, influencing public opinion, molding character, disseminating knowledge, and they are rapidly finding in social service a field where they can turn 'beliefs into energies.'"[88]

Despite these successful forays into settlement work, WMU Good Will Centers ultimately encountered defeating obstacles. The basic problem was lack of denominational support for women's efforts. Money for the centers largely flowed through the local churches. "Churches as a whole were not as willing to budget for good will centers as the women were."[89] Furthermore, the growing influence of women's ministries threatened the Southern Baptist Home Mission Board and the rest of convention leadership. In her 1924 presidential address to WMU, Minnie Kennedy commented, "Our Personal Service work, particularly in good will centers, has assumed such proportions that like the brethren in the days of 1874–88 some of the brethren today are wondering what they are going to do with this 'rising power.'"[90] As Good Will Center programs expanded, the expenses mounted. Local WMU societies often depended on funds from associations, state conventions, or most often from the Southern Baptist Home Mission Board. Citing financial reasons, in the 1940s WMU Good Will Centers were turned over, one by one, to the governance of the Southern Baptist Home Mission Board.

THE FOCUS OF PERSONAL SERVICE: WOMEN AND CHILDREN

Whether in work with immigrants, city dwellers, industrial workers, or concerns with public health, Baptist women focused their programs on women and children. The Baptist settlement house provided a "separate sphere" for women's work as an extension of the home.[91] Baptist Good Will Centers were distinctly feminine worlds. McLure's list of goals for settlement work does not mention men at all.[92] Ministry to mothers was a recurring theme in the pages of *Royal Service*. The Personal Service Committee urged local societies to establish Homemakers' Clubs, or mothers' meetings, primarily to convert women to Christianity and secondarily to educate women to be good mothers and wives. Through social ministry to women, WMU leadership continued to affirm ideals of evangelical womanhood. Women were perceived as the key for shaping the spiritual and moral condition of the family. They were, "when enlightened the truest leaven in the hand of the social worker for elevating the home."[93] They believed women could become ideal mothers through an imitation of Christ. This focus on the maternal role as motivation for missions and reform is not unique to WMU. Female reformers in the Progressive Era consistently modeled their public efforts on their domestic role. Ellen Carol Dubois argues that the first generation of women progressives—settlement workers and municipal reformers—consistently perceived their roles as public expressions of their maternal roles. "The aim of Homemakers' Clubs is to help mothers to gain a sense of the value of Christ to every human being, young or old," she insisted in *Royal Service*. "What blessing should we ask for the mothers? What do they, and we ourselves, need? Unselfish love, infinite patience, wisdom and insight, tact and sympathy, health to bear the daily strain, quiet nerves, a sense of humor that smoothes rough places, a sweet strong cheerfulness, a likeness to Christ that shall be reflected in the lives of all the household."[94]

WMU leadership also believed that mothers would be the key to converting entire families to Christianity, and they assumed that every woman wished to be a good homemaker. Mothers' clubs combined homemaking and discipleship. They offered information on good hygiene, sewing, first aid, and child care in addition to Bible study. The WMU recommended methods they considered "the true ideals of home making and child training."[95] "Educated motherhood is the demand of today, not only in our land but across the sea," insisted Mrs. James Pollard of Baltimore, Maryland. This education could be gained through "Homemakers' Clubs" where "problems of everyday life in the home are to be discussed; child welfare, training, care of infants, first aid to injured, household economies and problems of every kind."[96] Practical education complemented the missionary enterprise. "The purpose of the club is not only to bring cheer to the lives of the mothers; it is to help them to solve the many difficult problems they meet in the care of their homes and their children, and especially to give them the message of Christ's love."[97] One society in North Carolina explained that at their mothers' club "we teach [the mothers] fancy work as well as plain sewing. An interesting program is prepared. These meetings are especially attractive to the tired mothers, they bring their babies and one of our young girls goes each time to amuse them."[98] Although the tone of the instructions suggests an attitude of noblesse oblige, the clubs brought together women from different walks of life. Presumably these were rich and poor white women. Work with immigrants was typically discussed as a discrete category. As the chapter on race reveals, Baptist women did little to encourage social relationships between black and white women.

Cheer-All Clubs, devoted to helping young women working alone in urban areas, were also elements of WMU Personal Service work. "In Cheer-All Clubs girls are banded together to help, protect and encourage other girls and for the development and advancement of Christian young womanhood."[99] These clubs typically met on Friday evenings to entertain young women who worked all week. The meetings began with devotions and hymn singing then continued with various "bright and entertaining" programs. These might include games or stories read aloud while the girls worked on "embroidery, millinery, or basketry."[100]

In 1915 ninety societies out of 4,566 reported participating in Homemakers' Clubs and ninety-seven reported work with Cheer-All Clubs.[101] From 1915 until 1925 roughly 2 percent of the local societies reporting Personal Service work sponsored Homemakers' Clubs and Cheer-All Clubs. During this same period, 5 percent reported participation with a full Good Will Center program that included both programs.[102] If we assume the women did not duplicate their reports, then approximately 7 percent of reporting societies participated in work with mothers' clubs and young working women from 1915 until 1925.

Children's programs occupied the largest portion of the WMU plan of Personal Service. The handbook outlined instructions for story hours, circulating libraries, playgrounds, day nurseries, boys' clubs, girls' clubs, cooking classes, industrial schools, and Vacation Bible Schools. Playgrounds and libraries were usually associated with Good Will Houses. The model settlement in Louisville kept a playground open every day all summer long with library hours on Monday and Friday and a story hour on Saturday afternoons.[103] A report of Louisville settlement activities in 1921 contends that the ages of children on the playground ranged from ten months to fifteen years, and the average attendance for each day was 112.[104]

Boys' and girls' clubs attempted to instill such virtues as thrift, cleanliness, and patriotism in the children who attended and pervasively reinforced gender-specific roles. "Give the boy a hammer and saw," advised one writer, "give the girl a needle and thread or a chance in the kitchen and who can measure the lessons learned?"[105] Blue Bird Clubs, an organization of Camp Fire Girls, provided basic instruction on homemaking to girls from ages nine to thirteen with an emphasis on play. For example, little girls might learn to sew for their dolls, furnish dollhouses, or keep their dolls clean in order to develop the "motherly instinct."[106] *Royal Service* reported the comment of one eleven-year-old girl after a lesson in practical cooking: "Father enjoys the cocoa I make for supper and always wants me to make biscuits because mine are light while mama's are heavy and greasy."[107]

For boys' clubs the handbook encouraged WMU societies to find a male director. If a woman must teach them, she was warned not to "make girls of boys."[108] While girls were learning to cook and sew, boys were taught simple parliamentary procedure and woodworking. Although "if a carpenter's shop is a part of the Good Will Center equipment then a man should teach."[109] The handbook suggested the name "Good Will Heroes" for the boys' clubs, but there are indications that some clubs adopted the programs of the Boy Scouts of America.[110] It is interesting that more attention is given to instructions and reporting of boys' clubs. Fewer than three pages of the handbook were devoted to instructions for Blue Bird Clubs, half of which provided a sample program. Four pages of detailed instructions were provided for the boys' clubs. The assumption was that the women would know instinctively how to work with little girls. Also, no category was provided to report the numbers for younger girls' clubs while boys' clubs were listed from the first report in 1916. Fewer than 2 percent of societies reported work with boys' clubs beyond the work of Good Will Centers from 1915 to 1925.

Industrial schools taught practical skills to children from ages six to fifteen. Good Will Centers held classes for the neighborhood children in sewing, basketry, or chair caning.[111] Manual training had the potential to meet real needs in the neighborhoods by teaching marketable skills.[112] Skills in making buttonholes or operating sewing machines could increase the family income, particularly in textile mill districts.[113] WMU leadership promoted industrial schools because of their value in "moral and material uplift."[114] But their central interest was the belief that busy hands would be slow to mischief. About 1 percent of societies reported participation with industrial schools (apart from Good Will Centers) in the period 1915 to 1925. The most reported during those years was eighty-five societies out of the 10,615 involved in Personal Service. Far more societies reported "sewing for the poor" than teaching the poor to sew. Over one-fourth of all WMU societies who participated in Personal Service reported sewing garments for the poor from 1915 to 1925.[115]

A few more local women were involved in Vacation Bible Schools than other children's programs recommended by the Personal Service Committee during this period.[116] Daily Vacation Bible Schools (VBS) held summer Bible classes for children that met for two hours and thirty minutes, five days a week. VBS typically began the first week in July and continued for six weeks during the summer.[117] Children learned Bible stories through games, music, and crafts. An average of 168 societies reported their involvement with Vacation Bible Schools in the decade from 1915 to 1925. Interest in VBS continued to grow within Baptist circles. Baptist historian H. Leon McBeth reports that Southern Baptists began to embrace this program more widely after World War I. In 1935 Baptist churches conducted 1,044 Vacation Bible Schools across the South.[118]

PUBLIC HEALTH

Women and children were also the center of much of WMU's concern for public health. Personal Service leaders urged WMU societies to join the campaign for public health, mostly in response to the meetings of the Southern Sociological Congress. *Royal Service* reprinted the aims of the congress under the title "The Call of Human Need" and urged Southern Baptist women to attend the 1915 meeting of the congress that was devoted exclusively to health issues.[119] After the meeting, the Personal Service Committee shared the ideas propagated by the congress: "We quote from Dr. Samuel Zane Batten before the Southern Sociological Congress: . . . The churches must teach men . . . that it is just as wicked a thing to kill a family by renting them an unsanitary tenement as it is to throw strychnia in the milk bottle."[120] Personal Service writers took Batten's words to heart and offered a strong appeal for engaging in the battle for public health. First of all, the writers for Personal Service emphasized that the health campaign was genuine missionary service. "We must realize that this work of preventing social evils is religious and spiritual work. Men have always believed that it is a spiritual service to nurse the sick, to visit the prisoner, to feed the hungry family, to take care of the fatherless child. But many today do not see that it is just as spiritual service to study the causes of poverty, to organize a Board of Health, to start a crusade against dirt, to teach people the laws of health."[121] Note that Baptist women followed Batten's lead and categorized health problems as a "social evil" linked to poverty, filthy living conditions, and lack of education. Seemingly a campaign like "good health" could be introduced into the goals of WMU without raising cries of liberalism. These campaigns could open the door for discussion of broader social issues.

The campaign for public health represents a solid theological shift from a typical Southern Baptist focus on "mansions in the skies" to the present life and its problems.[122] Baptist women believed that God cared about the physical conditions of the living, insisted the writer of the March 1916 Personal Service column in *Royal Service*. The article began with quotes from the Southern Sociological Congress. "Fifty percent of the deaths in our country are preventable," said the congress. Furthermore, "the death of children is the defeat of God's purpose and their health—physical, mental and moral—should be the primary function and responsibility of the church."[123] The writer continued with a biblical precedent for social service. "No one can read the Mosaic Law and not be impressed with the careful provision that is made for conserving the health and physical well being of the Israelites. What sort of Christians can be made of a people whose surroundings are unsanitary, whose spirits are depressed by disease, witnessed and experienced, whose bodies are weakened and wasted by want and ignorance? They must be taught to live here as well as to lay hold on eternal life."[124] In speaking of diseases that were both "witnessed and experienced," the writer evokes an image of mothers watching sick babies suffer with preventable diseases. This typical maternal concern for sick children led the leadership of WMU to urge societies to apply the gospel in tangible ways.[125] The Personal Service Committee urged Baptist women to research the causes of social problems. "When you have learned the actual facts as to housing, sanitation, health, education, recreation, child labor, family conditions, industrial conditions, . . . you will then find what is the greatest need and where your society can best put its time and effort."[126]

Education was central to the WMU's efforts at health reform. Personal Service publications provided basic programs for teaching local societies about public health. Sample posters listed health regulations and urged communities to adopt them. One lesson concluded, "The things that breed disease are poverty, ignorance, over-crowding, immorality, unsanitary premises, neglect and malnutrition of children."[127] The involvement of local women in public health issues is difficult to assess. For one thing, Personal Service records do not contain a specific category to quantify the "battle for Health" touted in the pages of *Royal Service*. A category for "hours of nursing" appeared beginning in 1920, but this does not indicate how many societies were involved, nor does it clarify whether this is professional nursing for the community or personal nursing of sick church members. Another problem with quantifying health results is that good health efforts were incorporated into the agendas of related programs. For example, day nurseries were designed to help poor working mothers and to provide for the health of their children. The handbook stated that "arrangements should be made to have the children examined by a physician, and if the child is not well those in charge may follow him up." Further, "a doctor or trained nurse could be called in consultation on certain days and prescription and diet lists given."[128] Day nurseries were counted with kindergartens in the Personal Service record from 1918 until 1922 when they were given a separate category. In 1922, 175 societies reported work with day nurseries, 406 reported in 1923, 190 in 1924, and 424 in 1925.[129] Of course, many day nurseries were housed in Good Will Centers and were reported with that work. What is difficult to determine is whether or not individual day nurseries, independent or in Good Will Centers, emphasized the health issues that the national WMU recommended. The same trouble applies to assessing the health and sanitation emphases in the home economics programs of Homemakers' Clubs and Cheer-All Clubs.

Some local societies clearly supported the WMU program of public health. For instance, women of the Waco Baptist Association financed a city nurse for the Mexican population and investigated public institutions such as jails and county farms "with a view to bringing about better sanitary conditions."[130] A local society in North Carolina enlisted the help of civic groups in their town to support a city nurse. "As we were not able to support her alone," they explained, "we secured the cooperation of the Civic League and took subscriptions for her salary and equipment. The whole town is enthusiastic over the results of this work."[131] The Good Will Center in Meridian, Mississippi, boasted that "physicians, specialists and hospitals recognize the work that is being undertaken through Good Will Center, to the extent they cooperate with the director in every way."[132] These programs are easily identified with the goals of the national WMU, although they did not advocate legislative action. There is little evidence to indicate that the women who investigated public institutions lobbied for systemic change.

AMERICANIZATION

WMU leadership urged societies to help immigrant mothers become integrated into American society.[133] They hoped to lead immigrants to adopt Protestant Christianity, ideally in its Baptist form. Implied in this goal is that immigrants would abandon their Old World religion—particularly Catholicism. "The immigrant mother is the last member of the family to be reached by American influence," reported the May 1916 issue of *Royal Service*, "yet upon her and her ability to make her home correspond to American conditions and ideals depend the true Americanization of her family."[134] In 1918 WMU leadership included "Americanization" as a category for the Personal Service reports. "Americanization, now that immigration has stopped, is an important duty for all Christians," explained the 1918 Personal Service report at the annual meeting of WMU. "We interpret it in simplest terms—reaching the foreign born wife and mother."[135] The 1919 report on Personal Service urged all Baptist women to take the following pledge: "We pledge ourselves to Americanization by renewed efforts to reach the alien woman in her home and through the door of consecrated friendliness to lead her into close touch with our Christ. To this end friendly visiting, the class in English as well as the Homemakers' Club may be used."[136] By the time of this pledge, WMU had been promoting English classes for nearly a decade. "Classes in English will better equip the immigrant to make his way in the world," insisted the program for March 1911, in *Our Mission Fields*. "The women need help more than do the men. Confined to the four walls of their kitchen, and made to listen to the crying and the shouting of the children, isn't it a wonder that more of them do not become insane? Many of them do, but you probably never hear about it."[137] In spite of their implication that immigrant women were unstable, the writers for this program clearly sympathized with the plight of mothers in a strange country and believed the programs of WMU would ease the transition. In addition to English, immigrant mothers were taught to "save money and start bank accounts."[138] The July 1909 edition of *Our Mission Fields* used banking statistics as evidence of the success of an immigrant's integration into American culture. "Mr. Charles Stelzle of the Presbyterian Church's Department of the Church and Labor, has made a careful study of the foreigner and he says that seventy per cent of the depositors in New York City savings banks came as immigrants."[139] Investment in the American banking system was a measure of Americanization.

From the time the WMU began gathering separate reports on Americanization from 1918 until 1925, an average of 142 societies, about 3 percent, reported work with immigrants. Slightly more interest in Americanization occurred during and just after World War I. These numbers do not include the programs of Good Will Centers. The settlement near Birmingham, Alabama, had developed from a sewing school for Italian immigrants.[140] The Center at Pratt City was located near the Birmingham mill district and continued work with immigrants as a central part of its program. In addition to programs for children, they maintained a night school for adults.[141] The Good Will Center in Norfolk, Virginia, also grew out of work with immigrants.[142] The ultimate goal of Baptist work in Americanization was to help immigrant communities form a Baptist congregation. Thus, the Americanization goal of most Baptist women could better be described as assimilation rather than cultural pluralism.

LABOR AND INDUSTRIAL PROBLEMS

WMU literature also promoted concern for workers in industrial conditions, particularly women and children. *Our Mission Fields* and *Royal Service* writers focused on labor issues in home mission programs under "problems of the cities." Writers reminded WMU readers that many women filled the ranks of labor. "By the census of 1910 we learn that 25 per cent of the women of the United States over 10 years of age are wage earners," said the mission program from November 1912. These women "wage earners" worked as "domestic servants, stenographers and typewriters, workers in cotton mills, woolen mills, in the paper mills and shoe factories of New England, cotton fields of the South, hop fields of Oregon, canneries of California, the glassworks of Pittsburgh, the garment factories of New York," and in "cigar factories of Philadelphia and Baltimore."[143] Writers pointed out that the working conditions for women were terrible. Women worked long days, at "break-neck" speeds, in "over-crowded" shops and mills, explained the mission study, and had little wholesome entertainment to fill their evenings.[144] Periodicals also helped WMU members understand why they should be concerned about the plight of the workers. "Why should we care if women in factories are overworked and underpaid?" asked the writer of the October 1911 mission study. "Why should we be troubled that working men and women with twelve or fourteen hours' work a day, and sometimes seven days' work a week, are too exhausted to hear or listen to the message of Christ's gospel? The answer is partly, because we are human just as they are and we cannot ignore their injustices."[145] WMU members should care about the laborer, indicated this writer, not only because workers needed to hear "Christ's gospel" but also because basic human compassion required a stand against injustice.

WMU monthly studies also attempted to create empathy for southern cotton mill workers. "And what is this roar of marching and who are these who come pressing from this great building, weak little children, feeble bent women and men with vacant faces and gaunt forms? The cotton mills stand a call for Personal Service."[146] Most of the actions WMU suggested focused on aiding the individual worker rather than on union issues or institutional change. Clubs for young women workers, rest areas, and lunchrooms were the most typical recommendations.[147] Personal Service pamphlets advocated helping people find jobs who were "willing to work," in order to encourage "self reliance, " but the only direct labor action recommended was to "present the case of the underpaid to their employers."[148]

The Personal Service Department also called on southern women to take up the fight against child labor. WMU programs detailed the horrors that befell children in the workforce. "Child workers breathe coal dust in the breakers, lint in the cotton mills, sawdust in the furniture factories and alkaline dust in soap factories," reported *Our Mission Fields*. "In felt factories the air is filled with fibers of wool, in tobacco-houses with a fine, snuff-like poison-laden dust; the naphtha of rubber works, phosphorous of matches, the lead of type foundries—all attack the lungs of children who are exposed to them during the hours of the week."[149] They asked local women to investigate industries to make sure they complied with child labor legislation. *Royal Service* proclaimed that "the city needs salvation from the cruelty that ruins the lives of those whom Christ loves with special tenderness—children. . . . We should see that our states have and enforce laws against the employment of children under a certain age."[150]

The March 1916 issue of *Royal Service* issued a call for the protection of children. "Child labor means adult ignorance. . . . According to the census there are 40,000 children employed in cotton mills, many of which are in the South. Painful as the fact is, we are face to face with one of the serious social problems of the South. . . . When the noble mother heart of southern womanhood becomes stirred and burdened for defrauded childhood, this stigma will no longer rest upon us."[151] WMU leaders directed their call for social justice to "the noble mother heart," evoking maternal images to engage southern women in social reform.

WMU leadership occasionally recommended that its constituency cooperate with secular organizations that worked for industrial betterment, such as the Consumer's League. A 1913 issue of *Our Mission Fields* explained how local women could support industrial reform. "All factories and tenements that conduct their business under sanitary conditions, that do not employ little children, that use such modern inventions as protect life and limb, and that keep those hours of labor which are not destructive to the highest ideals of life, are furnished with a label which is placed upon the garments."[152] Women were encouraged to purchase goods marked with these labels and to further "demand" that dealers handle only such goods that were not "stained with the blood of little children and women."[153] WMU publications sometimes expressed bolder sentiments regarding urban problems. One writer complained about the negative influence of unregulated capitalism. "We are becoming familiar with the thought," she purported, "that because competition is strong, work hard to get and rents high, it is necessary that families be crowded into small and unhealthy quarters. We feel that it is the manufacturers business, not ours." But, she argued, it is the Christian's responsibility to make "public sentiment Christian in its view of other people's rights." Ultimately, "the city needs salvation from the un-Christlike spirit of selfish commercialism."[154]

Progressive social ideas appeared in unlikely places. On the header of each page of the *Handbook for Personal Service* there are proverb-style quotes. The quotes have nothing to do with the content of the page below. For example, on the header of the page devoted to organizing a Blue Bird Club for girls, the proverb reads: "The resources of the earth being the heritage of the people, should not be monopolized by the few to the disadvantage of the many."[155] Several of the quotes speak to workers' rights, such as: "Women who toil should receive equal pay with men for equal work."[156] "Every worker should have one day's rest in seven and reasonable time for recreation and family life."[157] Yet another quote argues: "Suitable provision should be made for the old age of workers and for those incapacitated by injury and sickness."[158] None of these sentiments is accompanied by demands for organized political action to bring about institutional change. There are only expressions of these subtle sympathies for the worker and the poor, which distinguish WMU leadership from the more conservative attitudes of such groups as the early Charity Organization Society or the Southern Baptist Home Mission Board. In most cases WMU publications aimed to awaken the conscience of Baptist women.

The one thing WMU leaders repeatedly asked local societies to do was study their communities. A progressive message was implicit in many of the admonitions to research social ills. "If the aim is to secure for the child a fair chance at life," argued the Personal Service columnist, "we must study its environment at close range to realize the deleterious effect on character and career of unsanitary and ungodly surroundings."[159] The Personal Service Committee published and circulated a social survey to help societies gather information on their communities. Progressive Era reformers promoted the survey as an instrument for social change. Reformers believed that knowledge of social problems would produce action.[160] WMU endorsed the use of the survey in *Royal Service*. Lulie Wharton, chair of the national WMU Personal Service Committee, explained the social survey in the October 1914 issue. "It is the careful scrutiny of a community in order to obtain accurate knowledge of its necessities, its advantages, its possibilities. Its aim is to create the desire to change conditions. Why is it necessary? Christian women need to be aroused to a full comprehension of the problems and difficulties that face humanity."[161] For example, careful examination of tenements offered insights into the causes for the slums. "It has been the habit to blame tenants for dirty and unsightly surroundings. How can they be clean if there are no water and drains," lamented the columnist. "And how can premises be kept in order if there is no provision for the disposal of garbage and refuse?"[162] Again, like many of their contemporaries in the Progressive Era, Southern Baptist women believed, naively, that information about social problems would naturally produce social activism.

Evidently some WMU leaders intended for societies to press for social change. After societies "diagnosed" the social illnesses around them, WMU recommended they take the next step to heal their community.[163] Wharton urged WMUs to begin by arranging lectures from various "experts" on topics such as social service, the playground movement, on scientific farming, and similar topics. Further, she urged them to use whatever political means they had at their disposal. "By the press, by the interest of officials, by the cooperation of landlords can be aroused the desire to better the conditions which surround the very poor."[164] A later column reiterated the need for political action: "The cause of distress should be sought and removed if possible through legislation, enforcement of laws or creation of public sentiment."[165] With perhaps the exception of Fannie Heck, WMU leaders generally did not model activism as did settlement workers. As a whole, the calls for political action to resolve social problems were rare.

WMU publications and local women's missionary societies typically responded to urban issues by reaching out to individuals. WMU promoted night schools connected with Good Will Centers to help educate children and adults working in factory conditions. "Hours should be suited to the pupils, all of whom will probably have to be up next morning before it is light," insisted the handbook. "Concentrate on reading, writing, and arithmetic."[166] The Good Will Center near Birmingham, Alabama, operated a night school for immigrants.[167] The center in Meridian, Mississippi, operated a night school for four years and was proved so needed and efficient that "the city took over this phase of the work."[168] A worker in a North Carolina WMU night school wrote: "I feel sure that our night school is one of our best efforts in missionary work and personal service." She explained that the pupils were "children of the streets and children we have clothed" to bring to Sunday school. When the women began working with the children in Sunday school, they realized many of them could not read. So, the WMU opened a night school with one teacher and four assistants.[169] In 1919 the WMU, SBC Annual Meeting featured a lecture on how to teach English as a foreign language.[170] The problem of widespread illiteracy in the South became a focus of WMU after 1921, marked by the addition of "Star Classes" to the plan of Personal Service.[171] Personal Service reports indicate twenty adult reading classes in 1921 rising to as many as 327 in 1926.[172]

WMU reached out to individual women in industry in several ways. The Cheer-All Clubs, for example, attempted to encourage single, working women. Kindergartens and day nurseries aided mothers who worked in factories. The Meridian Good Will Center stated that their day nursery predominately cared for children of mill workers.[173] Programs for boys and girls attempted to occupy children whose parents worked long hours. Playgrounds helped free children from the "crowded, stuffy rooms" of the tenements or the city streets where "undirected play" could lead them into trouble.[174] Still, the available data reveal few societies even became involved in these modest programs designed to ease urban stress. Between 1915 and 1925 not one of these programs averaged over 6 percent participation from *reporting* societies. If one calculates the numbers of societies involved against the actual number of WMU societies in existence, the percentages are more dismal. The figures bear out the notion that most local WMU societies did not share the vision of national leadership for eradicating urban problems.

At this point it is worth remembering that the majority of Southern Baptist women lived in rural areas. Urban problems did not touch most of them on a daily basis. The WMU offices were located in Baltimore, Maryland. Some of the divergence in social views can be attributed to the fact that many leaders during this period lived and worked in more urban areas on the Eastern Seaboard. Their constituents lived throughout the rural South. It is perhaps no surprise that few Southern Baptist women were engaged in reforms relating to child labor, immigration, and industrialism. The more remarkable story is that 6 percent of WMU societies did participate in some program to address urban problems.

CONCLUSION

The Woman's Missionary Union Training School educated the leaders of Personal Service in classrooms with Maud Reynolds McLure and in fieldwork at the Training School model settlement. McLure's courses at the Training School used the programs of settlement workers and the social work methods of Progressive Era reformers. When local societies embraced the aims of Personal Service and established the recommended social settlements, they tailored their work to the more traditional interests of Southern Baptists. The most complete programs of Personal Service emerged in urban societies or in societies exposed to urban issues such as immigration and industrialization.

Baptist Good Will Centers functioned more as urban missions than social settlements. They did not employ resident workers or launch systematic programs for urban reform. Baptist women did, however, borrow the organizational structures of the settlement movement such as day nurseries, public playgrounds, circulating libraries, night schools, and industrial schools. They used the social work methods of the Charity Organization Society and social settlements to help families around their Good Will Centers. They emphasized scientific study, casework, and statistical surveys, and they encouraged cooperation with other social service organizations. Baptist women borrowed the methods and organizational structures of these movements and imbued them with conservative missionary goals. Nonetheless, they deliberately identified themselves with the settlement movement by studying at Hull House, Chicago Commons, and the social settlements in Louisville, Kentucky.

Like other female reformers of the Progressive Era, Baptist women in the work of Good Will Centers attempted to inculcate poor women and children with middle-class Protestant values. Baptist women were nearly as interested in teaching poor women to be good mothers and housekeepers as they were in converting them. Children's programs pointedly fostered narrow gender roles. Boys were taught parliamentary procedure and woodworking. Girls were taught to sew and care for their dolls. Ironically, because of this emphasis on traditional roles, Baptist women carved out areas of ministry unoccupied by Southern Baptist men. They were able to turn their attention fully to social ministry with women and children. This enhanced WMU's commitment to professional social work at the WMU Training School and provided new opportunities in denominational service for Southern Baptist women.

Even though the Personal Service results fell short of a social gospel agenda, it is extremely significant that Southern Baptist women adopted any form of settlement work at all given the conservative religious context of their denomination. The presence of settlement houses added a progressive dimension to the work of WMU absent in the institutional life of the Southern Baptist Convention. Leaders who developed the WMU handbooks for organizing Baptist Good Will Centers depended on a variety of more progressive settlement sources such as the Southern Methodist women's handbook, and Chicago'S Hull House.[175] The language of social reform pervaded the pages of the WMU's *Handbook for Personal Service* and the columns devoted to Personal Service in *Royal Service*. These publications challenged Baptist women to battle against such problems as slum conditions and child labor, to campaign for public health, and to promote recreation for neighborhood youth. While conservative impulses prevented Baptist Good Will Centers from embodying all the characteristics of traditional social settlements, they provided the foundation for Baptist social work. The WMU Training School (under various names) educated Baptist students in professional social work for ninety years (1907–97). The influence of southern progressivism and the social gospel produced a commitment to church social work among Southern Baptists that shaped the denomination throughout the twentieth century.

Conclusion

NOT LONG AFTER I BEGAN my research on the WMU in the Progressive Era, I was sitting at a restaurant in Waco, Texas, overlooking the Brazos River. Several of my dinner companions were social work professors on the faculty of Baylor University. I was lamenting the fact that the social gospel influences in WMU waned in the late 1920s. I said, "What did all this matter if it didn't produce lasting results?" One of the social work professors put down his fork, looked me in the eye, and said, "What do you mean there were no results? Of course, there were results! Social work! Social work was the result!" The WMU Training School, renamed the Carver School of Missions and Social Work in 1953, became one of the first accredited schools of church social work in the United States. Hundreds of men and women received training in church social work because of the WMU programs. Social work alone makes the story of WMU and progressivism significant.

Still, there are other reasons that this story matters. The manner in which WMU leaders applied gender ideology in the Progressive Era explains some of the contradictions and inconsistencies of Southern Baptist womanhood. On one hand, WMU programs reinforced gender stereotypes, while on the other hand they empowered and educated thousands of young women who would, in due time, "step out of their place." Southern Baptist women appropriated and internalized true womanhood ideology with its requisite emphasis on women's innate piety, purity, submissiveness, and domesticity. While they accepted the cultural expectations of women and took these very seriously, women interpreted these expectations to broaden women's roles rather than limit them. Baptist women embraced the idea that women were inherently more pious than men and concluded that women would be more effective missionaries and social workers. WMU leaders essentially agreed with domesticity—the teaching that women should be responsible for all matters relating to the care of the household and children. While they may have agreed that women should be in charge of children and home, they also argued that the barriers between public and private spheres were fluid. Maternal concerns led WMU leaders to visualize a new "home without walls" in which women actively worked to improve the lives of every mother and child. Baptist women repeatedly affirmed their belief in submission to male authority and insisted that the vast women's missionary enterprise was a direct result of their obedience to pastors who exhorted them to share the "whole gospel with the whole world."

Ironically, the ideology became subversive because women so earnestly accepted its tenets. As Baptist women reconstructed the boundaries of true womanhood, they in turn restructured their social ethics. True womanhood not only provided the justification for women to accept public roles but also produced a distinctly feminine social ethic. Within the language of domesticity, WMU leaders discovered mandates for social action. Maternal concerns contributed to the theological presuppositions of Baptist women. Women's traditional roles—feeding, clothing, and nursing the family—dovetailed with concepts of nurture present in Christianity. As a result, women more readily identified with the mandates to feed, clothe, and "mother" society. In short, gender helped Southern Baptist women develop and justify an ethic of social responsibility.

The story of WMU is also important because it forces us to reconsider Southern Baptist history in the Progressive Era. The denomination was culturally, economically, and theologically diverse. WMU history exposes the complexity of the denomination's past that has often been related in one-dimensional patriarchal narratives. Early WMU leaders fought tirelessly to establish a missionary organization in the face of tremendous opposition from both Southern Baptist pastors and laypersons. They insisted God called women to aid the cause of missions and this divine call must take precedence over any objection that mere mortals might raise. After years of struggle, Southern Baptist women finally established their missionary organization in 1888. The leaders represented the aristocracy of the South. *Home without Walls* focuses primarily on the story of these WMU leaders. The circumstances of their lives reveal a cultural divide between the leadership and local members. WMU corresponding secretaries and presidents in the Progressive Era, almost to a person, hailed from wealthy, influential Southern Baptist families. They were well-educated women, well versed in the methods and rhetoric of the Progressive Era. WMU leaders, like other female Protestant reformers, were women who had the time and money to lead a voluntary organization. They were not as affected by the poverty and isolation that shaped so many of their Southern Baptist brothers and sisters. Wealth and education distanced them from the vast majority of the Southern Baptist women they hoped to lead. Annie Armstrong and Fannie Heck, for example, were independently wealthy women who lived in Baltimore and Raleigh respectively. Their financial independence and urban connections provided them with opportunities not readily available to the vast majority of Southern Baptists.

For the first thirty-three years, Baltimore served as the Union's headquarters. Until 1901 the Executive Council, which governed WMU between meetings, was made up of women from Baltimore. As a border city, Baltimore represented an intersection of northern and southern intellectual currents. This partially explains why WMU leaders demonstrated knowledge of a wide variety of social reform programs. Maud McLure, Emma Leachman, and Fannie Heck visited Jane Addams's Hull House and the Chicago Commons Settlement. They also visited programs in New York. Annie Armstrong and McLure spent summers in Chautauqua, New York. WMU leaders embraced the Protestant women's missionary jubilee celebrations and pleaded with the ecumenical committee to plan a southern tour. Fannie Heck presided over a joint meeting of Northern and Southern Baptist women in Jamestown and addressed a gathering of Baptist women at the Baptist World Alliance. Annie Armstrong opposed the founding of the WMUTS, in part, because she believed the Northern Baptist Missionary Training Schools in Chicago and Philadelphia could meet the needs of WMU, SBC. All of these are indications that WMU leaders moved comfortably in urban circles that were more deeply engaged with progressivism. The economic and cultural diversity complicated the relationship between WMU leaders and local members. Anne Firor Scott's summation of women's missionary societies holds true for the Woman's Missionary Union: "As local societies began to coalesce into regional and national organizations, a gap developed between leaders and followers, between what the most articulate leaders wanted to accomplish and what timid members of local organizations were willing to undertake."[1]

This study of WMU also exposes the social and theological diversity of Southern Baptists in the Progressive Era. WMU leaders were southern progressives sympathetic to the social gospel. The influence of the social gospel was evident in the progressive statements WMU published on specific social issues and their recommendations to local women concerning social problems. WMU leaders entered the battle for public health and insisted that health problems were caused by poverty, overcrowded living conditions, and lack of education. They recommended practical actions for local women to involve themselves in health reform such as hiring community nurses, sponsoring health education programs in their clubs, and providing children with free health care. Leaders also addressed the problem of immigration. They encouraged local women to sponsor programs to help educate and assimilate immigrants into American culture. Local societies taught English as a foreign language, sewing, cooking, and health classes to immigrant women and children. WMU leaders also took progressive stands on labor problems. They urged local WMU societies to study their local laws, investigate industries, and boycott manufacturers who employed children. Leaders criticized unregulated capitalism and in general sympathized with the plight of the worker.

Some leaders of Personal Service urged Baptist women toward more progressive views on race and attempted to undermine southern racial prejudices. Annie Armstrong, Fannie Heck, and Ella Broadus Robertson admonished Southern Baptist women to deal justly with people of all races. White Baptist women developed home economics programs and mothers' clubs for black women, but most often cooperated with black Baptist women on missionary endeavors.

Royal Service even made mildly progressive statements on race relations. For example, editors endorsed a Methodist publication that urged white women to establish "higher ideals in regard to the relation between the races; by standing for full and equal justice in all departments of life."[2] Unfortunately, Southern Baptist women did not develop a consistent ethical response to racial injustice and remained at their very best, profoundly paternalistic. They did not recognize lynching as a systemic evil. Southern Baptists, as a whole, did not renounce segregation or fight systems of racial oppression in the South. The failure of Southern Baptist women and men to acknowledge and reject white supremacy as *sin* would, of course, haunt them throughout the twentieth century. We have yet to determine if it will shatter their moral foundation completely in the twenty-first.

The Personal Service Department was the institutional expression of southern progressivism. The leadership of Personal Service imbibed reform ideas, social gospel theology, and social work methods through their ties with women of other denominations, through reform organizations, and through the literature of social gospel writers. WMU writers and editors used the work of social gospel advocates as source material. The names of Josiah Strong, Samuel Zane Batten, Graham Taylor, and Shailer Mathews appear in the pages of WMU publications as authorities on social problems. One Personal Service training study stated plainly that "the gospel is a message of social redemption as well as of personal rescue," and "there are social vices and virtues as well as individual sins and graces." The same study concluded with a quote from Shailer Mathews that proclaimed the "social gospel" as "the joyful message that the power of Jesus Christ, the Son of God, is sufficient to regenerate the social order."[3] *Royal Service* articles printed statements declaring that social reform was "religious and spiritual work"[4] and referred to Jesus as the "greatest social reformer who ever lived."[5] The WMU Training School included social work in its standard curriculum of Personal Service. The Personal Service Committee encouraged local societies to adopt the accepted practices of social work in their own communities such as social surveys, friendly visiting, and careful analysis of social problems.

WMU eventually established social settlements called Good Will Centers. WMU leaders observed settlement work in Louisville, Kentucky, and studied the programs of Hull House and Chicago Commons before embarking on their own programs. Within the scope of Southern Baptist settlement work, WMU promoted a myriad of social service programs. Baptist Good Will centers sponsored night schools, industrial schools, day nurseries, kindergartens, mothers' meetings, and clubs for boys and girls. Many centers provided circular libraries and maintained public playgrounds. All of these are examples of programs learned from the social settlement movement. The programs recommended by the national WMU were borrowed directly from the Progressive Era social reformers, including proponents of the social gospel. But WMU leaders had little success in persuading local societies to adopt sweeping social service programs. Personal Service columns often contained mixed messages and genuinely believed conservative theology would harmonize with progressive reform agendas. There is little evidence to indicate that local WMU societies consistently worked to alleviate social problems through the work of their organizations.

The emphasis on social work, then, remains the most important residual effect of southern progressivism on WMU. The training in social work combined with the Personal Service programs provided women with broader opportunities for service within a conservative denomination. Women took the social work skills they learned at the WMU Training School and applied them variously as directors of settlements, as teachers in mountain schools, or in work with immigrants or with cotton mill workers. Like other female reformers of the Progressive Era, Baptist women in the work of Good Will Centers attempted to inculcate poor women and children with middle-class Protestant values. Baptist women were nearly as interested in teaching poor women to be good mothers and housekeepers as they were in converting them. Children's programs pointedly fostered narrow gender roles. Boys were taught parliamentary procedure and woodworking. Girls were taught to sew and care for their dolls. Interestingly, because of this emphasis on traditional roles, Baptist women carved out areas of ministry unoccupied by Southern Baptist men. They were able to engage in more progressive ministries *because* they embraced separate spheres. This enhanced WMU's commitment to professional social work at the WMU Training School and provided new opportunities in denominational service for Southern Baptist women.

The presence of settlement houses added a progressive dimension to the work of WMU. Leaders who developed the WMU handbooks for organizing Baptist Good Will Centers depended on a variety of traditional settlement sources such as the Southern Methodist women's handbook and Chicago's Hull House.[6] The language of social reform pervaded the pages of the WMU's *Handbook for Personal Service* and the columns devoted to Personal Service in *Royal Service*. These publications challenged Baptist women to battle against slum conditions and child labor, to campaign for public health, and to promote recreation for neighborhood youth. While conservative impulses prevented Baptist Good Will Centers from embodying all the characteristics of traditional social settlements, they became centers of field training for Baptist social work. The WMU Training School (later known as the Carver School of Missions and Social Work) educated

Baptist students in professional social work for ninety years (1907–97). Church social work sprouted from the soil of progressivism and was nourished by the rich theological tradition of the social gospel. It is not surprising, therefore, that the Carver School of Missions and Social Work became one of the key battlegrounds in the theological controversies that consumed Southern Baptists in the 1980s, but that is another story.

Notes

Introduction

1. Lulie Wharton, *Royal Service* 9, no. 4 (October 1914): 24.

2. Lulie Wharton, *Royal Service* 20 (September 1925): 27.

3. Arthur S. Link, "The Progressive Movement in the South," *North Carolina Historical Review* 23 (April 1946): 172–205; Anne Firor Scott, "A Progressive Wind from the South, 1906–1913," *Journal of Southern History* 29 (February 1963): 53–70; William Link, *The Paradox of Southern Progressivism, 1880–1930* (Chapel Hill: University of North Carolina Press, 1992).

4. Dewey Grantham, *Southern Progressivism: The Reconciliation of Progress and Tradition* (Knoxville: University of Tennessee Press, 1983), xix–xx. See also Hugh C. Bailey, *Liberalism in the New South: Southern Social Reformers and the Progressive Movement* (Coral Gables, FL: University of Miami Press, 1969); John Patrick McDowell, *The Social Gospel in the South: The Woman's Home Mission Movement in the Methodist Episcopal Church, South, 1886–1939* (Baton Rouge: Louisiana State University Press, 1982); and Lawrence Goodwyn, *The Populist Movement: A Short History of the Agrarian Revolt in America* (New York: Oxford University Press, 1978).

5. Link, *Paradox of Southern Progressivism*, 322–24; John Dittmer, *Black Georgia in the Progressive Era, 1900–1920* (Urbana: University of Illinois Press, 1977); Edwin J. Cashin and Glenn T. Eskew, eds., *Paternalism in a Southern City: Race, Religion, and Gender in Augusta, Georgia* (Athens: University of Georgia Press, 2001); Morton Sosna, *In Search of the Silent South: Southern Liberals and the Race Issue* (New York: Columbia University Press, 1977).

6. Grantham, *Southern Progressivism*, 126; Link, *Paradox of Southern Progressivism*, 70; Bailey, *Liberalism in the New South*, 63, 150. In the Houston public schools, for example, "Jim Crow was an essential component to the success of the reform policies." In the 1920s under the leadership of superintendent E. E. Olberholtzer, Houston public schools launched a wide range of reforms. "Segregation allowed the district to use almost one hundred per cent of the money for curriculum reform on only seventy-five per cent of the population." See Karen Benjamin, "Progressivism Meets Jim Crow: Curriculum Revision and Development in Houston, Texas, 1924–1929," *Pedagogica Historica* 39

(August 2003): 457. See also James D. Anderson, *The Education of Blacks in the South, 1865–1935* (Chapel Hill: University of North Carolina Press, 1988).

7. Charles E. Wynes, *Forgotten Voices: Dissenting Southerners in an Age of Conformity* (Baton Rouge: Louisiana State University Press, 1967), 5, and Link, *Paradox of Southern Progressivism*, 126. Larry D. Hill, "Texas Progressivism: A Search for Definition," in *Texas through Time: Evolving Interpretations*, ed. Walter L. Buenger and Robert A. Calvert (College Station: Texas A&M University Press, 1991), 234–35. See also Evan Anders, *Boss Rule in South Texas: The Progressive Era* (Austin: University of Texas Press, 1977).

8. McKelway, quoted in Bailey, *Liberalism in the New South*, 65.

9. Bailey, *Liberalism in the New South*, 112.

10. James E. McCulloch, ed., *The Call of the New South* (Nashville: Southern Sociological Congress, 1912), 14.

11. John Lee Eighmy, "Religious Liberalism in the South during the Progressive Era," *Church History* 38 (September 1969): 367.

12. Rufus B. Spain, *At Ease in Zion: A Social History of Southern Baptists* (Nashville: Vanderbilt University Press, 1967). The title is a reference to the book of Amos where the prophet criticizes the powerful and elite for being comfortable with social injustice.

13. John Lee Eighmy, *Churches in Cultural Captivity: A History of the Social Attitudes of Southern Baptists* (Knoxville: University of Tennessee Press, 1972).

14. For an analysis of the ways that Southern Baptists attempted to aid individuals, see Keith Harper, *The Quality of Mercy: Southern Baptists and Social Christianity, 1890–1920* (Tuscaloosa: University of Alabama Press, 1996).

15. Samuel Hill recommended Linder's definitions in his introduction to Eighmy's book. Linder, quoted in Eighmy, *Churches in Cultural Captivity*, xi.

16. Wayne Flynt, "Dissent in Zion: Alabama Baptists and Social Issues," *Journal of Southern History* 35 (November 1969): 523–42; Wayne Flynt, "Alabama White Protestantism and Labor, 1900–1914," *Alabama Review* 25 (1972): 192–217; Wayne Flynt, *Alabama Baptists: Southern Baptists in the Heart of Dixie* (Tuscaloosa: University of Alabama Press, 1998). For additional sources on Southern Baptists in the Progressive Era, see Paul Harvey, *Freedom's Coming: Religious Culture and the Shaping of the South from the Civil War to Civil Rights* (Chapel Hill: University of North Carolina Press, 2005); Paul Harvey, "Southern Baptists and the Social Gospel: White Religious Progressivism in the South, 1900–1925," *Fides et Historia* 27 (Summer 1995): 59–77; Eighmy, *Churches in Cultural Captivity*; William Ellis, *"A Man of Books and a Man of the People": E. Y. Mullins and the Crisis of Moderate Baptist Leadership* (Macon, GA: Mercer University Press, 1985); Harper, *Quality of Mercy*; John Storey, *Texas Baptist Leadership and Social Christianity, 1900–1980* (College Station: Texas A&M University Press, 1986).

17. Patricia Summerlin Martin, "Hidden Work: Baptist Women in Texas, 1880–1920" (PhD diss., Rice University, 1982).

18. Link, *Paradox of Southern Progressivism*, 32.

19. See SBC *Annual Proceedings*, 1912, 76–77, and SBC *Annual Proceedings*, 1913, 73.

20. Storey, *Texas Baptist Leadership and Social Christianity*, 22; Eighmy, *Churches in Cultural Captivity*, 81.

21. Eighmy, *Churches in Cultural Captivity*, 53.

22. Quoted in Harvey, "Southern Baptists and the Social Gospel," 74.

23. John E. White, "Temperance and Reform in the South," in *The South in the Building of the Nation: A History of the Southern States Designed to Record the South's Part in the Making of the American Nation*, vol. 10 (Richmond, VA: Southern Historical Publication: 1909), 575.

24. White, "Temperance and Reform in the South," 578.

25. White, "Temperance and Reform in the South," 574.

26. White, "Temperance and Reform in the South," 581.

27. SBC *Annual Report*, 1912, 297.

28. Early attempts to understand the Social Gospel Movement focused on industrial regions of the country and virtually ignored the South. See Charles Howard Hopkins, *The Rise of the Social Gospel in American Protestantism, 1865–1915* (New Haven, CT: Yale University Press, 1940), 3; Aaron Ignatius Abell, *The Urban Impact on American Protestantism, 1865–1900* (Cambridge, MA: Harvard University Press, 1943); Henry F. May, *Protestant Churches and Industrial America* (New York: Harper and Bros. Publishing, 1949); and Paul A. Carter, *The Decline and Revival of the Social Gospel: Social and Political Liberalism in American Protestant Churches, 1920–1940* (Ithaca, NY: Cornell University Press, 1954). Little consensus has been reached about the nature of the social gospel in the South. Stephen Prescott's historiographical essay on the southern social gospel affirms that a major issue involves definitions. Stephen Prescott, "The Social Gospel and the American South: An Historiographic Appraisal," in *Perspectives on the Social Gospel* (Lewiston, NY: Edwin Mellen Press, 1999): 33–50.

29. Hugh Bailey's biography of Edgar Gardner Murphy, published in 1968, first suggested that the social gospel existed in the South. The next year Wayne Flynt supported Bailey's thesis with an article detailing the social reform activities of leading Alabama Baptists from 1900 to 1914. See Hugh Bailey, *Edgar Gardner Murphy: Gentle Progressive* (Coral Gables, FL: University of Miami Press, 1968); J. Wayne Flynt, "Dissent in Zion: Alabama Baptists and Social Issues, 1900–1914," *Journal of Southern History* 35 (Winter 1969): 523–42; Flynt, "'Feeding the Hungry and Ministering to the Broken Hearted': The Presbyterian Church in the United States and the Social Gospel, 1900–1920" in *Religion in the South*, ed. Charles Reagan Wilson (Jackson: University Press of Mississippi, 1985): 83–137.

30. Denominational studies have made significant contributions to southern social gospel scholarship. Sydney Ahlstrom concluded that the Methodist church was "the most powerful church in the South," and "the social gospel in the South was largely a Methodist phenomenon." Sydney Ahlstrom, *A Religious History of the American People* (New Haven, CT: Yale University Press, 1972), 717, 719. Ahlstrom cited Hunter D. Farish, who contended that Methodism was an extremely influential force for social reform in southern society. See Hunter Dickinson Farish, *The Circuit Rider Dismounts: A Social History of Southern Methodism* (New York: Da Capo Press, 1969), 104, and John Patrick McDowell, *The Social Gospel in the South: The Woman's Home Mission Movement in the Methodist Episcopal Church, South, 1886–1939* (Baton Rouge: Louisiana State University Press, 1982).

31. John Lee Eighmy, "Religious Liberalism in the South during the Progressive Era," *Church History* 38 (September 1969): 372.

32. Eighmy, "Religious Liberalism," 360.

33. James J. Thompson agreed with Eighmy. There was a social gospel voice among Southern Baptists, said Thompson, but "the case must not be overstated. . . . The Southern Baptist masses remained hostile to demands for social activism regardless of what a few professors or editors might say." James J. Thompson, *Tried as by Fire: Southern Baptists and the Religious Controversies of the 1920s* (Macon, GA: Mercer University Press, 1982), 34. Other scholars argue that the definition of the social gospel must be modified to include more conservative theology. Keith Harper argues in *The Quality of Mercy* that Southern Baptists were reformers in their efforts to improve individual morality and circumstances. "It is true that Southern Baptists emphasized individual conversion," he stated, "but to argue that they displayed no concern for society at large misses the point." Harper, *Quality of Mercy*, 118. The issue is even further complicated when one examines the vision of a "better society." Conversionists did not always maintain the same notion of a better society as liberal social gospelers, or northern progressives. "Better society," for most southern progressives, did not suggest economic equity. Industrial capitalism was too new to the South, and too crucial to Southern Progressives' notion of the "New South" to evoke widespread critique or provoke a socialist response. "Better society" did not connote social or economic equality for African Americans. In fact, "better society" meant the peaceful maintenance of "place" as Harper points out. In effect, Harper's argument circles directly back to Eighmy's contention that Southern Baptists as a denomination were in the business of reinforcing cultural norms, of providing a religious ethos to uphold the status quo. This does not mean they were uniformly cruel or callous people. They were not unmindful of the hungry, the sick, the orphaned, the uneducated, or the needy. However, a concern for suffering people did not necessarily translate into a belief in corporate sin. See Harper, *Quality of Mercy*.

34. Catherine Allen, *A Century to Celebrate: History of Woman's Missionary Union* (Birmingham, AL: Woman's Missionary Union, 1987).

35. Harvey, "Southern Baptist and the Social Gospel," 59–77: Harvey, "Saints but Not Subordinates: The Woman's Missionary Union of the Southern Baptist Convention," in *Women and Twentieth-Century Protestantism*, ed. Margaret Bendroth and Virginia Brereton (Urbana: University of Illinois Press, 2002), 4–24. See also Harvey's *Freedom's Coming*; Elizabeth Flowers, "Southern Baptist Evangelicals or Social Gospel Liberals?: The Woman's Missionary Union and Social Reform, 1888–1928," *American Baptist Quarterly* 19 (June 2000): 106–28.

36. In discussing the social attitudes of Texas Baptist leaders, John Storey distinguished between "social gospel" and "social Christianity." This book maintains the distinction between the "social gospel," a movement rooted in liberal theology, and "social Christianity," a reform impulse shaped by conservative theological presuppositions. To blur the line between the social gospel and a southern social Christianity would ignore the profound tensions in southern religious circles over the relationship between theology and reform, between evangelicalism and liberalism. If historians gloss over theological differences, then we muffle the voices of the men and women who worked so hard to

explain their faith in sermons, papers, pamphlets, and magazines. If the social gospel is *too* broadly defined as biblically motivated social reform, then it could obscure a basic issue that is present in the primary sources. Wayne Flynt noted that Frank L. Barnett's newspaper, *Alabama Baptist*, revealed both an endorsement of a broad social reform agenda and repeated warnings about the dangers of the social gospel. This propensity for caveats and explanation appears in WMU literature. It is difficult to believe that Barnett or the women feared Southern Baptists were poised to abandon evangelicalism. Rather, these southern progressives needed to make clear distinctions between the social Christianity they were advocating and a liberal social gospel because they needed to convince their constituencies that social reform did not *require* liberal theology. Social reform, they insisted, would not be a threat to their Bible believing, soul-saving, evangelical religion.

John Storey, *Texas Baptist Leadership and Social Christianity*, 5. Paul Harvey followed Storey by adopting the term "social Christianity" when referring to Southern Baptist social attitudes. Harvey examined Southern Baptist social attitudes within the broader context of Progressivism rather than what he called a theoretical "social gospel party line." Harvey, *Redeeming the South: Religious Cultures and Racial Identities among Southern Baptists, 1865–1925* (Chapel Hill: UNC Press, 1997), 198. Harvey, "Southern Baptists and the Social Gospel" 61.

37. 1 Corinthians 3:9.

Chapter 1

1. Annie W. Armstrong, *Women as Helpers in God's Kingdom* (Baltimore: Baptist Mission Rooms, 1900), in Sorrell, Box 2, Woman's Missionary Union Archives, Birmingham, Alabama (WMUA).

2. This is a reference to Exodus 1:17 in which the midwives feared God and did not obey the king of Egypt.

3. The earliest Protestant women's foreign missionary society was founded in 1861. See Patricia Hill, *The World Their Household: The American Woman's Foreign Missionary Movement and Cultural Transformation* (Ann Arbor: University of Michigan Press, 1985). Presbyterian women in the South had no denomination-wide organization until 1912. See R. Pierce Beaver, *All Loves Excelling: American Protestant Women in World Missions* (Grand Rapids, MI: Eerdmans, 1968), 47–48, and Susan Hill Lindley, *"You Have Stept Out of Your Place": A History of Women and Religion in America* (Louisville: Westminster John Knox Press, 1996), 78.

4. Juliette Mather, *Light Three Candles: History of Virginia Woman's Missionary Union, 1874–1973* (Richmond: Virginia Woman's Missionary Union, 1973), 3. For studies of American women's foreign mission societies, see Hill, *World Their Household*, and Dana Robert, *American Women in Mission: A Social History of Their Thought and Practice* (Macon, GA: Mercer University Press, 1996).

5. Beaver, *All Loves Excelling*, 14–19. By 1829 the Boston Female Society had become purely Baptist, donating its gifts to Baptist causes.

6. On Ann Judson, see Joan Jacobs Brumberg, *Mission for Life: The Story of the Family of Adoniram Judson* (New York: Free Press, 1980), and Courtney Anderson, *To the Golden Shore: The Life of Adoniram Judson* (Valley Forge, PA: Judson Press, 1987).

7. Minutes of the Charleston Baptist Association, 5, in Helen Emery Falls, "Baptist Women in Missions Support in the Nineteenth Century," *Baptist History and Heritage* 12 (January 1977): 27. Methodist women established their first missionary society in New York in 1819. Alma Hunt, *History of Woman's Missionary Union* (Nashville: Convention Press, 1964), 7–8; Catherine Allen, *A Century to Celebrate: History of Woman's Missionary Union* (Birmingham, AL: Woman's Missionary Union, 1987), 16; Rosalind Robinson Levering, *Baltimore Baptists, 1773–1973: A History of the Baptist Work in Baltimore during 200 Years* (Baltimore: Baltimore Baptist Association, 1973), 43.

8. Even though Montgomery made her assessment about the reasons for the rise of the women's foreign missionary movement in 1910, her analysis has endured the test of modern scholarship. Helen Barrett Montgomery, *Western Women in Eastern Lands: An Outline Study of Fifty Years of Woman's Work in Foreign Missions* (New York: Macmillan, 1910). Susan Hill Lindley echoed Montgomery's reasoning in *"You Have Stept Out of Your Place,"* 76–79. Lisa Joy Pruitt's *A Looking-Glass for Ladies: American Protestant Women and the Orient in the Nineteenth Century* (Macon, GA: Mercer University Press, 2005) examines the ways Protestant women's literature in America depicted Eastern women in the nineteenth century and explains the impact of these images on missionary activity.

9. Montgomery, *Western Women*, 5. See also Kendal P. Mobley, *Helen Barrett Montgomery: The Global Mission of Domestic Feminism* (Waco, TX: Baylor University Press, 2009).

10. Hill, *World Their Household*, 35.

11. Lindley, *"You Have Stept Out of Your Place,"* 76–77.

12. Fannie E. S. Heck, *In Royal Service* (Richmond, VA: Foreign Mission Board, SBC, 1913), 73–74. The page numbers listed for *In Royal Service* correlate to the hardback version of this work unless otherwise noted. There is also a paperback version issued by Broadman Press with no date.

13. Further, Judson mandated instruction suited to "discipline and adorn the mind, to cultivate the heart, improve the manners, to form habits of order, industry, and economy and universal benevolence." Elizabeth Barber Young, *A Study of the Curricula of Seven Selected Women's Colleges of the Southern States* (New York: Teachers College, 1932), 24–26. See also Robert, *American Women in Mission*, 92–114.

14. *Alabama Baptist* editorial, quoted in Wayne Flynt, *Alabama Baptists: Southern Baptists in the Heart of Dixie* (Tuscaloosa: University of Alabama Press, 1998), 91.

15. Heck, *In Royal Service*, 73–74. Judson Baptist College is located in Marion, Alabama. The archival records for the Bessie Tift College, later known as Tift College, are located in the Jack Tarver Library at Mercer University. There are still other Baptist women's colleges with antebellum origins: Mary Sharpe College in Tennessee, Stephens College and Baptist College for Women in Missouri, and Keachie Female College in Louisiana.

16. Lori Bateman, "Separation, Coordination, and Coeducation: Southern Baptist Approaches to Women's Higher Education," *Baptist History and Heritage* 38 (Summer/Fall 2003): 91. The men moved to Waco and joined with the existing Waco College to become Baylor University. After a large donation from the Hardin family during the De-

pression, Baylor Female College was renamed Mary Hardin-Baylor. It became coeducational in 1971 and in 1978 adopted its present name, University of Mary Hardin-Baylor. Anne Luther Bagby graduated from Baylor Female College in 1879 and was the daughter of one of the early presidents. She taught literature there before her appointment with the Foreign Mission Board to Brazil. Two of her daughters received degrees from Baylor Female College then returned to Brazil to help their mother as teachers in a school for women in São Paulo, which they referred to as Baylor College of the Southern Cross. The Bagbys hold the distinction of being the longest-serving foreign missionaries in the history of the Southern Baptist Convention. The majority of these institutions that survived either merged with a male counterpart or became coeducational in the twentieth century. Judson is the only Baptist institution chartered before the Civil War that has retained its identity as a woman's college.

17. *Thirty-Third Annual Catalogue, Baylor College, 1878–79*, Musick Alumni Center and Museum, University of Mary Hardin-Baylor, Belton, Texas.

18. Nancy Hardesty makes a persuasive argument that Charles Grandison Finney galvanized women for social reform and eventually for women's rights by challenging them to be "useful" in the Kingdom of God during his revival meetings. *Women Called to Witness: Evangelical Feminism in the 19th Century* (Knoxville: University of Tennessee Press, 1999).

19. Lindley, *You Have Stept Out of Your Place*, 77.

20. Heck, *In Royal Service*, 88, and Montgomery, *Western Women*, 10.

21. J. M. Carroll, *History of Texas Baptists* (Dallas: Baptist Standard Publishing, 1923), 9, quoted in Patricia Summerlin Martin, "Hidden Work: Baptist Women in Texas, 1880–1920" (PhD diss., Rice University, 1982), 107.

22. A. C. Dayton, "A Noble Woman," *Tennessee Baptist*, August 3, 1861.

23. Heck, *In Royal Service*, 85–86, paperback.

24. Heck, *In Royal Service*, 86, paperback.

25. Heck, *In Royal Service*, 126.

26. Robert, *American Women in Mission*, 130–37.

27. Heck, *In Royal Service*, 90, paperback.

28. Annie Armstrong, *Women as Helpers in God's Kingdom* (1900), 7. WMUA.

29. Heck, *In Royal Service*, 91, paperback.

30. Bobbie Sorrill, *Annie Armstrong: Dreamer in Action* (Nashville: Broadman Press, 1984), 40.

31. Minute Book, Woman's Mission to Woman, Maryland Baptist Historical Society, quoted in Allen, *Century to Celebrate*, 25.

32. Heck, *In Royal Service*, 126.

33. See Roberts, *American Women in Mission*, 130.

34. Blanche Sydnor White, *Our Heritage: History of Woman's Missionary Union, Auxiliary to the Maryland Baptist Union Association, 1742–1958* (Baltimore: Woman's Missionary Union of Maryland, 1959), 28.

35. White, *Our Heritage*, 27–28.

36. White, *Our Heritage*, 28. Most of the funds were sent directly to missionaries in the field before 1878. Some of their work was conducted in cooperation with the

Southern Baptist Convention's Foreign Mission Board. When the Baltimore branch of Woman's Mission to Woman became the Maryland branch of WMW in 1878, all of the society's funds were channeled through the FMB with the stipulation that their designations would be respected.

37. White, *Our Heritage*, 28–29.

38. Heck, *In Royal Service*, 102.

39. Lottie Moon to H. A. Tupper (February 11, 1884), in Keith Harper, *Send the Light: Lottie Moon's Letters and Other Writings* (Macon, GA: Mercer University Press, 2002), 104. For more information on Lottie Moon, see Catherine Allen, *The New Lottie Moon Story* (Nashville: Broadman Press, 1980), and Regina Sullivan, *Lottie Moon: A Southern Baptist Missionary to China in History and Legend* (Baton Rouge: Louisiana State University Press, 2011).

40. Allen, *Century to Celebrate*, 25–27; Spain, *At Ease in Zion*, 170–71; Hunt, *History of Woman's Missionary Union*, 15.

41. Heck, *In Royal Service*, 105.

42. Heck, *In Royal Service*, 106.

43. Minutes, Baptist Women Mission Workers of Texas (November 21–22, 1911).

44. Minutes of the Annual Meeting of the Rio Grande Baptist Association (1923), n.p., Texas Collection, Baylor University, Waco, Texas.

45. Mrs. W. J. J. Smith, *A Centennial History of the Baptist Women of Texas, 1830–1930* (Dallas: Woman's Missionary Union, 1933), 27.

46. Heck, *In Royal Service*, 145. Foy Johnson Farmer, *Hitherto: History of North Carolina Woman's Missionary Union* (Raleigh: North Carolina Woman's Missionary Union, 1952), 21–22.

47. Mrs. W. J. J. Smith, *A Centennial History of the Baptist Women of Texas, 1830–1930* (Dallas: Woman's Missionary Union, 1933), 49–50.

48. Annie Armstrong to R. J. Willingham (May 25, 1895), in Keith Harper, ed., *Rescue the Perishing: Selected Correspondence of Annie W. Armstrong* (Macon, GA: Mercer University Press, 2004), 91.

49. *Western Recorder*, December 6, 1888.

50. *Biblical Recorder*, February 10, 1892.

51. Minutes, Baptist Women Mission Workers of Texas (November 21–22, 1911).

52. Minutes of the Woman's Missionary Societies, Auxiliary to Baptist State Convention of North Carolina (Raleigh, 1892), 35, North Carolina Woman's Missionary Union.

53. Smith, *Centennial History of the Baptist Women of Texas*, 35. The first chapter of the *Centennial* relates numerous stories of Texas women and their struggles on the frontier.

54. Smith, *Centennial History of the Baptist Women of Texas*, 35.

55. Allen, *Century to Celebrate*, 4.

56. *Baptist Argus*, March 16, 1898, quoted in Allen, *Century to Celebrate*, 35.

57. Allen, *Century to Celebrate*, 38.

58. Charles Reagan Wilson gave Jones this moniker in chapter 6 of his book *Baptized in Blood: The Religion of the Lost Cause, 1865–1920* (Athens: University of Georgia Press, 1980). Heck, *In Royal Service*, 111. Catherine Allen identified the speaker as Williams in *Century to Celebrate*, 37.

59. H. Leon McBeth, "The Role of Women in Southern Baptist History," *Baptist History and Heritage* 12 (January 1977): 14.

60. Catherine Allen determined this unilateral transfer of administrative authority to be a blow to women's work. Alma Hunt wrote of the event as an endorsement of women's work. See Allen, *Century to Celebrate*, 39, and Hunt, *History of the Women's Missionary Union*, 20–21.

61. Allen, *Century to Celebrate*, 41.

62. Ethlene Boone Cox, *Following in His Train* (Nashville: Broadman Press, 1938), 55.

63. Quoted in Cox, *Following in His Train*, 56.

64. Cox, *Following in His Train*, 56.

65. Annie Armstrong, *Women as Helpers in God's Kingdom* (Baltimore: Baptist Mission Rooms, 1900), 7, WMUA.

66. Alice Armstrong, "Woman's Obligation to Spread the Gospel," 11–12. Annie Armstrong Notebooks, WMUA.

67. *Baptist Basket*, June 1888.

68. Heck, *In Royal Service*, 133.

69. Alice Armstrong, "Woman's Missionary Union, Auxiliary to SBC, 1888–1898," 5, WMUA.

70. The first corresponding secretary was Annie Armstrong (1888–1906). Armstrong refused payment for her work throughout her service with WMU. During the tenure of Edith Campbell Crane (1907–11), WMU began paying a salary for the work of corresponding secretary. In 1901, WMU began paying the travel expenses of the president and other executive officers. See Allen, *Century to Celebrate*, 55 and 442.

71. There were ten member states at WMU's founding in 1888, thus there were ten state presidents who served automatically as national WMU vice presidents.

72. *Baptist Basket*, June 1888.

73. Allen, *Century to Celebrate*, 55.

74. James B. Crooks, *Politics and Progress: The Rise of Urban Progressivism in Baltimore, 1895–1911* (Baton Rouge: Louisiana State University Press, 1968), 194.

75. Allen, *Century to Celebrate*, 68.

76. Allen, *Century to Celebrate*, 67.

77. Bobbie Sorrill notes that James Armstrong's "firm offered for sale seventeen-pound boxes of tobacco, smoking pipes, Garrett's snuff, fifty different brands of imported cigars, and 1,500,000 other good, medium and low priced cigars." *Annie Armstrong: Dreamer in Action* (Nashville: Broadman Press, 1984), 23–24.

78. Flynt, *Alabama Baptists*, 294.

79. Fannie's father, Colonel Jonathan Heck, was a devout Southern Baptist and "believed in every phase of the work of the denomination." For years he was superintendent of the Sunday school in First Baptist Church, Raleigh. He served as the president of the North Carolina State Sunday School Convention, as president of the State Baptist Convention of North Carolina, vice president of the Foreign Mission Board, and on the board of trustees for both Wake Forest College and Southern Baptist Theological Seminary. Hunt, *History of Woman's Missionary Union*, 31.

80. Mrs. W. C. James [Minnie Kennedy], *Fannie E. S. Heck: A Study of the Hidden Springs in a Rarely Useful and Victorious Life* (Nashville: Broadman Press, 1939), 4.

81. "Fannie E. S. Heck," *Window of Young Women's Auxiliary* clipping from WMU Offices, Baptist State Convention of North Carolina, Carey, North Carolina. "Editorial," *Royal Service* (October 1915): 4–5; Heck wrote a pamphlet on the Ecumenical Conference in New York called *A Great Event* published by the Maryland Mission Rooms in 1900; Catherine Allen, *Laborers Together with God: 22 Great Women in Baptist Life* (Birmingham, AL: Woman's Missionary Union, 1987), 26–37.

82. Her great-uncle William Crane sponsored the education and commissioning of Lott Carey and Collin Teague, African American missionaries to Liberia, and was one of the founders of the Maryland Baptist Missionary Union. Her second cousin William Carey Crane served as president of Baptist colleges in Mississippi, Louisiana, and Texas and founded some of the earliest Baptist periodicals in those states. In her four years of service, she traveled 50,000 miles, gave 426 speeches, and visited every member state of the SBC. She attended the World Missionary Conference in Edinburgh in 1910 as the representative of WMU and was elected recording secretary of the women's meeting of the Baptist World Alliance in 1911. Crane also served as the southern advisory chair of the Jubilee of Missions celebrating the fiftieth anniversary of organized interdenominational women's work for foreign missions. In 1911 Edith Crane offered her resignation to WMU due to health problems caused by complete exhaustion. She married Methodist layman Samuel Tucker Lanham in 1912 and moved to his home in Spartanburg, South Carolina. Together they had two daughters. Soon after moving to Spartanburg, she joined Bethel Methodist Church and became president of the Woman's Missionary Society. Edith Campbell Crane Lanham died in 1933 at the age of fifty-seven. See Claris I. Crane, *Daughter of the Covenant: Edith Campbell Crane, 1876–1933* (Baltimore: Woman's Missionary Union, Auxiliary to the Baptist Convention of Maryland, 1966), 2–11. Also Fannie Heck to R. J. Willingham (May 27, 1907), Training School Collection, Southern Baptist Historical Library and Archives (SBHLA), Nashville, Tennessee.

83. In 1921 the WMU executive offices relocated to Birmingham, Alabama, taking Mallory back to her home state where she served until her retirement in 1948. *Buhlmaier to Brinkley: A History of the Mallory Baptist Center, 1915–1975* (Baltimore: Baptist Convention of Maryland, n.d.), 3. Pamphlet in Historical Library, Baptist Convention of Maryland.

84. Flynt, *Alabama Baptists*, 294; Allen, *Century to Celebrate*, 491.

85. Interestingly, Bell later served as assistant corresponding secretary of the Foreign Mission Board and as head of the Sunday School Board. Their daughter, Ada Carol, became a missionary to China in 1914, and Martha Bell joined her there in 1918. In 1921 the two women returned to the United States and became involved in social work. Ada Carol Bell established a Good Will Center in Ridgecrest, North Carolina, in 1923. Allen, *Laborers Together with God*, 17–25.

86. "Miss Fannie Heck Enters Her Rest," *Raleigh News and Observer*, August 26, 1915, Fannie Heck papers, Box 1, Folder 4, North Carolina Baptist Historical Collection, Z. Smith Reynolds Library, Wake Forest University, Winston-Salem, North Carolina (hereafter NCBHC).

87. Allen, *Laborers Together with God.*

88. I have not been able to discover where she attended school in Virginia.

89. They had nine children. Allen, *Laborers Together with God*, 38–44. Cox, *Following in His Train*, 74.

90. Illness forced her to return to the United States where her husband became a pastor. She opposed the WMU Training School and resigned her presidency with Annie Armstrong. Fannie Heck returned to office again after Barker resigned and remained WMU president until her death in 1915. Allen, *Laborers Together with God*, 52–56.

91. Allen, *Laborers Together with God*, 61.

92. Heck, *In Royal Service*, 142–43.

93. Paul Harvey, "Saints but Not Subordinates: The Woman's Missionary Union of the Southern Baptist Convention," in Margaret Lamberts Bendroth and Virginia Lieson Brereton, eds., *Women and Twentieth-Century Protestantism* (Urbana: University of Illinois Press, 2002), 5.

94. Hill, *World Their Household*, 5, 3.

Chapter 2

1. Fannie Exile Scudder Heck, *In Royal Service* (Richmond, VA: Foreign Mission Board, SBC, 1913).

2. Heck, *In Royal Service*, 8.

3. Heck, *In Royal Service*, 8.

4. Heck, *In Royal Service*, 298.

5. Heck, *In Royal Service*, 298.

6. In her study of Baptist women, Patricia Summerlin Martin stated, "the central theme of change in Baptist women's role was power—the assumption of personal power and the exercise of institutional power." Patricia Summerlin Martin, "Hidden Work: Baptist Women in Texas, 1880–1920" (PhD diss., Rice University, 1982), 10. "In the nineteenth century," noted historian Paul Harvey, "Southern Baptist churchwomen increasingly chafed at quietist prescriptions for female piety even while continuing to work within the language of 'the refined Southern woman.'" Paul Harvey, "Saints but Not Subordinates: The Woman's Missionary Union of the Southern Baptist Convention," in *Women and Twentieth-Century Protestantism*, ed. Margaret Lamberst Bendroth and Virginia Lieson Brereton (Urbana: University of Illinois Press, 2002), 8. For a detailed analysis of Baptist women's missionary writings, see Melody Maxwell, *The Woman I Am: Southern Baptist Women's Writings, 1906–2006* (Tuscaloosa: University of Alabama Press, 2014). See also Elizabeth Flowers, *Into the Pulpit: Southern Baptist Women and Power since World War II* (Chapel Hill: University of North Carolina Press, 2014).

7. Catherine Allen, *A Century to Celebrate: History of Woman's Missionary Union* (Birmingham, AL: Woman's Missionary Union Press, 1987), 237. After the nineteenth amendment passed, however, WMU leaders boldly encouraged women to vote. See Allen, *Century to Celebrate*, 237.

8. Historians have studied these various perceptions of womanhood in the nineteenth century that Fannie Heck described. Barbara Welter's groundbreaking study found the "cult of true womanhood" pervasive not only in the literature of the mid-nineteenth century but also deeply ingrained in the public consciousness. "If anyone, male or female, dared to tamper with the complex of virtues which made up True Womanhood," Welter

noted, "he was damned immediately as an enemy of God, of civilization and of the Republic." See Barbara Welter, "The Cult of True Womanhood, 1820–1860," *American Quarterly* 18 (Summer 1966): 152.

9. Betty DeBerg noted that "by the middle of the nineteenth century . . . the cult of true womanhood represented the dominant values and code of behavior for the middle class and all others who sought upward mobility and middle class respectability." Betty DeBerg, *Ungodly Women: Gender and the First Wave of American Fundamentalism* (Minneapolis: Fortress Press, 1990), 19.

10. Welter's research is based predominately on national women's magazines published in the Northeast. For further studies of the "cult of domesticity," see Gerda Lerner, "The Lady and the Mill-Girl: Changes in the Status of Women in the Age of Jackson," *Mid-Continent American Studies Journal* 10 (1969): 5–15; Ann Douglas Wood, "Mrs. Sigourney and the Sensibility of Inner Space," *New England Quarterly* 45 (1972): 163–81; Kathryn Kish Sklar, *Catharine Beecher: A Study in American Domesticity* (New Haven, CT: Yale University Press, 1973); and Nancy F. Cott, *The Bonds of Womanhood: "Woman's Sphere" in New England, 1780–1835* (New Haven, CT: Yale University Press, 1977).

11. Cott, *Bonds of Womanhood*, 3.

12. Ruth Bordin reports that in many places in the 1880s, women comprised 30 to 40 percent of the industrial labor force. Thus, the ideal was fashioned around middle- and upper-middle-class women. The leisure time not only presented women with a new ideological identity but also provided them with the time they would need to organize as reformers in the decades after the Civil War. Ruth Bordin, *Woman and Temperance: The Quest for Power and Liberty, 1873–1900* (Philadelphia: Temple University Press, 1981), 10.

13. Betty DeBerg, *Ungodly Women: Gender and the First Wave of American Fundamentalism* (Minneapolis: Fortress Press, 1990), 19.

14. William R. Taylor suggests that southern views were transported from England. Margaret Ripley Wolfe concurs that "transplanted Englishmen" determined the role of women in the South during the seventeenth and early eighteenth centuries. "In the southern colonies," explains Wolfe, "they relegated women—red, white, and black—to perhaps even more pronounced positions of inferiority [than in the north]." See William R. Taylor, *Cavalier and Yankee: The Old South and American National Character* (Garden City, NY: Anchor Books, 1963), 143, and Margaret Ripley Wolfe, *Daughters of Canaan: A Saga of Southern Women* (Lexington: University Press of Kentucky, 1995), 11. Historian Nancy Cott believes the attitudes most likely developed locally. Northern and Southern ideologies separate native traditions with shared causes or they could be "separate, indigenous traditions with different origins." Cott, *Bonds of Womanhood*, 11. Whether these ideas were imported or native, Cott rightly emphasizes that a separate sphere for women was not created entirely by the rise of industrial capitalism. Women were already conducting their lives largely within the realm of the household. Rather, the rise of capitalism caused the domestic sphere to "become more conspicuous and more clearly articulated" as the nineteenth century wore on. Cott, *Bonds of Womanhood*, 199.

15. Elizabeth Fox-Genovese, "Family and Female Identity in the Antebellum South:

Sarah Gayle and Her Family," in *In Joy and Sorrow: Women, Family, and Marriage in the Victorian South, 1830–1900*, ed. Carol Bleser (New York: Oxford University Press, 1991), 11.

16. Heck, *In Royal Service*, 9.

17. Anne Scott reports that one young woman wrote she "longed to die because she had not found a husband" and if given a chance "would make a faithful, obedient wife, loving with all my heart, yielding entire trust to my husband." Anne Firor Scott, *Southern Lady: From Pedestal to Politics, 1830–1930* (Chicago: University of Chicago Press, 1970), 7.

18. Suzanne D. Lebsock, "Radical Reconstruction and the Property Rights of Southern Women," in *Half Sisters of History: Southern Women and the American Past*, ed. Catherine Clinton (Durham, NC: Duke University Press, 1994), 113.

19. *Texas Baptist Herald*, March 30, 1870, 1.

20. Judith Tomlin to Virginia Savage, in Catherine Clinton, *The Plantation Mistress: Woman's World in the Old South* (New York: Pantheon Books, 1982), 85.

21. Tomlin to Savage, in Clinton, *Plantation Mistress*, 85.

22. George C. Rable, *Civil Wars: Women and the Crisis of Southern Nationalism* (Urbana: University of Illinois Press, 1989), 8. Rebecca Sharpless's study of Texas cotton farms also confirms the typical pattern of birth as two years apart persisted into the early decades of the twentieth century. Sharpless, *Fertile Ground, Narrow Choices: Women on Texas Cotton Farms, 1900–1940* (Chapel Hill: University of North Carolina Press, 1999), 42.

23. Sharpless, *Fertile Ground*, 39.

24. Sharpless, *Fertile Ground*, 41.

25. Rable, *Civil Wars*, 9.

26. These statistics are drawn from the years 1765–1815. See Clinton, *Plantation Mistress*, 235.

27. Elizabeth Fox-Genovese explained that antebellum defenders of slavery linked that institution with the role of women. "Religious and secular pro-slavery theorists alike forcefully insisted that all social relations—notably those of slavery—depended upon and were grounded in the natural and divinely sanctioned subordination of women to men." Fox-Genovese, "Family and Female Identity in the Antebellum South." Eugene Genovese points out that religious theorists applied the same biblical literalism that defended slavery to the issue of women. "Suffice it to note that pro-slavery rested, above all, on biblical sanction," comments Genovese, "the justification of black slavery derived from the general justification of slavery, regardless of race, as ordained of God, and all class stratification derived from the prior divine command that women should submit to men—racial subordination derived from class subordination, which derived from gender subordination. For the mouth of the Lord hath spoken it." Eugene Genovese, "Toward a Kinder and Gentler America: The Southern Lady in the Greening of the Politics of the Old South," in *In Joy and Sorrow: Women, Family, and Marriage in the Victorian South, 1830–1900*, ed. Carol Bleser (New York: Oxford University Press, 1991), 127.

28. For further discussion of female purity and white supremacy see Catherine Clinton, "Southern Dishonor: Flesh, Blood, Race, and Bondage," in *In Joy and Sorrow:*

Women, Family, and Marriage in the Victorian South, 1830–1900, ed. Carol Bleser (New York: Oxford University Press, 1991), 52–68.

29. Frederick A. Ross, quoted in Eugene Genovese, "Toward a Kinder and Gentler America," 127.

30. William Harper, "Harper's Memoir on Slavery," in *The Pro-Slavery Argument: As Maintained by the Most Distinguished Writers of the Southern States* (Philadelphia: Lippencott, 1853), 214–215.

31. Virginia Kent Anderson Leslie, "A Myth of the Southern Lady: Antebellum Proslavery Rhetoric and the Proper Place of Woman," in *Southern Women*, ed. Caroline M. Dillman (New York: Hemisphere, 1988), 19. "It is no accident," Anne Scott commented wryly, "that the most articulate spokesmen for slavery were also eloquent exponents of the subordinate role of women." Anne Firor Scott, *The Southern Lady: From Pedestal to Politics*, (Chicago: University of Chicago Press, 1970), 17.

32. Scott, *Southern Lady*, 21. Scott does not give a direct citation for her paraphrase of George Fitzhugh.

33. Charles Reagan Wilson, *Baptized in Blood: The Religion of the Lost Cause, 1865–1920* (Athens: University of Georgia Press, 1980).

34. Quoted in Scott, *Southern Lady*, 5.

35. Wilson, *Baptized in Blood*, 46–48.

36. See Drew Gilpin Faust, *Mothers of Invention: Women of the Slaveholding South in the American Civil War* (New York: Vintage Books, 1997).

37. Anne Scott noted that "when plantations broke up and people began to move to town, the image [of 'true womanhood'] as a real force in women's lives was doomed." Scott, *Southern Lady*, 228.

38. For information regarding revivalism and gender, see Sarah Evans, *Born for Liberty: A History of Women in America* (London: Collier Macmillan, 1989), and Nancy Hardesty, *Women Called to Witness: Evangelical Feminism in the 19th Century* (Knoxville: University of Tennessee Press, 1999). In *The Feminization of American Culture* (New York: Alfred A. Knopf, 1977), Ann Douglas contends that the relationship between the clergy and women was extremely strong because disestablishment relegated religion to the private sphere, thus reinforcing true womanhood notions of the "inherently religious" woman. The Anglican presence in the colonial South contributed similar notions of piety and submissiveness to the cultural pool. See Alice E. Matthews, "The Religious Experience of Southern Women," in *Women and Religion in America*, vol. 2, *The Colonial and Revolutionary Periods*, ed. Rosemary Radford Ruether and Rosemary Skinner Keller (San Francisco: Harper and Row, 1983), 193–232.

39. Nathan Hatch argues that "if American religion is anything writ large, it springs from a Methodist rather than a Puritan kernel." Nathan Hatch, *The Puzzle of American Methodism*, American Society of Church History Papers (Portland, OR: TREN, 1994). Gregory Schneider expounds on the influence of Methodism in American culture with particular reference to Victorian gender ideology in *The Way of the Cross Leads Home* (Bloomington: Indiana University Press, 1993). "American Methodism," states Catherine Albanese, "laid the foundations in white people's experience for the adoption of an evangelical version of Victorian domestic ideology." Catherine Albanese, introduction to Schneider, *Way of the Cross Leads Home*, xxii.

40. Reverend Richard Allestree, *The Whole Duty of Man*, excerpts in Matthews, "Religious Experience of Southern Women," 207.

41. *Religious Herald* (Richmond), February 20, 1868, 2, quoted in Rufus B. Spain, *At Ease in Zion: Social History of Southern Baptists, 1865–1900* (Nashville: Vanderbilt University Press, 1967), 168.

42. *Religious Herald*, February 20, 1868, 2.

43. *Religious Herald* (Richmond) January 5, 1899, 1.

44. *Christian Index* (Atlanta), May 28, 1885, 8, quoted in Spain, *At Ease in Zion*, 167.

45. *Texas Baptist Herald*, May 17, 1871, 1.

46. Heck, *In Royal Service*, 8.

47. Nancy Cott's study of New England women concludes that religion, particularly Calvinism, served "to elevate women as religion's supporters and . . . to reaffirm women's subordination to men." Cott, *Bonds of Womanhood*, 159. It is important to note that the Puritan ethos carried with it a reverence for education. The majority of women in New England were literate because of Puritanism, and this shaped women's self-understanding as well as the evolution of gender roles in New England.

48. George W. McDaniel, "Christ and Woman," *Home and Foreign Fields* 2 (July 1918): 4.

49. *Texas Baptist Herald*, May 17, 1871, 1. The phrase "shoving the plain" may be a reference to woodworking: smoothing out a piece of wood. But, if so, it is misspelled (it should be "plane," not "plain").

50. *Texas Baptist Herald*, May 17, 1871, 1.

51. Donald G. Mathews, *Religion in the Old South* (Chicago: University of Chicago Press, 1977), 113. Sara Evans noted, "Christ appeared as the epitome of feminine virtue: loving, forgiving, suffering and sacrificing for others. Thus, the notion of female moral superiority received further reinforcement as the ideals of femininity and of Christianity appeared to coalesce." Evans, *Born for Liberty*, 73.

52. *Royal Service* (February 1915): 12.

53. The model of separate domestic spheres has been questioned because of its narrow focus on privileged white women. Scholars have begun to question its relevance for women of other races and classes. For treatments of gender identities that take class and race into broader consideration, see Susan Tank Lesser's biographical essay "Paradigms Gained: Further Readings in the History of Women in the Progressive Era" in *Gender, Class, Race, and Reform in the Progressive Era*, ed. Noralee Frankel and Nancy S. Dye (Lexington: University Press of Kentucky, 1991), 180–93, and Sarah Eisenstein, *Give Us Bread but Give Us Roses: Working Women's Consciousness in the United States, 1890 to the First World War* (Boston: Routledge, 1983).

54. Rev. Rufus Weaver, "The Problem of the City," Home Mission Board Leaflet Series No. 15, 1906–1907. Southern Baptist Library and Archives, Nashville, Tennessee.

55. *Royal Service* (September 1921): 28.

56. Anne Firor Scott, "Women's Perspective on the Patriarchy in the 1850s," in *Half Sisters of History: Southern Women and the American Past*, ed. Catherine Clinton (Durham, NC: Duke University Press, 1994), 86.

57. Barbara Welter, "The Cult of True Womanhood, 1820–1860," *American Quarterly* 18 (Summer 1966): 174.

58. Alice Armstrong, "Woman's Obligation to Spread the Gospel," 9–11. Annie Armstrong Notebooks, WMUA.

59. Armstrong, "Woman's Obligation," 9–11.

60. Minutes, Rehoboth Baptist Association (1913), 17. Texas Collection, Carroll Library Building, Baylor University, Waco, Texas.

61. Mary Hill Davis, "San Antonio, 1907," in *Living Messages: Official Addresses of Mrs. F. S. Davis, 1907–1931* (Dallas: Woman's Missionary Union of Texas, 1935), 2.

62. *Texas Baptist Herald*, May 17, 1871, 1.

63. Ann Judson to Richmond Female Judson Society (Washington, DC, April 26, 1823), quoted in Heck, *In Royal Service*, 49.

64. *Our Mission Fields* (January, February, March, 1912): 20–21.

65. *Our Mission Fields* (January, February, March, 1912): 40.

66. Ann Judson to Richmond Female Judson Society, in Heck, *In Royal Service*, 49.

67. Minutes, Woman's Missionary Society, Auxiliary to the Baptist State Convention of North Carolina, December 9, 1892 (Raleigh: Edwards and Broughton, 1893).

68. Davis, "San Antonio, 1907," 2.

69. Elizabeth Blackwell, the first woman to receive a formal medical degree in America, argued that a woman's nature made her ideally suited for the medical profession. Blackwell believed that female physicians were needed to treat women within their own sphere. Charlotte G. Borst and Kathleen W. Jones, "As Patients and Healers: The History of Women and Medicine," *OAH Magazine of History* 19 (September 2005): 24. See also Charlotte G. Borst, *Catching Babies: The Professionalization of Childbirth, 1870–1920* (Cambridge, MA: Harvard University Press, 1995); Regina Markell Morantz, *Sympathy and Science: Women Physicians in American Medicine* (New York: Oxford University Press, 1985); Ellen Singer More and Maureen A. Milligan, eds., *The Empathic Practitioner: Empathy, Gender, and Medicine* (New Brunswick, NJ: Rutgers University Press, 1994).

70. Helen Barrett Montgomery, *Western Women in Eastern Lands: An Outline Study of Fifty Years of Woman's Work in Foreign Missions* (New York: Macmillan, 1910), 124.

71. Montgomery, *Western Women*, 122.

72. Montgomery, *Western Women*, 126.

73. *Our Mission Fields* (April, May, June 1913): 47–49.

74. *Our Mission Fields* (April, May, June 1913): 51. The doctor's name was Ida Fay Levering of Secunderabad, India. It is possible that Levering was related to Joshua Levering, but I have not found the connection. I do not know what reaction WMU may have received from Levering's comment that the women come "two by two to preach."

75. Franklin T. Fowler, "The History of Southern Baptist Medical Missions," *Baptist History and Heritage* (October 1, 1975): 196. On the voyage to China she met J. A. Thompson, a representative of the National Bible Society of Scotland, who was serving in Japan. Ruth McGowan later married him and left the service of the Foreign Mission Board.

76. Fowler, "History of Southern Baptist Medical Missions," 197.

77. Fowler, "History of Southern Baptist Medical Missions," 198.

78. Other UMHB alumni listed in this pamphlet who became doctors were Dr. Alma

Freeman (1922); Dr. Pearl Smith (1923); Dr. Estella Ginsberg Strayer (1924); Dr. Lois Norman (1930); Dr. Margaret Alex Vance (1931); Dr. Sally Provence (1937). Dorothea Lohoff Gingrich, ed., *By Their Fruits Ye Shall Know Them*, UMHB Centennial Series Pamphlet (Belton, TX: University of Mary Hardin-Baylor, 1944), 23–28, located in the Musick Alumni Center and Museum at the Parker House, University of Mary Hardin-Baylor, Belton, Texas.

79. *Album of Southern Baptist Foreign Missionaries, 1926*, SBHLA.

80. See T. Laine Scales, *"All That Fits a Woman": Training Southern Baptist Women for Charity and Mission, 1907–1926* (Macon, GA: Mercer University Press, 2000).

81. See Mathews, *Religion in the Old South*, 115–20, for a description of the Evangelical social impulse among antebellum women.

82. Sarah Jessie Stakely, "Annual Address of the President," Report of the Fourteenth Annual Meeting of WMU, SBC (1902), 7.

83. Greg Vickers, "Woman's Place: Images of Womanhood in the SBC, 1888–1929" (master's thesis, Vanderbilt University, 1986), 82. Vickers concluded that WMU leadership held "ethical tenets which were not shared by the men and which resulted in behavior historians have not found prevalent among Southern Baptist males." Vickers, "Woman's Place," 90.

84. Rosemary Skinner Keller noted this in her study of the Methodist deaconess movement. "The language of family and Mother House at the heart of the deaconess movement is undeniably quaint to the ears of feminists at the turn of the 21st century," Keller wrote. "However . . . advocates of deaconess orders were speaking in a language to make their radical moves as the first professional women in the churches justifiable to national authorities, and grassroots members of local congregations, as well as to themselves." Rosemary Skinner Keller, "Creating a Sphere for Women: The Methodist Episcopal Church, 1869–1906," in *Women in New Worlds: Historical Perspectives on the Wesleyan Tradition*, ed. Hilah F. Thomas, Rosemary Skinner Keller, and Louise L. Queen (Nashville: Abingdon, 1981), 84.

85. Lulie Wharton, *Royal Service* (September 1925): 27.

86. Maud Reynolds McClure, *A Glimpse of Settlement Work* (May 1913), pamphlet in the Personal Service Notebooks, WMUA.

87. *Royal Service* (December 1920): 30.

88. "Personal Service Survey," ca. 1912, Personal Service Notebooks, WMUA.

89. This was common to women's literature in that era. In her study of female reformers in Atlanta, Georgina Hickey found that "throughout these case studies, social workers and reformers promoted the image of women as the key to a family's survival." Georgina Hickey, "Disease, Disorder, and Motherhood: Working-Class Women, Social Welfare, and the Process of Urban Development in Atlanta" in *Before the New Deal: Social Welfare in the South, 1830–1930*, ed. Elna C. Green (Athens: University of Georgia Press, 1999), 184.

90. *Annual Report*, Woman's Missionary Union, Auxiliary to the Southern Baptist Convention (May 1916), 52.

91. *Royal Service* (February 1915): 12.

92. Susan Hill Lindley contends that most female middle-class social gospel activists focused their attention on women and children by organizing such works as kindergar-

tens, day nurseries, and mothers' classes. See Lindley's discussion of the social gospel in *"You Have Stept Out of Your Place:" A History of Women and Religion in America* (Louisville: Westminster John Knox Press, 1996), 135–47.

93. *Royal Service* (February 1915): 12.

94. *Our Mission Fields* (October, November, December, 1913): 32. This focus on the maternal role as motivation for missions and reform is not unique to WMU. Female reformers in the Progressive Era consistently modeled their public efforts on their domestic role. Ellen Carol Dubois argues that the first generation of women progressives—settlement workers and municipal reformers—consistently perceived their roles as public expressions of their maternal roles. See Ellen Carol Dubois, "Harriet Stanton Blatch and the Transformation of Class Relations among Women Suffragists," in *Gender, Class, Race, and Reform in the Progressive Era*, ed. Noralee Frankel and Nancy S. Dye (Lexington: University Press of Kentucky, 1991), 162–79.

95. *Royal Service* (February 1915): 11.

96. *Royal Service* (February 1915): 12.

97. *Royal Service* (August 1917): 12.

98. *Royal Service* (October 1915): 27.

99. *A Handbook for Personal Service* (Baltimore: Woman's Missionary Union, n.d.), 34. Personal Service Notebooks, WMUA, 28.

100. *Handbook for Personal Service*, 28.

101. Anne Firor Scott contends that members of women's clubs were the first to initiate programs to address the problems of the cities and in so doing, virtually *invented* Progressivism. Scott, *Natural Allies: Women's Associations in American History* (Urbana: University of Illinois Press, 1992), 141–74. Nancy Dye observed that "when we view reform through women's eyes, re-defining the relationship between home and community—the private and the public—emerges as central to progressivism. Nancy S. Dye, Introduction to *Gender, Class, Race, and Reform in the Progressive Era*, ed. Noralee Frankel and Nancy S. Dye (Lexington: University Press of Kentucky, 1991), 4.

102. *Texas Baptist Herald*, November 3, 1869.

103. *Royal Service* (March 1916): 10.

104. Wharton was the director of the Personal Service department of WMU, which was the center of their social service agenda.

105. Lulie Wharton, *Royal Service* 9, no. 4 (October 1914): 24.

106. Minutes, Woman's Missionary Society, Aux. to Baptist State Convention of North Carolina (December 9, 1892), 35.

107. *Our Mission Fields* 6, no. 3 (January, February, March 1912), 15.

108. Mrs. John Stout, *Shall the Baptists of the South Organize for Mission Work?* (Baltimore: Maryland Baptist Mission Rooms, 1888). In WMU historical scrapbook.

109. Lottie Moon to H. A. Tupper, July 17, 1885, in Keith Harper, ed., *Send the Light: Lottie Moon's Letters and Other Writings* (Macon, GA: Mercer University Press, 2002), 114–15.

110. Annie Armstrong to J. M Frost, July 24, 1896, in Harper, *Send the Light*, 94–95.

111. Annie Armstrong to R. J. Willingham, January 28, 1903, in Harper, *Send the Light*, 54.

112. *Baptist Standard*, October 16, 1913, 14, quoted in Martin, "Hidden Work," 147.

113. *Royal Service* (July 1922): 4–5.

114. Wharton, *Royal Service* 20 (September 1925): 27.

Chapter 3

1. Elizabeth Marshall Evans, *Annie Armstrong* (Birmingham, AL: WMU Press, 1963), 8.

2. Fannie Exile Scudder Heck, *In Royal Service: The Mission Work of Southern Baptist Women* (Richmond: Foreign Mission Board, 1913), 139–40.

3. See Susan M. Yohn, "'Let Christian Women Set the Example in Their Own Gifts': The 'Business' of Protestant Women's Organizations," in *Women and Twentieth-Century Protestantism*, ed. Margaret Lamberts Bendroth and Virginia Lieson Brereton (Urbana: University of Illinois Press, 2002), 213–35; Burton Bledstein, *The Culture of Professionalism: The Middle Class and the Development of Higher Education in American* (New York: W. W. Norton, 1978); and Paul Harvey, "The Ideal of Professionalism and the White Southern Baptist Ministry, 1870–1920," *Religion and American Culture* 5 (Winter 1995): 99–123.

4. Catherine Allen, *A Century to Celebrate: History of Woman's Missionary Union* (Birmingham, AL: Woman's Missionary Union Press, 1987), 482–87. Allen provides a chart of WMU contributions in the back of her centennial history of WMU. I have included the box contribution amounts in my totals. $2,418, 924 translates to over $30 million dollars in 2018.

5. Elizabeth Marshall Evans, *Annie Armstrong* (Birmingham, AL: Woman's Missionary Union, SBC, 1963).

6. Evans, *Annie Armstrong*, 9–10.

7. Sorrill, *Annie Armstrong*, 39.

8. Shannon Baker, "Following in the Footsteps of Annie Armstrong in Baltimore," *Baptist Life: News Journal of the Baptist Convention of Maryland/Delaware* (March 2006): 1, 6; Harriett S. Levering, "A Sketch of Miss Annie," *Window of Y.W.A.* (March 1935): 9–10, 32.

9. Heck, *In Royal Service*, 139–40.

10. Helen Barrett Montgomery, *Western Women in Eastern Lands: An Outline Study of Fifty Years of Woman's Work in Foreign Missions* (New York: Macmillan, 1910), 38.

11. Evans, *Annie Armstrong*, 33–34.

12. Blanche Sydnor White, *Our Heritage: History of Woman's Missionary Union, Auxiliary to the Maryland Baptist Union Association, 1742–1958* (Baltimore: Woman's Missionary Union of Maryland, 1959), 37. See also W. Loyd Allen, *You Are a Great People: Maryland Delaware Baptists, 1742–1998* (Franklin, TN: Providence House Publishers, 2000), 139–40.

13. Heck, *In Royal Service*, 141. Brick cards were small collectible cards with the names and pictures of missionaries on them. They were sold to finance new church buildings in Cuba.

14. White, *Our Heritage*, 37.

15. Alice Armstrong, "*WMU, SBC 1888–1898*," 12. Pamphlet in Annie Armstrong Box 2, WMUA.

16. Evans, *Annie Armstrong*.

17. In 1985, periodical sales constituted 62 percent of WMU's $8.6 million budget. In 2005, WMU reported a combined income of periodical subscriptions and literature sales of over $9.7 million—80 percent of their revenue for that year. See Allen, *Century to Celebrate*, 498–505. SBC *Annual Report* (2006), 424.

18. Alice Armstrong, "*WMU, Auxiliary to SBC, 1888–1898*," 7. Pamphlet in Annie Armstrong Box 2, WMUA.

19. Keith Harper edited and compiled many of Armstrong's letters in *Rescue the Perishing: Selected Correspondence of Annie Armstrong* (Macon, GA: Mercer University Press, 2004). His work was extremely helpful to this project.

20. Annie Armstrong to R. M. Inlow (January 15, 1903), in Harper, *Rescue the Perishing*, 120.

21. Susan M. Yohn, "'Let Christian Women Set the Example in Their Own Gifts': The 'Business' of Protestant Women's Organizations," in *Women and Twentieth-Century Protestantism*, ed. Margaret Lamberts Bendroth and Virginia Lieson Brereton (Urbana: University of Illinois Press, 2002), 214–15. Evans, *Annie Armstrong*, 177.

22. Montgomery, *Western Women*, 38.

23. Alice Armstrong, "*WMU, SBC 1888–1898*," 12.

24. Annie W. Armstrong, *Women as Helpers in God's Kingdom* (Baltimore: Baptist Mission Rooms, 1900), in Sorrell Box 2, WMUA, 12.

25. Montgomery, *Western Women*, 38.

26. Alice Armstrong, "*WMU, SBC 1888–1898*," 12.

27. White, *Our Heritage*, 45.

28. Annie Armstrong to I. T. Tichenor (June 24, 1899), in Harper, *Rescue the Perishing*, 104.

29. Annie Armstrong to I. T. Tichenor (September 7, 1899), in Harper, *Rescue the Perishing*, 109.

30. Armstrong, *Women as Helpers in God's Kingdom*, 9.

31. Annie Armstrong to J. M Frost (July 1, 1901), in Harper, *Rescue the Perishing*, 79.

32. SBC *Annual Report, WMU Report* (1913), 65.

33. Annie Armstrong to J. M. Frost (April 21, 1899), in Harper, *Rescue the Perishing*, 28.

34. Annie Armstrong to I. T. Tichenor (June 24, 1899) in Harper, *Rescue the Perishing*, 105; Annie Armstrong to R. J. Willingham (March 7, 1899), in Harper, *Rescue the Perishing*, 25.

35. Armstrong to A. J. Barton (1899), in Harper, *Rescue the Perishing*, 60.

36. Armstrong to E. E. Bomar (November 17, 1902), in Harper, *Rescue the Perishing*, 13–15.

37. Armstrong to J. M. Frost (no day, 1901), in Harper, *Rescue the Perishing*, 24.

38. White, *Our Heritage*, 47.

39. Allen, *Century to Celebrate*, 181.

40. Armstrong to Frost (December 30, 1903), in Harper, *Rescue the Perishing*, 9.

41. Armstrong to Frost (February 14, 1900), in Harper, *Rescue the Perishing*, 63.

42. Armstrong to J. M. Frost (April 13, 1904), in Harper, *Rescue the Perishing*, 260.

43. Armstrong to J. M. Frost (September 1, 1898), in Harper, *Rescue the Perishing*, 55.

44. Armstrong to J. M. Frost (April 21, 1899), in Harper, *Rescue the Perishing*, 29.

45. Armstrong to A. J. Barton (September 3, 1898); Armstrong to R. J. Willingham (January 24, 1899); Armstrong to R. J. Willingham (July 5, 1902), in Harper, *Rescue the Perishing*, 57, 59, 69.

46. Annie Armstrong to R. J. Willingham (January 19, 1894), WMUA.

47. Annie Armstrong to R. J. Willingham (January 27, 1894), WMUA.

48. Armstrong to I. T. Tichenor (May 31, 1899), in Harper, *Rescue the Perishing*, 238–39.

49. Armstrong to Frost (October 8, 1900); Armstrong to Frost (October 9?, 1900), in Harper, *Rescue the Perishing*, 61–62.

50. Armstrong to Frost (February 14, 1900), in Harper, *Rescue the Perishing*, 63.

51. Armstrong to A. J. Barton (1899), in Harper, *Rescue the Perishing*, 60.

52. T. P. Bell to J. M. Frost (December 23, 1897), in Harper, *Rescue the Perishing*, 64.

53. Annie Armstrong to R. J. Willingham (November 10, 1903), in Harper, *Rescue the Perishing*, 113.

54. Fannie Heck to R. J. Willingham (May 25, 1898), in Harper, *Rescue the Perishing*, 187.

55. Annie Armstrong to I. T. Tichenor (April 8, 1899), in Harper, *Rescue the Perishing*, 195; and Armstrong to R. J. Willingham (February 7, 1899), in Harper, *Rescue the Perishing*, 202.

56. Annie Armstrong to R. J. Willingham (April 26, 1905), WMUA. See Sorrill, *Annie Armstrong*, 266. Armstrong concluded that "it will cause friction should I take part in the work at any point." Evans, *Annie Armstrong*, 179.

57. Evans, *Annie Armstrong*, 176.

58. Evans, *Annie Armstrong*, 176.

59. SBC *Annual Report* of 1913; Catherine Allen compiled comprehensive financial charts for the centennial history of WMU, *Century to Celebrate*, 482–506.

60. Sorrill, *Annie Armstrong*, 279–80.

61. Annie Armstrong, *Women as Helpers in God's Kingdom* (1900), 11. WMUA.

Chapter 4

1. Nannie Helen Burroughs to Rev. W. Clyde Atkins (January 28, 1939), Una Roberts Lawrence Papers, SBHLA.

2. Burroughs to Atkins (January 28, 1939).

3. Burroughs to Atkins (January 28, 1939).

4. Evelyn Brooks Higginbotham, *Righteous Discontent: The Woman's Movement in the Black Baptist Church, 1880–1920* (Cambridge, MA: Harvard University Press, 1993), 89.

5. Dewey Grantham, *Southern Progressivism: The Reconciliation of Progress and Tradition* (Knoxville: University of Tennessee Press, 1983), 126; William Link, *The Paradox of Southern Progressivism, 1880–1930* (Chapel Hill: University of North Carolina Press, 1992), 70.

6. Hugh Bailey, *Liberalism in the New South: Southern Social Reformers and the Progressive Movement* (Coral Gables, FL: University of Miami Press, 1969), 112.

7. For more on the origins of black Baptists, see James Melvin Washington, *Frustrated Fellowship: The Black Baptist Quest for Social Power* (Macon, GA: Mercer University Press, 2004); Leroy Fitts, *A History of Black Baptists* (Nashville: Broadman Press, 1985); and Paul Harvey, *Redeeming the South: Religious Cultures and Racial Identities among Southern Baptists, 1865–1925* (Chapel Hill: University of North Carolina Press, 1997).

8. Washington, *Frustrated Fellowship*, 12.

9. Rufus B. Spain, *At Ease in Zion: A Social History of Southern Baptists, 1865–1900* (Nashville: Vanderbilt University Press, 1967), 51.

10. Washington, *Frustrated Fellowship*, 138.

11. Washington, *Frustrated Fellowship*, 139.

12. Higginbotham, *Righteous Discontent*, 154.

13. Washington, *Frustrated Fellowship*, 137.

14. Frederick Douglass, "The Color Line in America," *North American Review* 132 (June 1, 1881): 568.

15. C. Vann Woodward, *The Strange Career of Jim Crow* (1955; repr., New York: Oxford University Press, 1966), 98.

16. In her study of Jim Crow practices in the rural South, Melissa Walker noted that "rural southerners described a highly articulated racial etiquette that differed from place to place and from person to person." See Walker, "Shifting Boundaries: Race Relations in the Rural Jim Crow South," in *African American Life in the Rural South, 1900–1950*, ed. R. Douglas Hurt (Columbia: University of Missouri Press, 2003), 81.

17. Avery Downing, quoted in Walker, "Shifting Boundaries," 89.

18. For an in-depth study of lynching, see the Equal Justice Initiative's *Lynching in America: Confronting the Legacy of Racial Terror* (Montgomery, AL: Equal Justice Initiative, 2015).

19. *Baptist Home Mission Monthly* 11 (November 1889): 295–96. See also Washington, *Frustrated Fellowship*, 148–49.

20. J. M. Frost, quoted in Washington, *Frustrated Fellowship*, 165.

21. Another "betrayal" was the failure to include black Baptists in the Fortress Monroe Conference in September 1894. At that meeting Southern Baptists met with Northern Baptists to determine which group would control education and missions for black southerners.

22. For further discussion of Richard Henry Boyd and the National Baptist Publishing Board, see Harvey, *Redeeming the South*, 243–50.

23. Higginbotham, *Righteous Discontent*, 6, and C. Eric Lincoln and Lawrence H. Mamiya, *The Black Church in the African American Experience* (Durham, NC: Duke University Press, 1998), 28.

24. Nannie Helen Burroughs's papers can be found in the Burroughs Collection, Library of Congress, Manuscript Division, Washington, DC.

25. Burroughs, quoted in Higginbotham, *Righteous Discontent*, 150.

26. Broughton, quoted in Higginbotham, *Righteous Discontent*, 70.

27. Higginbotham, *Righteous Discontent*, 73.

28. Higginbotham, *Righteous Discontent*, 155.

29. Annie Armstrong to R. J. Willingham (January 6, 1897), in Keith Harper, *Rescue the Perishing: Selected Correspondence of Annie W. Armstrong* (Macon, GA: Mercer University Press, 2004), 339–40.

30. Annie Armstrong to J. M. Frost (January 26, 1897), in Harper, *Rescue the Perishing*, 341.

31. Elizabeth Marshall Evans, *Annie Armstrong* (Birmingham, AL: Woman's Missionary Union, SBC, 1963), 21.

32. Evans, *Annie Armstrong*, 30.

33. Evans, *Annie Armstrong*, 30–31.

34. Annie Armstrong to J. M Frost (January 26, 1897), in Harper, *Rescue the Perishing*, 340.

35. Annie Armstrong to J. M Frost, (January 26, 1897), in Harper, *Rescue the Perishing*, 341.

36. Annie Armstrong to J. M. Frost (July 2, 1897), in Harper, *Rescue the Perishing*, 345.

37. Annie Armstrong to R. J. Willingham (January 6, 1897), in Harper, *Rescue the Perishing*, 339–40. I am grateful to Bill Sumners, director of the Southern Baptist Historical Library and Archives in Nashville, Tennessee, for bringing some of these letters to my attention. See Bill Sumners, "Bridge Builders: Baptist Women and Race Relations at the Turn of the Twentieth Century," *Journal of African American Southern Baptist History* (June 2004): 72–81.

38. Annie Armstrong to J. M Frost (January 26, 1897), in Harper, *Rescue the Perishing*, 341.

39. See Link, *The Paradox of Southern Progressivism, 1880–1930.*

40. Annie Armstrong to R. J. Willingham (June 2, 1902), in Harper, *Rescue the Perishing*, 350.

41. J. M. Frost, *The Sunday School Board: Its History and Work*, in *A Sourcebook for Baptist Heritage*, by H. Leon McBeth (Nashville: Broadman Press, 1990), 301.

42. Harvey, *Redeeming the South*, 244.

43. Annie Armstrong to J. M. Frost (July 2, 1897), James Marion Frost Papers, SBHLA.

44. Annie Armstrong to J. M. Frost (July 2, 1897), James Marion Frost Papers, SBHLA.

45. Mrs. V. W. Broughton, "The Development of Christian Homes, the Hope of the Negro Race," (Baltimore: Mission Literature Department, Southern Baptist Convention, ca. 1901), WMUA. It is interesting that this speech included concepts of gender equality amid the advice on the development of Christian homes. Broughton stated that Christian homes represented the pinnacle of family life where "the woman is no longer the slave or the gaudy toy; but man's equal—his worthy helper, companion, and friend."

46. Annie Armstrong notebooks, No. 6 side 2, WMUA.

47. Minutes, Woman's Convention, Auxiliary to the National Baptist Convention (September 12, 1901).

48. S. W. Layten, Minutes, Woman's Convention, Auxiliary to the National Baptist Convention (Birmingham, AL, 1902), copy in Una Roberts Lawrence papers, Southern Baptist Convention Library and Archives, Nashville, Tennessee.

49. S. W. Layten, Minutes, Woman's Convention, Auxiliary to the National Baptist Convention (Chicago, 1905), copy in Una Roberts Lawrence papers, Southern Baptist Convention Library and Archives, Nashville, Tennessee.

50. S. W. Layten, Minutes, Woman's Convention, Auxiliary to the National Baptist Convention (Chicago, 1905) copy in Una Roberts Lawrence papers, Southern Baptist Convention Library and Archives, Nashville, Tennessee.

51. S. W. Layten, Minutes, Woman's Convention, Auxiliary to the National Baptist Convention (Chicago, 1905) copy in Una Roberts Lawrence papers, Southern Baptist Convention Library and Archives, Nashville, Tennessee.

52. R. H. Boyd, Minutes, National Baptist Convention (Birmingham, Alabama, 1903), 4, Una Roberts Lawrence Papers, SBHLA).

53. R. H. Boyd, Minutes, National Baptist Convention (Birmingham, Alabama, 1903), 4, Una Roberts Lawrence Papers, SBHLA.

54. S. W. Layten, Minutes, Woman's Convention, Auxiliary to the National Baptist Convention (Philadelphia, 1903).

55. Nannie Helen Burroughs, Minutes, Woman's Convention, NBC (Philadelphia, 1903).

56. Nannie Helen Burroughs, Minutes, Woman's Convention, NBC (Philadelphia, 1903).

57. Sandy Martin, *Black Baptists and African Missions: The Origins of a Movement, 1880–1915* (Macon, GA: Mercer University Press, 1998), 13.

58. Atticus G. Haygood, quoted in Ralph Luker, *The Social Gospel in Black and White: American Racial Reform, 1885–1912* (Chapel Hill: University of North Carolina Press, 1991), 33.

59. Emanuel Love, quoted in Washington, *Frustrated Fellowship*, 137.

60. Annie Armstrong to R. J. Willingham (January 6, 1897), in Harper, *Rescue the Perishing*, 340.

61. Annie Armstrong to J. M. Frost (January 26, 1897), in Harper, *Rescue the Perishing*, 342.

62. Annie Armstrong notebooks, No. 6, side 2, WMUA.

63. Annie Armstrong, introduction to Broughton, "Development of Christian Homes."

64. Minutes, Woman's Convention, NBC (Chicago, 1905).

65. When Una Roberts Lawrence became chairperson of personal service in 1929, she resumed the relationship of WMU with Nannie Helen Burroughs. In 1932 WMU formed a committee to consider relationships with National Baptist women with Lawrence as chairwoman. In 1934, Burroughs wrote Lawrence and commended her because "at last" she had "begun to think colored." Nannie Helen Burroughs to Una Roberts Lawrence, August 18, 1934, Una Roberts Lawrence papers, Southern Baptist Library and Archives, Nashville, Tenn.

66. Higginbotham, *Righteous Discontent*, 2.

67. Nannie Helen Burroughs papers, Library of Congress, Washington, DC, http://hdl.loc.gov/loc.mss/eadmss.ms003010, accessed July 21, 2011.

68. Higginbotham, *Righteous Discontent*, 211.

69. Bettye Collier-Thomas notes that "between 1910 and 1940, almost three fourths of all African American women were employed as domestic servants." Bettye Collier-Thomas, *Jesus, Jobs, and Justice: African American Women and Religion* (New York: Alfred A. Knopf, 2010), 281. Paula Giddings reports that there were basically two professions open to black women: teaching in "colored schools" or domestic service. See Giddings, *When and Where I Enter: The Impact of Black Women on Race and Sex in America* (New York: Bantam Books, 1984), 101–2. See also Jacqueline Jones, *Labor of Love, Labor of Sorrow: Black Women, Work, and the Family from Slavery to the Present* (New York: Basic Books, 1985).

70. Pamela Smoot, "African American Baptist Women: Making a Way Out of No Way," *Baptist History and Heritage* 42 (Summer 2007): 26.

71. Black women believed "they were 'the fundamental agency under God in the regeneration . . . of the race, as well as the groundwork and starting point of its progress upward,' wrote Anna Julia Cooper in her *Voice of the South* (1892), one of the best-written books of the period." Cooper believed that this was a tremendous responsibility because "only the BLACK WOMAN can say 'when and where I enter . . . then and there the whole Negro race enters with me.'" Cooper, quoted in Giddings, *When and Where I Enter*, 82.

72. Collier-Thomas, *Jesus Jobs, and Justice*, 281.

73. Collier-Thomas, *Jesus Jobs, and Justice*, 286, and Higginbotham, *Righteous Discontent*, 182.

74. S. W. Layten, Minutes, Woman's Convention, NBC (Philadelphia, 1903).

75. Higginbotham, *Righteous Discontent*, 193.

76. Broughton, "Development of Christian Homes."

77. Nannie Helen Burroughs, "New and Old Paths to Fertile Fields" (Washington, DC: Woman's Convention of the National Baptist Convention, n.d.), 12, in Una Roberts Lawrence papers, SBHLA.

78. WMU literature often displayed crass paternalism, calling domestic laborers the "white woman's burden." Catherine Allen, *A Century to Celebrate: History of Woman's Missionary Union* (Birmingham, AL: Woman's Missionary Union, 1987), 242.

79. Minutes of the Annual Meeting of the Woman's Missionary Societies, Auxiliary to Baptist State Convention of North Carolina (Raleigh, 1895), 15. The Home Mission Board was still competing with the American Baptist Home Mission Society for control of the South during the period of the 1880s and 1890s. The race issue remained a point of contention. The Home Mission Board encouraged WMU to initiate work with African Americans partially because Southern Baptists resented the presence of northern missionaries in the South.

80. II Chronicles 19:7; or "God shows no partiality," Galatians 2:6, New American Standard Bible.

81. Minutes of Woman's Missionary Societies, North Carolina (Raleigh, 1896), 15.

82. See, for example, *Our Mission Fields* (January 1910): 43; *Our Mission Fields* (October, November, December, 1910): 38; *Our Mission Fields* (January, February, March 1911): 18; *Royal Service* (February 1915): 11.

83. Ronald C. White Jr. defined romantic racialism as "a belief in racial differences but

not necessarily racial inferiority." See *Liberty and Justice for All: Racial Reform and the Social Gospel, 1877–1925* (San Francisco: Harper and Row, 1990), 47.

84. *Our Mission Fields* (January, February, March 1911): 18.

85. See Spain, *At Ease in Zion*, 76.

86. *Our Mission Fields* (January, February, March 1911): 18.

87. *Our Mission Fields* (January, February, March 1911): 18.

88. *Our Mission Fields* (January, February, March 1911): 18.

89. *Our Mission Fields* (January, February, March 1911): 18.

90. *Our Mission Fields* (October, November, December 1910): 38. This article cited Josiah Strong and Shailer Mathews as experts on the "problems of the cities" but also stated that "individual salvation, and that alone" could solve the problems of the "negro" in the cities.

91. *Our Mission Fields* (January 1910): 43.

92. *Royal Service* (August 1924): 17.

93. *Royal Service* (August 1925): 33.

94. Rev. Robert Ryland, DD, "The Colored People" (Baltimore: Baptist Mission Rooms, 1898), 7, WMUA.

95. Fannie E. S. Heck to Lulie Wharton, ca. 1912. WMUA.

96. Fannie Heck to Lulie Wharton, ca. 1912. Heck papers, WMUA.

97. *Royal Service* (February 1915): 11.

98. *Royal Service* (February 1915): 11.

99. Samuel S. Hill Jr., Charles H. Lippy, and Charles Reagan Wilson, eds., *Encyclopedia of Religion in the South* (Macon, GA: Mercer University Press, 1984), s.v. "Commission on Interracial Cooperation," by Morton Sosna.

100. Allen, *Century to Celebrate*, 246.

101. John Patrick McDowell, *The Social Gospel in the South: The Woman's Home Mission Movement in the Methodist Episcopal Church, South, 1886–1939* (Baton Rouge: Louisiana State University Press, 1982), 91.

102. *Royal Service* (December 1923): 28.

103. *Royal Service* (December 1922): 16.

104. *Royal Service* (October 1922): 18.

105. Ella Broadus Robertson, *Royal Service* (January 1923): 28.

106. *Royal Service* (January 1923): editorial.

107. *Royal Service* (December 1923): 28.

108. *Royal Service* (December 1923): 28.

109. *Royal Service* (August 1925): 33.

110. *Royal Service* (December 1922): 29.

111. *Annual Report of the Woman's Missionary Union, Auxiliary to Louisiana Baptist Convention*, 1923, 18–19.

112. *Royal Service* (August 1924): 12.

113. *Royal Service* (August 1924): 10.

114. *Royal Service* (August 1924): 11.

115. *Royal Service* (August 1924): 11.

116. *Royal Service* (August 1924): 11.

117. *Royal Service* (August 1924): 14.

118. *Royal Service* (August 1924): 15.

119. Allen, *Century to Celebrate*, 244–45.

120. Quoted in Higginbotham, *Righteous Discontent*, 223.

121. *Thirteenth Annual Report of the Woman's Convention, National Baptist Convention* 1913, 33, quoted in Higginbotham, *Righteous Discontent*, 222.

122. *Journal of the Eighteenth Annual Session of the Woman's Convention, Auxiliary to the National Baptist Convention, Held in St. Louis, Missouri, September 4–9, 1918* (Nashville: Sunday School Publishing Board, 1919), 169, quoted in Higginbotham, *Righteous Discontent*, 223.

123. Ronald C. White Jr. discussed the role of both Christian and civic scriptures in the writings of social gospel leaders. See White, *Liberty and Justice for All*, 112.

124. *Royal Service* (August 1924): 12.

125. Emma M. Whitefield, *Royal Service* (December 1923): 28; (January 1924): 25.

126. *Royal Service* (August 1924): 13.

127. Allen, *Century to Celebrate*, 247.

128. For details on WMU's racial attitudes after 1930, see Allen, *Century to Celebrate*, 248–57.

129. Allen, *Century to Celebrate*, 247.

130. Allen, *Century to Celebrate*, 247.

131. Nannie Helen Burroughs, "The Dawn of a New Day in Dixie," in *Think on These Things* (Washington, DC, privately published, 1956), quoted in Allen, *Century to Celebrate*, 245.

132. Charlotte Hawkins Brown, quoted in Kendal P. Mobley, "'What a Chasm There Is between Us': Charlotte Hawkins Brown and White Protestant Progressives, 1901–1952," in *Baptist History and Heritage* 42 (Summer/Fall 2007): 42.

Chapter 5

1. *Annual Report* (1912), 51. Catherine Allen believes WMU avoided using the term "social service" directly in connection with personal service to avoid "antagonizing opponents of the social gospel." Catherine Allen, *A Century to Celebrate: History of Woman's Missionary Union* (Birmingham, AL: Woman's Missionary Union, 1987), 215.

2. *Report of the Annual Meeting of Woman's Missionary Union, Auxiliary to Southern Baptist Convention* (1913), 41. Subsequently referred to as *Annual Report*.

3. Walter Rauschenbusch to Munson Ford (June 30, 1886), in Winthrop Hudson, ed., *Walter Rauschenbusch: Selected Writings* (New York: Paulist Press, 1984), 58.

4. Christopher Evans, *The Kingdom Is Always but Coming: A Life of Walter Rauschenbusch* (Grand Rapids, MI: Eerdmans, 2004), 61.

5. Evans, *Kingdom*, 67.

6. Evans, *Kingdom*, 197.

7. Washington Gladden, quoted in Gary Dorrien, "Social Salvation: The Social Gospel as Theology and Economics," in *The Social Gospel Today*, ed. Christopher Evans (Louisville: Westminster John Knox, 2001), 107.

8. Sydney E. Ahlstrom, *A Religious History of the American People* (New Haven, CT:

Yale University Press, 1972), 791. The earliest histories of the social gospel largely focused on these men and identified their common theological and ethical themes.

9. Strong, quoted in Charles Howard Hopkins, *The Rise of the Social Gospel in American Protestantism, 1865–1915* (New Haven, CT: Yale University Press, 1940), 205.

10. Christopher Evans has edited an excellent collection of articles that seek to fill this gap in scholarship. The bibliographies for each article contain a treasure trove of primary and secondary sources. See Evans, *Social Gospel Today*.

11. Mathews, quoted in Hopkins, *Rise of the Social Gospel*, 3.

12. Shailer Mathews, *The Individual and the Social Gospel* (New York: Missionary Education Movement and Laymen's Missionary Movement, 1914), 21.

13. Walter Rauschenbusch, *A Theology for the Social Gospel* (Nashville: Abingdon Press, 1917), 5.

14. Rauschenbusch, *Theology for the Social Gospel*, 5.

15. Rauschenbusch, *Theology for the Social Gospel*, 5–6.

16. Rauschenbusch, *Christianizing the Social Order*, in *Walter Rauschenbusch: Selected Writings*, ed. Winthrop Hudson (New York: Paulist Press, 1984), 179.

17. John Dillenberger and Claude Welch, *Protestant Christianity: Interpreted through Its Development*, 2nd ed. (New York: Macmillan, 1988), 225–26.

18. Walter Rauschenbusch, *The New Evangelism*, quoted in Robert T. Handy, *The Social Gospel in America, 1870–1920* (New York: Oxford University Press, 1966), 325.

19. Rauschenbusch, *New Evangelism*, 327.

20. Washington Gladden, *The Church and the Modern Life* (Boston: Houghton, Mifflin, 1908), 155.

21. Gladden, *Church and the Modern Life*, 157.

22. Gladden, *Church and Modern Life*, 22.

23. Walter Rauschenbusch, *Christianizing the Social Order* (New York: Macmillan, 1919), 60.

24. See Jane Addams, "Jane Addams on the Need for Social Settlements, 1892," in *Major Problems in the Gilded Age and the Progressive Era*, ed. Leon Fink (Lexington, MA: D. C. Heath, 1993), 302.

25. Walter Rauschenbusch, *Christianity and the Social Crisis* (New York: Macmillan, 1907), 422.

26. Rauschenbusch, *Christianizing the Social Order*, 49.

27. Rauschenbusch, "Kingdom of God," in Handy, *Social Gospel in America*, 267.

28. Rauschenbusch, "Kingdom of God," in Handy, *The Social Gospel in America*, 267.

29. Ahlstrom, *Religious History*, 802.

30. Elias B. Sanford, ed., Inter-Church Conference on Federation, *Church Federation* (New York, 1906), 33–34.

31. Hopkins, *Rise of the Social Gospel*, 302.

32. Hopkins, *Rise of the Social Gospel*, 163.

33. Jesse L. Hurlbut, *The Story of Chautauqua* (New York: G. P. Putnam's Sons, 1921), 395–98.

34. Lewis L. Gould, *The Progressive Era* (Syracuse, NY: Syracuse University Press, 1974), 9.

35. Hopkins, *Rise of the Social Gospel*, 299.

36. Walter Rauschenbusch, quoted in Katherine Amato-von Hemert, "Battle between Sin and Love in Social Work History," in *Christianity and Social Work: Readings on the Integration of Christian Faith and Social Work Practice*, ed. Beryl Hugen and T. Laine Scales (Botsford, CT: North American Association of Social Work, 2002), 50–51.

37. John Lee Eighmy, *Churches in Cultural Captivity: A History of the Social Attitudes of Southern Baptists* (Knoxville: University of Tennessee Press, 1972), 110.

38. "Report of the Committee on Social Service," Minutes of the Eighty-Ninth Annual Session of the Baptist General Association of Virginia, Petersburg, Virginia, November 14–19, 1912, SBHLA, 112.

39. *Annual of the Alabama State Convention* (1933), 24, quoted in Eighmy, *Churches in Cultural Captivity*, 110.

40. *Annual of the Baptist General Convention of Texas* (1920), (Texas Baptist Historical Collection, Waco) 80.

41. Eighmy, *Churches in Cultural Captivity*, 110.

42. Harvey, "Southern Baptists and the Social Gospel: White Religious Progressivism in the South, 1900–1925." *Fides et Historia* 27 (Summer 1995): 65.

43. Eighmy, *Churches in Cultural Captivity*, 89–90.

44. J. M. Price, *Christianity and Social Problems* (Nashville, 1928), 90–103, 224–39. See also Eighmy, *Churches in Cultural Captivity*, 131.

45. William Brackney notes that Walter Rauschenbusch spoke at the Baptist Congress in 1904 held at Broadway Baptist Church in Louisiville, Kentucky. See Brackney, "The Frontier of the Free Exchange of Ideas: The Baptist Congress as a Forum for Baptist Concerns, 1881–1912," *Baptist History and Heritage* 38 (Summer/Fall 2003): 8–27.

46. *Our Mission Fields* (January, February, March 1912): 19.

47. Fannie E. S. Heck to Mattie Heck, April 24, 1900. Heck papers, NCBHC.

48. F. E. S. Heck, "A Great Event," 12. Woman's Missionary Union Library and Archives, WMU Headquarters, Birmingham, Alabama.

49. *Biblical Recorder* (March 29, 1911): 1, 5.

50. *Foreign Mission Journal* (February 1912): 247–51.

51. *Annual Report* (1917), 93.

52. John Patrick McDowell, *The Social Gospel in the South: The Woman's Home Mission Movement in the Methodist Episcopal Church, South, 1886–1939* (Baton Rouge: Louisiana State University Press, 1982), 3.

53. McDowell, *Social Gospel*, 20, and Francis A. Downs, "The Greatest Woman of Southern Methodism," *Methodist Review* 64 (April 1915).

54. Between 1900 and 1920, WMU met in four Methodist churches, four Presbyterian churches, one Congregational church, nine Baptist churches, two hotels, and one YMCA. See *Annual Report* (1900–1920).

55. See Minutes of Woman's Missionary Union, Auxiliary to the Baptist State Convention of North Carolina, North Carolina Woman's Missionary Union Offices, Baptist State Convention of North Carolina, Cary, North Carolina.

56. Annie Armstrong to T. P. Bell, March 3, 1894. SBHLA.

57. For descriptions of early Methodist settlement houses, see Sara Estelle Haskins,

Woman and Missions in the Methodist Episcopal Church, South (Nashville: Methodist Episcopal Church, 1920), 202.

58. Carrie Littlejohn, *History of Carver School of Missions and Social Work* (Nashville: Broadman Press, 1958), 64.

59. *A Handbook of Personal Service*, n.d. Personal Service Notebooks, WMU Library and Archives, Birmingham, Alabama.

60. *Proceedings of the Birmingham Baptist Association*, 1913, 32. SBHLA.

61. Unpublished manuscript, Heck papers, NCBHC. Pamphlets published after her death in Baltimore by Woman's Missionary Union. For advertisement, see *Royal Service* (January 1921): back cover.

62. Unpublished notes, Heck papers, NCBHC.

63. Fannie E. S. Heck to Lulie Wharton, ca. 1912. WMU Library and Archives, Birmingham, Alabama.

64. M. R. McClure to Fannie E. S. Heck, February 8, 1915, Heck papers, NCBHC.

65. McLure to Heck, February 8, 1915.

66. *Proceedings of the Twenty-Fifth Annual Meeting of the Baptist Women Mission Workers of Texas* (November 21–22, 1911), 34. Texas Collection, Carroll Library Building, Baylor University, Waco, Texas.

67. Annie Armstrong Notebooks, WMUA. For more detailed discussion of the WMU's attitude toward temperance, see Allen, *Century to Celebrate*, 238–41; Rosalie Beck, Kay Shurden, and Catherine Allen, "The Impact of Southern Baptist Women on Social Issues: Three Viewpoints," *Baptist History and Heritage* 12 (July 1987): 29–49.

68. Ruth Bordin, *Woman and Temperance: The Quest for Power and Liberty, 1873–1900* (Philadelphia: Temple University Press, 1981), 110.

69. *The Survey*, n.d. Personal Service Notebooks, WMUA.

70. Allen, *Century to Celebrate*, 238.

71. Carolyn Weatherford insists that "Woman's Missionary Union and women in Southern Baptist life are synonymous. If women had leadership roles outside of Woman's Missionary Union, history is silent." I would agree that from its founding in 1888 until the 1960s, leadership roles for women in local Baptist churches were typically limited to Woman's Missionary Union, although there were some Baptist churches in the South that had female deacons prior to the founding of WMU and continued to have them into the twentieth century. Furthermore, women have been the principal leaders of the Sunday schools in Southern Baptist churches since the nineteenth century. This role should not be overlooked when assessing the influence of Baptist women in the South. Carolyn Weatherford, "Shaping of Leadership among Southern Baptist Women," *Baptist History and Heritage* (July 1987): 15; Charles W. Deweese, "Deaconesses in Baptist History: A Preliminary Study," *Baptist History and Heritage* (January 1977): 52–57. See also Elizabeth Flowers, *Into the Pulpit: Southern Baptist Women and Power since World War II* (Chapel Hill: University of North Carolina Press, 2014).

72. This is unpublished research noted in correspondence between historians Ruth Provence and Catherine Allen, cited in Allen, *Century to Celebrate*, 240.

73. Allen, *Century to Celebrate*, 238.

74. Allen, *Century to Celebrate*, 240.

75. Fannie Breedlove Davis, handwritten memoir, Biographical File, Musick Alumni Center and Museum, University of Mary Hardin-Baylor, Belton, Texas.

76. *Royal Service* (August 1925): 29.

77. *Royal Service* (September 1925): 27.

78. J. E. McCulloch to F. E. S. Heck, March 3, 1913. Heck papers, NCBHC.

79. J. E. McCulloch, ed., *Democracy in Earnest: The Southern Sociological Congress, 1916–1918* (Nashville: Southern Sociological Congress, 1918), 318.

80. Ronald C. White Jr. and C. Howard Hopkins, *The Social Gospel: Religion and Reform in Changing America* (Philadelphia: Temple University Press, 1976), 93–94.

81. A full report on the Southern Sociological Congress is included in *Royal Service* (May 1915): 26. See also *Royal Service* (March 1916): 8–14.

82. Samuel Zane Batten, "Modern Miracles of the Church in Health Conservation," in *The New Chivalry—Health*, ed. James E. McCulloch (Nashville: Southern Sociological Congress, 1915). Speeches given at the Southern Sociological Congress May 8–11, 1915, Houston, Texas.

83. *Royal Service* (March 1916): 13.

84. *Royal Service* (March 1916): 13.

85. Victor I. Masters, *Southern Problems for Southern Baptists* (Atlanta: Home Mission Board of the Southern Baptist Convention, 1910), SBHLA.

86. *Royal Service* (March 1916): 13–14.

87. *Royal Service* (March 1916): 14.

88. Victor I. Masters, *The Home Board and Social Service* (Atlanta: Publicity Department of the Southern Baptist Convention, n.d.), SBHLA.

89. *A Handbook of Personal Service*, revised (Baltimore: Woman's Missionary Union, nd), 4. Personal Service Notebooks, WMUA. Paul Harvey points out that the terms "efficiency" and "uplift" connote the progressive emphasis on "scientific management." Shailer Mathews applied "scientific management" to church organization. The elements of efficiency in church programs appealed to Southern Baptists. See Paul Harvey, *Redeeming the South: Religious Cultures and Racial Identities among Southern Baptists, 1865–1925.* (Chapel Hill: University of North Carolina Press, 1997), 197.

90. Alma Hunt, *History of Woman's Missionary Union* (Nashville: Convention Press, 1964), 31.

91. Catherine Allen, *Laborers Together with God: 22 Great Women in Baptist Life* (Birmingham, AL: Woman's Missionary Union, 1987). See also Mrs. W. C. James [Minnie Kennedy], *Fannie E. S. Heck: A Study of the Hidden Springs in a Rarely Useful and Victorious Life* (Nashville: Broadman Press, 1939), 59–60.

92. "Editorial," *Royal Service* (October 1915): 4–5; Allen, *Laborers Together with God*, 26–37.

93. Allen, *Century to Celebrate*, 104.

94. Allen, *Century to Celebrate*, 196.

95. Nimmo to F. E. S. Heck, February 11, 1915, Heck papers, NCBHC.

96. Nimmo to F. E. S. Heck, February 4, 1915, Heck papers, NCBHC.

97. Clippings, Heck papers, NCBHC.

98. Fannie E. S. Heck, from *The Window of Young Woman's Auxiliary*, clipping, Fan-

nie Heck papers, North Carolina Woman's Missionary Union, Baptist State Convention of North Carolina, Cary, North Carolina.

99. Fannie E. S. Heck, "Address to Associated Charities of Raleigh, North Carolina—20 Months after Organization" (copy of unpublished manuscript, ca. 1905), n.p. Heck papers, NCBHC. Heck wrote this address by hand and scribbled the informal title across the back of one of the pages. Associated Charities of Raleigh was founded in June 1903. This address must have been given in February 1905. For information on the founding of Associated Charities of Raleigh, see *Annual Report of the Associated Charities of Raleigh* (1904), 2. North Carolina State Archives, Raleigh, North Carolina. The Charity Organization Society of London was founded in 1869 by Octavia Hill and Canon Barnett to coordinate charity efforts in that city. Canon Barnett was also one of the founders of Toynbee Hall. See Elizabeth A. Ferguson, *Social Work: An Introduction* (New York: J. B. Lippincott, 1963), 62.

100. Heck, "Address to Associated Charities," n.p.

101. Heck, "Address to Associated Charities," n.p.

102. As Stanley P. Caine notes, the social gospel was "built on the premise that social justice and Christianity were synonymous." See Caine, "The Origins of Progressivism," in *The Progressive Era*, ed. Lewis L. Gould (Syracuse, NY: Syracuse University Press, 1974), 13.

103. Minutes, Woman's Missionary Societies, Auxiliary to Baptist State Convention of North Carolina (1898), 16.

104. The 1925 personal service report to the Annual Meeting of the WMU, SBC, offers a farewell to Lulie Wharton as chair of the Personal Service Department. *Annual Report* (1925), 61.

105. Allen, *Century to Celebrate*, 215.

106. Allen, *Century to Celebrate*, 215; Hunt, *History of the Woman's Missionary Union*, 125.

107. *Annual Report* (1915), 60–61.

108. *Annual Report* (1912), 51.

109. Joyce E. Williams and Vicky M. MacLean, *Settlement Sociology in the Progressive Years: Faith, Science, and Reform* (Leiden: Brill, 2015), 77.

110. *Our Mission Fields* (October, November, December 1913): 29.

111. *Our Mission Fields* (October, November, December 1912): 34.

112. *Royal Service* (September 1925): 26–27.

113. Williams and MacLean, *Settlement Sociology*, 62–63.

114. *Our Mission Fields* (October, November, December 1912): 20.

115. *Handbook of Personal Service*, n.d., WMUA.

116. *Annual Report* (1913), 42.

117. *The Survey*, n.d. Personal Service Notebooks, WMUA.

118. Williams and MacLean, *Settlement Sociology*, 28.

119. *Royal Service* (November 1921): 30. There are two different publications called *The Survey*. One was a publication of Baptist women designed to help local societies gather information about their communities. The other was the magazine of the Charity Organization Society movement, and the first social work publication in the United

States, published from 1907 until 1952. I believe the writer is referring to the latter in this instance. Ferguson, *Social Work*, 67.

120. *Royal Service* (November 1921): 30.

121. Williams and MacLean, *Settlement Sociology*, 28.

122. *Royal Service* (November 1921): 30.

123. *Royal Service* (November 1921): 30.

124. *Jubilate Program* (1913), Personal Service Notebooks, WMUA.

125. *Royal Service* (October 1914): 24.

126. *A Handbook of Personal Service*, n.d. Personal Service Notebooks, WMUA.

127. E. Y. Mullins, *Axioms of Religion* (Philadelphia: Griffith and Rowland Press, 1908), 16–17.

128. Minutes, Corpus Christi Missionary Baptist Association (1913), Texas Collection, Baylor University, Waco, Texas, 18; Minutes, Portsmouth Baptist Association (1913), 25, SBHLA.

129. *Annual Report* (1912), 52.

130. *Annual Report* (1912), 52.

131. *Annual Report* (1912), 53.

132. *Annual Report* (1915), 65.

133. "Chairman" was the word used by the WMU at that time.

134. "Personal Service Report," *Annual Report of Woman's Missionary Union, Auxiliary to Louisiana Baptist Convention* (1920), 30. Louisiana Baptist Convention Archives, Alexandria, Louisiana. Interestingly, the national records indicate that Louisiana supported two Good Will Centers in 1920. But the state records do not mention Baptist settlement work at all. *Annual Report* (1920), 78.

135. "Personal Service Report," *Annual Report of Woman's Missionary Union, Auxiliary to Louisiana Baptist Convention* (1921), 25.

136. "Personal Service Report," *Annual Report of Woman's Missionary Union, Auxiliary to Louisiana Baptist Convention* (1922), 26; (1923), 18.

137. *Annual Report* (1915), 65.

138. *Annual Report of Woman's Missionary Union, Auxiliary to Louisiana Baptist Convention* (1921), 26–27.

139. *Annual Report* (1911), 42.

140. The numbers of societies reporting were drawn from the Personal Service Reports of WMU Annual Meetings from 1916 to 1930. These numbers were compared to Catherine Allen's table of member organizations from 1915 to 1929 to arrive at percentages of societies reporting. The lowest percentage was fourteen in 1917. See Allen, *Century to Celebrate*, 479.

141. Fannie Heck, *The Manual of Personal Service*, revised (Baltimore: Woman's Missionary Union, n.d.), 4. Personal Service Notebooks, WMUA.

142. *Manual of Personal Service*, 4.

143. *Handbook of Personal Service*, 2.

144. Minutes, Wichita Baptist Association (1925), 26. Texas Collection, Carroll Library Building, Baylor University, Waco, Texas.

145. In the 1940s "Personal Service" was reorganized as "community missions." Allen, *Century to Celebrate*, 215.

146. *A Manual of Personal Service* (Baltimore: Woman's Missionary Union Auxiliary to the Southern Baptist Convention, ca. 1911). *The Handbook of Personal Service*, revised (Baltimore: Woman's Missionary Union, n.d.), WMUA.

147. *Handbook of Personal Service*, 4.

148. Minutes, Texarkana Missionary Baptist Association (1916), 22. Texas Collection, Baylor University.

149. Minutes of the Lauderdale County Baptist Association (1920), 5, SBHLA.

150. Minutes, Portsmouth Baptist Association (1917), 25, SBHLA.

151. *Annual Report* (1915), 64.

152. *Annual Report* (1915), 65.

Chapter 6

1. William Owen Carver, *Out of His Treasure: Unfinished Memoirs* (Nashville: Broadman Press, 1956), 69.

2. Carver, *Out of His Treasure*, 69. See also Mark Robert Wilson, *William Owen Carver's Controversies in the Baptist South* (Macon, GA: Mercer University Press, 2010).

3. Edward Bagby Pollard and Mrs. H. M. (Lulie) Wharton, *Our Duty to the Community: A Course of Six Studies* (Baltimore: Woman's Missionary Union, 1915). Personal Service Notebooks, WMUA.

4. Edward Bagby Pollard and Lulie Pollard Wharton were either brother and sister or cousins. I have not been able to determine their precise relationship.

5. Pollard and Wharton, *Our Duty to the Community*, n.p.

6. Rauschenbusch follows this same pattern. Walter Rauschenbusch, *A Theology for the Social Gospel* (Nashville: Abingdon Press, 1917).

7. Pollard, "First Study: The Social Teachings of the Scriptures," *Our Duty to the Community*, n.p.

8. Pollard, "First Study," n.p.

9. Pollard, "First Study," n.p.

10. Pollard, "Second Study: The Place of Social Service in the Christian Life," *Our Duty to the Community*, n.p.

11. Pollard, "Second Study," n.p.

12. Pollard, "Second Study," n.p.

13. Pollard, "Fifth Study: Studying a Town—Essential Facts," *Our Duty to the Community*, n.p.

14. Lulie Wharton to Fannie E. S. Heck (March 23, 1915). Fannie Heck correspondence, WMUA.

15. Wharton, "Fourth Study: Woman's Organizations in Social Service," *Our Duty to the Community*, n.p.

16. Wharton, "Fourth Study," n.p.

17. Wharton, "Fourth Study," n.p.

18. Good Will Centers were the Woman's Missionary Union version of social settlements.

19. Wharton, "Sixth Study: Applying the Remedy," *Our Duty to the Community*, n.p.

20. Wharton, "Sixth Study," n.p.

21. *Royal Service* (January 1918): 21.

22. John Eighmy referred to Poteat as the "foremost Darwinist" among Southern Baptists. See *Churches in Cultural Captivity: A History of the Social Attitudes of Southern Baptists* (Knoxville: University of Tennessee Press, 1972), 127.

23. Eighmy, *Churches in Cultural Captivity: A History of the Social Attitudes of Southern Baptists* (Knoxville: University of Tennessee Press, 1972), 84–85.

24. W. O. Carver said Armstrong's main objection was the fear that the school would become a "matrimonial-bureau." Carrie Littlejohn, *History of Carver School of Missions and Social Work* (Nashville: Broadman Press, 1958), 13.

25. Catherine Allen, *A Century to Celebrate: History of Woman's Missionary Union* (Birmingham, AL: Woman's Missionary Union, 1987), 263.

26. For a full discussion of the debate over the Training School, see Allen, *Century to Celebrate*, 263–69; Littlejohn, *History of Carver School*, 1–43.

27. Carver, *Out of His Treasure*, 68.

28. Carver, *Out of His Treasure*, 76.

29. Carver, *Out of His Treasure*, 76.

30. T. Laine Scales, *"All That Fits a Woman": Training Southern Baptist Women for Charity and Mission, 1907–1926* (Macon, GA: Mercer University Press, 2000), 150.

31. Sources do not indicate how many summers McLure actually spent at the Chautauqua Assembly.

32. Jesse L. Hurlbut, *The Story of Chautauqua* (New York: G. P. Putnam's Sons, 1921), 395–98.

33. *Handbook for Personal Service*, 4, 48.

34. The names of Personal Service Committee members listed on Personal Service reports during Lulie Wharton's tenure included Mrs. F. T. Grady, Mrs. A. J. Clark, Kathleen Mallory, Mrs. George Stevens, Susan Bancroft Tyler [Mrs. James Pollard], Mrs. James W. Kirkman, Mrs. W. H. Baylor, Mrs. Oscar G. Levy, and Mrs. A. J. Fristoe. In 1924 Mrs. Peyton A. Eubank took over as chair of the Personal Service Committee. The women were listed by their married names in the literature, and I have not been able to ascertain the given names of all the women.

35. The chairman of the Northern Baptist Social Service Commission, Samuel Zane Batten, offered the BWA resolution calling on other Baptist groups to organize social action committees. These commissions were organized on both the state and national level but functioned independently of one another. See Eighmy, *Churches in Cultural Captivity*, 82.

36. Eighmy, *Churches in Cultural Captivity*, 87.

37. Eighmy, *Churches in Cultural Captivity*, 88.

38. Eighmy, *Churches in Cultural Captivity*, 123. Eighmy is referring to more than a juxtaposition of "souls" with "society." Southern Baptist progressives appeared, at times, to espouse opposing theological systems, one embracing individual conversion as the only solution to social problems and the other applying salvation to both individuals and to society.

39. *Our Mission Fields* (July 1909): 9.

40. *Royal Service* (March 1916): 14.

41. *A Handbook for Personal Service* (Baltimore: Woman's Missionary Union, n.d.), 34. Personal Service Notebooks, WMUA.

42. *Handbook for Personal Service*, 36.

43. *Handbook for Personal Service*, 39.

44. *Handbook for Personal Service*, 137.

45. Minutes of the Woman's Missionary Societies, Auxiliary to Baptist State Convention of NC (1898), 16; *Royal Service* 17 (March 1923): 10.

46. Sydney Ahlstrom, *A Religious History of the American People* (New Haven, CT: Yale University Press, 1972), 613.

47. *Royal Service* (February 1915): 10.

48. *Report of the Annual Meeting of Woman's Missionary Union, Auxiliary to the Southern Baptist Convention* (May 1915), 59. Subsequently referred to as *Annual Report*.

49. *Royal Service* (August 1917): 8–10.

50. *Our Mission Fields* (October, November, December 1913): 29.

51. For anti-social-gospel sentiment among Southern Baptist leaders, see chapter 3 of James J. Thompson Jr., *Tried as by Fire: Southern Baptists and Religious Controversies of the 1920s* (Macon, GA: Mercer University Press, 1982).

52. *Royal Service* (October 1921): 28.

53. *Annual Report* (1912), 51.

54. Eighmy, *Churches in Cultural Captivity*, 110.

55. *A Handbook of Personal Service*, n.d., 9. Personal Service Scrapbooks, WMUA.

56. Walter Rauschenbusch, "The Kingdom of God," in *The Social Gospel in America, 1870–1920*, by Robert Handy (New York: Oxford University Press, 1966), 267.

57. *A Handbook of Personal Service*, n.d., 7, WMUA.

58. *Royal Service* (October 1921): 28.

59. *Royal Service* (February 1915): 9.

60. Rauschenbusch, "Kingdom of God," 267.

61. Shailer Mathews, quoted in Charles Howard Hopkins, *The Rise of the Social Gospel in American Protestantism, 1865–1915* (New Haven, CT: Yale University Press, 1940), 3.

62. Fannie Heck, "Pageant of the Golden Rule" (copy of early manuscript), Heck papers, NCBHC.

63. "Some Questions Answered" (1913), Personal Service Notebooks, WMUA.

64. Rauschenbusch, Gladden, Mathews, and other social gospel writers affirmed the necessity of both individual and social salvation.

65. *A Handbook of Personal Service*, n.d., 12–13. Personal Service Notebooks, WMUA.

66. *Annual Report* (1913), 41.

67. Josiah Strong, quoted in "Wisdom of the Moderns," *Harper's Bazar*, April 1912, 1.

68. Washington Gladden, *The Church and Modern Life* (Boston: Houghton, Mifflin, 1908), 155, 157.

69. *Our Mission Fields* (July 1909): 6.

70. *Our Mission Fields* (July 1909): 8.

71. *Our Mission Fields* (July 1909): 8.

72. *Royal Service* (October 1921): 28.

73. Manuscript of speech, 1910, Heck papers, NCBHC.

74. Fannie Heck, speech to the Woman's Missionary Union, Auxiliary to the Baptist State Convention of North Carolina (April 18, 1911), unpublished manuscript, Heck papers, WMU Offices, Baptist State Convention of North Carolina, Cary, North Carolina.

75. *Annual Report* (1915), 59–60.

76. Grace N. Kimball, quoted in James Shepard Dennis, *Christian Missions and Social Progress: A Sociological Study of Foreign Missions* (New York: Fleming H. Revell, 1897), 48. This book was based on a series of lectures by Dennis at Princeton Theological Seminary in 1896.

77. Walter Rauschenbusch, in *Walter Rauschenbusch: Selected Writings*, ed. Winthrop S. Hudson (New York: Paulist Press, 1984), 124.

Chapter 7

1. *Report of the Baptist Training School Settlement, 1914*, quoted in *Royal Service* (February 1915): 10.

2. See T. Laine Scales, *"All That Fits a Woman": The Education of Southern Baptist Women for Missions and Social Work at the Woman's Missionary Union Training School, 1907–1926* (Macon, GA: Mercer University Press, 2000).

3. Patricia Madoo Lengermann and Gillian Niebrugge, *The Women Founders: Sociology and Social Theory, 1830–1930* (Long Grove, IL: Waveland Press, 2007), 72.

4. Laine Scales demonstrates the differences between Baptist Good Will Centers and traditional social settlements. Her arguments are persuasive. Scales, *"All That Fits a Woman."*

5. Allen F. Davis, *Spearheads of Reform: The Social Settlements and the Progressive Movement, 1890–1914* (New York: Oxford University Press, 1967), 3.

6. Davis, *Spearheads of Reform*, 12.

7. Lengermann and Niebrugge, *Women Founders*, 67.

8. Davis, *Spearheads of Reform*, 16.

9. Joyce E. Williams and Vicky M. MacLean, *Settlement Sociology in the Progressive Years: Faith, Science, and Reform* (Leiden: Brill, 2015), 17.

10. Williams and MacLean, *Settlement Sociology*, 50–51.

11. Williams and MacLean, *Settlement Sociology*, 20.

12. Mina Carson, *Settlement Folk: Social Thought and the American Settlement Movement, 1885–1930* (Chicago: University of Chicago Press, 1990), 176–77.

13. Davis, *Spearheads of Reform*, 12–13.

14. Williams and MacLean, *Settlement Sociology*, 57.

15. Jane Addams, "Jane Addams on the Need for Social Settlements, 1892," in *Major Problems in the Gilded Age and the Progressive Era*, ed. Leon Fink (Lexington, MA: D. C. Heath, 1993), 302.

16. Davis, *Spearheads for Reform*, 6.

17. Williams and MacLean, *Settlement Sociology*, 91.

18. Stanley Caine, "The Origins of Progressivism," in *The Progressive Era*, ed. Lewis L. Gould (Syracuse, NY: Syracuse University Press, 1974), 14.

19. Addams, quoted in Williams and MacLean, *Settlement Sociology*, 95.

20. Addams, in Fink, *Major Problems*, 302.

21. Williams and MacLean, *Settlement Sociology*, 98.

22. Williams and MacLean, *Settlement Sociology*, 58.

23. Graham Taylor, quoted in Williams and MacLean, *Settlement Sociology*, 70.

24. Harry Lurie, quoted in Elizabeth A. Ferguson, *Social Work: An Introduction* (New York: J. B. Lippincott, 1963), 67.

25. Mary Agnes Dougherty, "The Social Gospel According to Phoebe: Methodist Deaconesses in the Metropolis, 1885–1918," in *Perspectives on American Methodism*, ed. Russell E. Richey, Kenneth E. Rowe, and Jean Miller Schmidt (Nashville: Kingswood Books, 1993), 362.

26. Ferguson, *Social Work*, 68.

27. Katherine Amato-von Hemert, "Battle between Sin and Love in Social Work History," in *Christianity and Social Work*, ed. Beryl Hugen and T. Laine Scales (Botsford, CT : North American Association of Christians in Social Work, ca. 2002), 47.

28. Davis, *Spearheads for Reform*, 21.

29. Anne Firor Scott, *Southern Lady: From Pedestal to Politics* (Chicago: University of Chicago Press, 1970), 142.

30. Sara Estelle Haskins, *Women and Missions in the Methodist Episcopal Church, South* (Nashville: Methodist Episcopal Church, 1920), 202.

31. *History of Woman's Work* (History Committee of the Woman's Missionary Society, North Texas Conference, Methodist Episcopal Church, South, 1929), 86.

32. Haskins, *Women and Missions*, 204.

33. Carrie Littlejohn, *History of Carver School of Missions and Social Work* (Nashville: Broadman Press, 1958), 64.

34. Littlejohn, *History of Carver School*, 64.

35. Scales, *"All That Fits a Woman,"* 191–92.

36. The other was Kingsley House in New Orleans. Davis, *Spearheads for Reform*, 23.

37. It is now the New York School of Social Work affiliated with Columbia University. Ferguson, *Social Work*, 65–66.

38. Littlejohn, *History of Carver School*, 65.

39. Scales, *"All That Fits a Woman,"* 182–84.

40. *Report of the Baptist Training School Settlement, 1914*, quoted in *Royal Service* (February 1915): 10.

41. Littlejohn, *History of Carver School*, 193–94.

42. *Royal Service* (March 1921): 30.

43. *Royal Service* (November 1921): 30.

44. Catherine Allen, *A Century to Celebrate: History of Woman's Missionary Union* (Birmingham, AL: Woman's Missionary Union, 1987), 222.

45. *Annual Report* (1914) 59.

46. Minutes of Woman's Missionary Union Auxiliary to Birmingham Baptist Association (1919), 21. Southern Baptist Convention Archives, Nashville, Tennessee.

47. *Royal Service* (May 1923): 17.

48. Five members of the graduating class planned to become foreign missionaries, and the final eight were married and thus did not indicate career plans. *Annual Report* (1915), 49.

49. *Royal Service* (October 1921): 28.

50. *Our Mission Fields* (October, November, December 1912): 34.

51. *Royal Service* (October 1921): 28.

52. *Royal Service* (February 1915): 10.

53. *Royal Service* (February 1915): 10, and Allen, *Century to Celebrate*, 220–21.

54. *Royal Service* (June 1919): 27.

55. Minutes of the Baptist General Association of Virginia (1910), SBHLA, 73.

56. Rees Watkins, *The House of Happiness: A Ministry of Love* (Richmond, VA: Woman's Missionary Union, Auxiliary to Richmond Baptist Association, 1981), 8.

57. Watkins, *House of Happiness*, 15.

58. Watkins, *House of Happiness*, 11.

59. *Buhlmaier to Brinkley: A History of the Mallory Baptist Center, 1915–1975* (Baltimore: Baptist Convention of Maryland, n.d.). Pamphlet in Historical Library, Baptist Convention of Maryland.

60. *Annual Report* (1918), 55.

61. Minutes of the Waco Baptist Association (1912), 6–7.

62. Minutes of the Waco Baptist Association (1913), 30.

63. Minutes of the Waco Baptist Association (1913), 30; (1915), 29. This is an example of local women who embraced a progressive program before WMU recommended it. However, the influence of southwestern culture in Texas makes it difficult to assess their relationships with national WMU as compared to those of other southern states. For example, Texas Baptists, under the leadership of R. C. Buckner, began supporting a woman's missionary training program in Dallas as early as the fall of 1906. The seminary at Baylor University in Waco, Texas, began enrolling women in their classes in 1907. When the Waco seminary moved to Fort Worth and became Southwestern Baptist Theological Seminary, their charter provided for the education of women. In 1910, the two programs from Waco and Dallas merged as the Woman's Missionary Training School at Fort Worth. The Baptist Women Mission Workers of Texas raised $50,000 to build facilities for the Training School. In 1934 the Missionary Training degree was merged with the curriculum of the seminary's school of education. Thus the training and education of local Texas women diverged somewhat from the Louisville Training School. See Robert A. Baker, *Tell the Generations Following: A History of Southwestern Baptist Theological Seminary, 1908–1983* (Nashville: Broadman Press, 1983), 137, 157, 267.

64. The proceedings of the National Conference of Charities and Correction reveal the activities of the Charity Organization Society. See Davis, *Spearheads for Reform*, 21.

65. *Handbook of Personal Service*, 48.

66. Scales, *"All That Fits a Woman,"* 186–87.

67. *Handbook of Personal Service*, 2.

68. *Royal Service* (February 1915): 10. The use of the phrase "in this case" may suggest that the management felt a secular approach to settlement work was acceptable in certain instances.

69. Maud Reynolds McLure, *A Glimpse of Settlement Work* (Baltimore: Woman's Missionary Union, 1913), 2. WMUA.

70. Addams, in Fink, *Major Problems*, 302.

71. McLure, *Glimpse of Settlement Work*, 2.

72. McLure, *Glimpse of Settlement Work*, 4.

73. *Handbook of Personal Service*, 18.

74. *Handbook of Personal Service*, 19. Residents of Hull House founded the first public playground in Chicago in 1893. See Davis, *Spearheads for Reform*, 61.

75. *Handbook for Personal Service*, 25, 29.

76. *Handbook for Personal Service*, 33.

77. *Handbook of Personal Service*, 20–23.

78. *Handbook for Personal Service*, 8–9.

79. One of the proverbs in the heading of the handbook says: "If you want to realize yourself, you must enter this great army of relief and service—the friendly visitors." *Handbook for Personal Service*, 11.

80. *Handbook for Personal Service*, 15.

81. *Handbook for Personal Service*, 10; McLure, *Glimpse of Settlement Work*; *Royal Service* (August 1917): 9.

82. Littlejohn, *History of Carver School*, 65.

83. *Royal Service* (December 1922): 12.

84. *Royal Service* (December 1922): 12.

85. *Royal Service* (December 1922): 13.

86. Watkins, *House of Happiness*, 18.

87. Carver, *Out of His Treasure*, 68.

88. *Annual Report* (1913), 42.

89. Allen, *Century to Celebrate*, 223.

90. Allen, *Century to Celebrate*, 223.

91. For discussion of social settlements as a "separate sphere," see Vicky MacLean and Joyce Williams, "'Ghosts of Sociologies Past': Settlement Sociology in the Progressive Era at the Chicago School of Civics and Philanthropy," *American Sociologist* 43 (September 2012): 241.

92. McLure, *Glimpse of Settlement Work*, 2.

93. *Our Mission Fields* (October, November, December 1913): 32. See Ellen Carol Dubois, "Harriet Stanton Blatch and the Transformation of Class Relations among Women Suffragists," in *Gender Class, Race and Reform in the Progressive Era*, ed. Noralee Frankel and Nancy S. Dye (Lexington: University Press of Kentucky, 1991): 162–79.

94. *Royal Service* (February 1915): 12.

95. *Royal Service* (February 1915): 11.

96. *Royal Service* (February 1915): 12.

97. *Royal Service* (August 1917): 12.

98. *Royal Service* (October 1915): 27.

99. *Handbook for Personal Service*, 28.

100. *Handbook for Personal Service*, 28.

101. *Annual Report* (1916), 56, and Allen, *Century to Celebrate*, 478.

102. An average of 49 percent of societies filed personal service reports during those years.

103. *Royal Service* (September 1921): 27.

104. *Royal Service* (September 1921): 27.

105. *Royal Service* (April 1923): 27.

106. *Handbook for Personal Service*, 34.

107. *Royal Service* (April 1923): 27.

108. *Handbook for Personal Service*, 20.

109. *Handbook for Personal Service*, 21.

110. *Handbook for Personal Service*, 20–21. The Good Will Center at Pratt City adopted the Boy Scout program. See Minutes of WMU, Birmingham Baptist Association (1914), 28.

111. *Handbook for Personal Service*, 29.

112. Industrial training was an integral part of the broader social settlement movement. Hull House, for example, offered classes in pottery, metalwork, enameling, wood carving, weaving, dressmaking, sewing, millinery, and cooking. Davis, *Spearheads for Reform*, 47.

113. Davis, *Spearheads for Reform*, 47.

114. *Handbook for Personal Service*, 29.

115. Personal Service Reports, *Annual Report* (1916–26).

116. WMU referred local women to Robert G. Boville of the Association Bible House for Vacation Bible School information. *Handbook for Personal Service*, 25.

117. *Handbook for Personal Service*, 24–25.

118. H. Leon McBeth, *The Baptist Heritage* (Nashville: Broadman Press, 1987), 647.

119. *Royal Service* (May 1915): 26.

120. *Royal Service* (March 1916): 13.

121. *Royal Service* (March 1916): 14.

122. Texas Baptist Social Service Commission Report, quoted in John Lee Eighmy, *Churches in Cultural Captivity: A History of the Social Attitudes of Southern Baptists* (Knoxville: University of Tennessee Press, 1972), 109.

123. *Royal Service* (March 1916): 12.

124. *Royal Service* (March 1916): 12.

125. For a discussion of feminine thinking in light of the maternal, see Sara Ruddick, *Maternal Thinking: Toward A Politics of Peace* (New York: Ballantine, 1989).

126. *Royal Service* (November 1921): 30.

127. *Royal Service* (July 1920): 24.

128. *Handbook for Personal Service*, 18.

129. Personal Service Reports in *Annual Reports*, 1916–26.

130. Minutes of the Waco Baptist Association (1915), 29; and (1916), 35.

131. *Royal Service* (October 1915): 27.

132. *Royal Service* (April 1922): n.p.

133. *Royal Service* (May 1916): 25.

134. *Royal Service* (May 1916): 25.

135. *Annual Report* (1918), 57.

136. *Annual Report* (1919), 61.

137. *Our Mission Fields* (March 1911): 49.

138. *Royal Service* (March 1922): 29.

139. *Our Mission Fields* (July 1909): 11.

140. *Royal Service* (June 1919): 27.

141. Minutes of the Woman's Missionary Union, Auxiliary to the Birmingham Baptist Association (1915), 32; (1918), 17; and (1919), 21.

142. Minutes of the Baptist General Association of Virginia (1910), 73.

143. *Our Mission Fields* (October, November, December 1912): 33.

144. *Our Mission Fields* (October, November, December 1912): 33.

145. *Our Mission Fields* (October, November, December 1911): 17.

146. *Annual Report* (1911), 43. Southern women were not strangers to industrial conditions. J. Dowd Hall points out that by the end of World War II, 70 percent of American rayon production took place in the southern states. See Jacqueline Dowd Hall, "Disorderly Women: Gender and Labor Militancy in the Appalachian South," in *Half Sisters of History*, ed. Catherine Clinton (Durham, NC: Duke University Press, 1994), 183.

147. *Our Mission Fields* (October, November, December 1913): 33. The presence of women working outside the home was not foreign to the experience of southern women. Jacqueline Dowd Hall points out, for example, that the 1910 manuscript census for Elizabethtown, Tennessee, showed 20 percent of women over the age of fourteen engaged in paid occupations. See Hall, "Disorderly Women," 185.

148. *Handbook for Personal Service*, 37, WMUA. See also Mrs. G. W. Peyton, *Personal Service* (Louisiana State WMU, 1912), n.p. Pamphlet, WMUA.

149. *Our Mission Fields* (October, November, December 1912): 32.

150. *Our Mission Fields* (July 1909): 9.

151. *Royal Service* (March 1916): 10–11.

152. *Our Mission Fields* (October, November, December 1913): 34.

153. *Our Mission Fields* (October, November, December 1913): 34.

154. *Our Mission Fields* (July 1909): 8–9.

155. *Handbook for Personal Service*, 34.

156. *Handbook for Personal Service*, 37.

157. *Handbook for Personal Service*, 36.

158. *Handbook for Personal Service*, 39.

159. *Royal Service* (December 1914): 25.

160. Williams and MacLean, *Settlement Sociology*, 28.

161. Wharton, *Royal Service* (October 1914): 24.

162. *Royal Service* (December 1914): 25.

163. *Royal Service* (November 1914): 26.

164. *Royal Service* (December 1914): 25.

165. *Royal Service* (March 1923): 51.

166. *Handbook for Personal Service*, 25.

167. Minutes of the Birmingham Baptist Association (1915), 32.

168. Personal Service clipping from *Royal Service* (April 1922), n.p., in Personal Service Notebooks, WMUA.

169. *Royal Service* (October 1915): 27.

170. Allen, *Century to Celebrate*, 227.

171. Star classes were adult literacy classes and were called "adult classes" beginning in 1922. *Annual Report* (1922), 69–71.

172. *Annual Report* (1922), 71; (1927), 90.

173. Personal Service clippings from *Royal Service* (April 1922): n.p.

174. *Handbook for Personal Service,* 18–19.

175. *Handbook for Personal Service,* 48.

Conclusion

1. Anne Firor Scott, *Natural Allies: Women's Associations in American History* (Urbana: University of Illinois Press, 1991), 85.

2. *Royal Service* (February 1915): 11.

3. Edward Bagby Pollard and Mrs. H. M. Wharton, *Our Duty to the Community: A Course of Six Studies* (Baltimore: Woman's Missionary Union, 1915), n.p. Personal Service Notebooks, WMUA.

4. *Royal Service* (March 1916): 14.

5. *Royal Service* (October 1921): 28.

6. *Handbook for Personal Service,* 48.

Bibliography

PRIMARY SOURCES

Manuscript Collections

Annie Armstrong Notebooks, Woman's Missionary Union Archives, Birmingham, Alabama.

Armstrong-Frost Correspondence, Home Mission Board Collection, Southern Baptist Historical Library and Archives, Nashville, Tennessee.

Armstrong Papers, Woman's Missionary Union Archives, Birmingham, Alabama.

Associated Charities of Raleigh, North Carolina State Archive, Raleigh. Nannie Helen Burroughs Papers, Library of Congress, Washington, DC.

Fannie E. S. Heck Papers, North Carolina Baptist Historical Society, Z. Smith Reynolds Library, Wake Forest University, Winston-Salem, North Carolina.

Heck Correspondence, Woman's Missionary Union Archives, Birmingham, Alabama.

Personal Service Scrapbooks, Woman's Missionary Union Archives, Birmingham, Alabama.

Texas Collection, Carroll Library Building, Baylor University, Waco, Texas.

Una Roberts Lawrence Collection, Southern Baptist Historical Library and Archives, Nashville, Tennessee.

University of Mary Hardin-Baylor Papers, Musick Alumni Center and Museum, University of Mary Hardin-Baylor, Belton, Texas.

WMU Historical Scrapbook, WMU Files of Baptist Convention of Maryland/Delaware Historical Collection, Columbia, MD.

WMU Papers, North Carolina Woman's Missionary Union Offices, Baptist State Convention of North Carolina, Cary, North Carolina.

Institutional Reports

Annual Proceedings of the Southern Baptist Convention, 1885–1930.

Annual Reports of the Woman's Missionary Union, Auxiliary to Louisiana Baptist Convention, 1900–1925.

Annual Reports of the Woman's Missionary Union, Auxiliary to the Southern Baptist Convention, 1888–1930.

Minutes of the Annual Meeting of the Woman's Missionary Societies, Auxiliary to Baptist State Convention of North Carolina, 1890–1915.

Minutes of the Annual Meetings of the Woman's Missionary Union, Auxiliary to the Southern Baptist Convention, 1888–1930.

Minutes of the Baptist Women Mission Workers of Texas, 1910–11.

Minutes of the Woman's Convention, Auxiliary to the National Baptist Convention, 1901–25.

Periodicals

Baltimore Baptist. Baltimore, Maryland.

Baptist Argus (later published as *Baptist World*). Louisville, Kentucky.

Baptist Basket. Louisville, Kentucky.

Baptist Home Mission Monthly. American Baptist Home Missionary Society.

Biblical Recorder. Cary, North Carolina: Baptist State Convention of North Carolina.

Christian Index. Atlanta, Georgia.

Foreign Mission Journal (later published as *Home and Foreign Fields*). Sunday School Board, Nashville, Tennessee.

Heathen Helper. Louisville, Kentucky.

Home Field (later published as *Home and Foreign Fields*). Sunday School Board, Nashville, Tennessee.

Our Mission Fields. Baltimore: Woman's Missionary Union, 1906–14.

Raleigh News and Observer. Raleigh, North Carolina.

Royal Service. Birmingham, Alabama: Woman's Missionary Union.

Tennessee Baptist. Nashville: Tennessee Baptist Convention.

Texas Baptist Herald. Waco, Texas.

Western Recorder. Louisville: Kentucky Baptist Convention.

Books and Articles

Abbot, Lyman. *Christianity and Social Problems*. Boston: Houghton, Mifflin, 1896.

Batten, Samuel Zane. *The Social Task of Christianity*. New York: Fleming H. Revell, 1911.

Broadus, John A. *Should Women Speak in Mixed Public Assemblies?* Louisville: Baptist Book Concern, 1904.

Brunner, Edmund de Schweinitz. *Church Life in the Rural South*. New York: George H. Doran, 1923.

Buhlmaier to Brinkley: A History of the Mallory Baptist Center, 1915–1975. Baltimore: Baptist Convention of Maryland, n.d., 3.

Buhlmaier, Marie. *Along the Highway of Service*. Atlanta: Home Mission Board of the Southern Baptist Convention, 1924.

Carroll, J. M. *A History of Texas Baptists*. Dallas: Baptist Standard Publishing, 1923.

Carver, W. O. *Out of His Treasure: Unfinished Memoirs*. Nashville: Broadman Press, 1956.

Davis, Mary Hill. *Living Messages: Official Addresses of Mrs. F. S. Davis, 1907–1931*. Dallas: Woman's Missionary Union of Texas, 1935.

Dennis, James Shepherd. *Christian Missions and Social Progress: A Sociological Study of Foreign Missions*. New York: Fleming H. Revell, 1897.

Downs, Francis A. "The Greatest Woman of Southern Methodism." Methodist Review 64 (April 1915).

Eisenstein, Sarah. *Give Us Bread but Give Us Roses: Working Women's Consciousness in the United States, 1890 to the First World War*. Boston: Routledge, 1983.

Gardner, Charles S. "The Accumulation of Wealth." *Review and Expositor* 11 (April 1914): 204–16.

———. *The Ethics of Jesus and Social Progress*. New York: George H. Doran, 1914.

———. "The Relation of the Individual to Society." *Review and Expositor* 26 (January 1929): 3–26.

Gladden, Washington. *The Church and Modern Life*. Boston: Houghton, Mifflin, 1908.

Harper, Keith. *Rescue the Perishing: Selected Correspondence of Annie W. Armstrong*. Macon, GA: Mercer University Press, 2004.

———. *Send the Light: Lottie Moon's Letters and Other Writings*. Macon, GA: Mercer University Press, 2002.

Haskins, Sara Estelle. *Women and Missions in the Methodist Episcopal Church, South*. Nashville: Methodist Episcopal Church, 1920.

Hatch, Nathan. *The Puzzle of American Methodism*. American Society of Church History Papers. Portland, OR: TREN, 1994.

Heck, Fannie E. S. *In Royal Service: The Mission Work of Southern Baptist Women*. Richmond: Foreign Mission Board, 1913.

Hudson, Winthrop, ed. *Walter Rauschenbusch: Selected Writings*. New York: Paulist Press, 1984.

Hurlbut, Jesse L. *The Story of Chautauqua*. New York: G. P. Putnam's Sons, 1921.

Masters, Victor I. *Baptist Home Missions*. Atlanta: Home Mission Board of the Southern Baptist Convention, 1914.

———. *Baptist Missions in the South*. Atlanta: Home Mission Board of the Southern Baptist Convention, 1915.

———. *The Call of the South*. Atlanta: Home Mission Board of the Southern Baptist Convention, 1918.

———. *Country Church in the South*. Atlanta: Home Mission Board of the Southern Baptist Convention, 1917.

———, ed. *The Home Mission Task*. Atlanta: Home Mission Board of the Southern Baptist Convention, 1912.

———. *Making America Christian*. Atlanta: Home Mission Board of the Southern Baptist Convention, 1921.

Mathews, Shailer. *The Individual and the Social Gospel*. New York: Missionary Education Movement and Laymen's Missionary Movement, 1914.

McCulloch, James E., ed. *Battling for Social Betterment*. Nashville: Southern Sociological Congress, 1914.

———. *The Call of the New South*. Nashville: Southern Sociological Congress, 1912.

———. *Democracy in Earnest: The Southern Sociological Congress, 1916–1918*. Nashville: Southern Sociological Congress, 1918.

———. *The New Chivalry—Health*. Nashville: Southern Sociological Congress, 1915.

———. *The South Mobilizing for Social Service*. Nashville: Southern Sociological Congress, 1913.

Montgomery, Helen Barrett. *Western Women in Eastern Lands: An Outline Study of Fifty Years of Woman's Work in Foreign Missions*. New York: Macmillan, 1910.

Mullins, E. Y. *Axioms of Religion*. Philadelphia: Griffith and Rowland Press, 1908.

Price, J. M. *Christianity and Social Problems*. Nashville, 1928.

Rauschenbusch, Walter. *Christianizing the Social Order*. New York: Macmillan, 1919.
———. *A Rauschenbusch Reader: The Kingdom of God and the Social Gospel*. Compiled by Benson Y. Landis. New York: Harper and Row, 1957.
———. *A Theology for the Social Gospel*. Nashville: Abingdon Press, 1917.
Sanford, Elias B. *Church Federation*. New York, 1906.
Seale, Tenie. *Personal Service Interpreted*. Virginia: Woman's Missionary Union, 1917.
Strong, Josiah. *Our Country*. New York: Baker and Taylor, 1885, 1891.
Watts, Joseph T. *The Rise and Progress of Maryland Baptists*. State Mission Board of the Maryland Baptist Union Association, Baltimore: Maryland Baptist Union Association, [1953].
Wharton, Lulie P. *Fruits of the Years: The Story of Woman's Missionary Union and Home Missions*. Atlanta: Home Mission Board of the Southern Baptist Convention, 1938.
White, John E. "Temperance and Reform in the South." In *The South in the Building of the Nation: A History of the Southern States Designed to Record the South's Part in the Making of the American Nation*. Vol. 10. Richmond, VA: Southern Historical Publication, ca. 1909–13.

SECONDARY SOURCES

Abbot, Shirley. *Womenfolks: Growing Up Down South*. New York: Ticknor and Fields, 1983.
Abell, Aaron Ignatius. *The Urban Impact on American Protestantism, 1865–1900*. Cambridge, MA: Harvard University Press, 1943.
Abernathy, Mollie C. "Southern Women, Social Reconstruction, and the Church in the 1920s." *Louisiana Studies* 13 (1974): 289–312.
Ahlstrom, Sydney. *A Religious History of the American People*. New Haven, CT: Yale University Press, 1972.
Allen, Catherine. *A Century to Celebrate: History of Woman's Missionary Union*. Birmingham, AL: Woman's Missionary Union, 1987.
———. *Laborers Together with God: 22 Great Women in Baptist Life*. Birmingham, AL: Woman's Missionary Union, 1987.
———. *The New Lottie Moon Story*. Nashville: Broadman Press, 1980.
Allen, W. Loyd. *You Are a Great People: Maryland Delaware Baptists, 1742–1998*. Franklin, TN: Providence House Publishers, 2000.
Ammerman, Nancy. *Baptist Battles: Social Change and Religious Conflict in the Southern Baptist Convention*. New Brunswick, NJ: Rutgers University Press, 1990.
Anders, Evan. *Boss Rule in South Texas: The Progressive Era*. Austin: University of Texas Press, 1977.
Anderson, Courtney. *To the Golden Shore: The Life of Adoniram Judson*. Valley Forge, PA: Judson Press, 1987.
Anderson, James D. *The Education of Blacks in the South, 1865–1935*. Chapel Hill: University of North Carolina Press, 1988.
Ayers, Edward L. *The Promise of the New South: Life after Reconstruction*. New York: Oxford University Press, 1992.
Bailey, Hugh C. *Edgar Gardner Murphy: Gentle Progressive*. Coral Gables, FL: University of Miami Press, 1968.

———. *Liberalism in the New South: Southern Social Reformers and the Progressive Movement*. Coral Gables, FL: University of Miami Press, 1969.

Bailey, Kenneth K. *Southern White Protestantism in the Twentieth Century*. New York: Harper and Row, 1964.

Baker, Robert A. *A Baptist Sourcebook*. Nashville: Broadman Press, 1966.

———. *Relations between Northern and Southern Baptists*. 1954. Reprint, New York: Arno Press, 1980.

———. *The Southern Baptist Convention and Its People, 1607–1972*. Nashville: Broadman Press, 1974.

———. *Tell the Generations Following: A History of Southwestern Baptist Theological Seminary, 1908–1983*. Nashville: Broadman Press, 1983.

Baker, Shannon. "Following in the Footsteps of Annie Armstrong in Baltimore." *Baptist Life: News Journal of the Baptist Convention of Maryland/Delaware* (March 2006).

Barclay, Wade Crawford. *The Methodist Episcopal Church: Widening Horizons, 1845–1895*. New York: Board of Missions, Methodist Church, 1957.

Bateman, Lori Brand. "Separation, Coordination, and Coeducation: Southern Baptist Approaches to Women's Higher Education." *Baptist History and Heritage* 38 (Summer/Fall 2003): 88–99.

Beaver, R. Pierce. *All Loves Excelling: American Protestant Women in World Missions*. Grand Rapids, MI: William B. Eerdmans, 1968.

Beck, Rosalie, Kay W. Shurden, and Catherine B. Allen. "The Impact of Southern Baptist Women on Social Issues: Three Viewpoints." *Baptist History and Heritage* 12 (July 1987): 29–40.

Bendroth, Margaret Lamberts, and Virginia Lieson Brereton, eds. *Women and Twentieth-Century Protestantism*. Urbana: University of Illinois Press, 2002.

Benjamin, Karen. "Progressivism Meets Jim Crow: Curriculum Revision and Development in Houston, Texas, 1924–1929." *Pedagogica Historica* 39 (August 2003): 457–76.

Berthoff, Rowland T. "Southern Attitudes toward Immigration, 1865–1914." *Journal of Southern History* 17 (1951): 328–60.

Bledstein, Burton. *The Culture of Professionalism: The Middle Class and the Development of Higher Education in America*. New York: W. W. Norton, 1978.

Bleser, Carol, ed. *In Joy and Sorrow: Women, Family, and Marriage in the Victorian South, 1830–1900*. Oxford: Oxford University Press, 1991.

Blevins, Caroline DeArmond. "Patterns of Ministry among Southern Baptist Women." *Baptist History and Heritage* (July 1987): 40–49.

Blocker, Jack S. *"Give to the Winds Thy Fears": The Women's Temperance Crusade, 1873–1874*. Westport, CT: Greenwood Press, 1985.

Bloom, Harold. *The American Religion: The Emergence of the Post-Christian Nation*. New York: Simon and Schuster, 1992.

Bode, Frederick A. *Protestantism in the New South: North Carolina Baptists and Methodists in Political Crises, 1894–1902*. Charlottesville: University Press of Virginia, 1975.

Boles, John. *The Great Revival, 1787–1895: The Origins of the Southern Evangelical Mind*. Lexington: University Press of Kentucky, 1972.

Bordin, Ruth. *Woman and Temperance: The Quest for Power and Liberty, 1873–1900*. Philadelphia: Temple University Press, 1981.

Borst, Charlotte G. *Catching Babies: The Professionalization of Childbirth, 1870–1920*. Cambridge, MA: Harvard University Press, 1995.

Borst, Charlotte G., and Kathleen W. Jones. "As Patients and Healers: The History of Women and Medicine." *OAH Magazine of History* 19 (September 2005): 23–26.

Brackney, William. "The Frontier of the Free Exchange of Ideas: The Baptist Congress as a Forum for Baptist Concerns, 1881–1912." *Baptist History and Heritage* 38 (Summer/Fall 2003): 8–27.

Brimm, Hugh A. "The Social Consciousness of Southern Baptists in Relation to Some Regional Problems, 1910–1935." ThD thesis, Southern Baptist Theological Seminary, 1944.

Brumberg, Joan Jacobs. *Mission for Life: The Story of the Family of Adoniram Judson*. New York: Free Press, 1980.

Buenger, Walter L., and Robert A. Calvert, eds. *Texas through Time: Evolving Interpretations*. College Station: Texas A&M University Press, 1991.

Calkins, Gladys Gilkey. *Follow Those Women: Church Women in the Ecumenical Movement*. New York: National Council of Churches, 1961.

Carson, Mina. *Settlement Folk: Social Thought and the American Movement, 1885–1930*. Chicago: University of Chicago Press, 1990.

Carter, Paul A. *The Decline and Revival of the Social Gospel: Social and Political Liberalism in American Protestant Churches, 1920–1940*. Ithaca, NY: Cornell University Press, 1954.

Cash, Wilbur J. *The Mind of the South*. New York: Vintage Books, 1941.

Cashin, Edwin J., and Glenn T. Eskew, eds. *Paternalism in a Southern City: Race, Religion, and Gender in Augusta, Georgia*. Athens: University of Georgia Press, 2001.

Catt, Carrie Chapman, and Nettie Rogers Shuler. *Woman Suffrage and Politics: The Inner Story of the Suffrage Movement*. New York: Charles Scribner, 1923.

Chatfield, E. Charles, Jr. "The Southern Sociological Congress: Organization of Uplift." *Tennessee Historical Quarterly* 19 (December 1960): 328–47.

Clark, Norman. *Deliver Us from Evil: An Interpretation of American Prohibition*. New York: Norton, 1976.

Clark, Thomas D., and Albert D. Kirwan. *The South since Appomattox: A Century of Regional Change*. New York: Oxford University Press, 1967.

Clinton, Catherine, ed. *Half Sisters of History: Southern Women and the American Past*. Durham, NC: Duke University Press, 1994.

———. *The Plantation Mistress: Woman's World in the Old South*. New York: Pantheon Books, 1982.

———. "'Southern Dishonor': Flesh, Blood, Race, and Bondage." In *In Joy and Sorrow: Women, Family, and Marriage in the Victorian South, 1830–1900*, edited by Carol Bleser, 52–68. New York: Oxford University Press, 1991.

Collier-Thomas, Bettye. *Jesus, Jobs, and Justice: African American Women and Religion*. New York: Alfred A. Knopf, 2010.

Conkin, Paul. *Cane Ridge: America's Pentecost*. Madison: University of Wisconsin Press, 1990.

Cott, Nancy F. *The Bonds of Womanhood: "Woman's Sphere" in New England, 1780–1835*. New Haven, CT: Yale University Press, 1977.

Cox, Ethlene Boone. *Following in His Train*. Nashville: Broadman Press, 1938.

Crane, Claris I. *Daughter of the Covenant: Edith Campbell Crane, 1876–1933*. Baltimore: Woman's Missionary Union of Maryland, 1966.

Croly, Mrs. J. C. *The History of the Woman's Club Movement in America*. New York: H. G. Allen, 1898.

Crooks, James B. *Politics and Progress: The Rise of Urban Progressivism in Baltimore, 1895–1911*. Baton Rouge: Louisiana State University Press, 1968.

Crowther, Edward R., and Keith Harper, eds. *Between Fetters and Freedom: African American Baptists since Emancipation*. Macon, GA: Mercer University Press, 2015.

Crumpler, Carolyn Weatherford. "The Role of Women in Baptist Missions." *Baptist History and Heritage* (July 1992): 25–33.

Culver, Dwight W. *Negro Segregation in the Methodist Church*. New Haven, CT: Yale University Press, 1953.

Curtis, Susan. *A Consuming Faith: The Social Gospel in Modern American Culture*. Columbia: University of Missouri Press, 2001.

Dabney, Virginius. *Liberalism in the South*. Chapel Hill: University of North Carolina Press, 1932.

Davidson, Elizabeth H. *Child Labor Legislation in the Southern Textile States*. Chapel Hill: University of North Carolina Press, 1939.

Davis, Allen F. *Spearheads for Reform: The Social Settlements and the Progressive Movement, 1890–1914*. New York: Oxford University Press, 1967.

Davis, C. Anne. "Guest Editorial: Women in Southern Baptist History." *Baptist History and Heritage* (July 1987): 2–3.

———. "History of the Carver School of Church Social Work." *Review and Expositor* (Spring 1988): 209–20.

DeBerg, Betty A. *Ungodly Women: Gender and the First Wave of American Fundamentalism*. Minneapolis: Fortress Press, 1990.

Deweese, Charles W. "Deaconesses in Baptist History: A Preliminary Study." *Baptist History and Heritage* (January 1977): 52–57.

Dillenberger, John, and Claude Welch. *Protestant Christianity: Interpreted through Its Development*. 2nd ed. New York: Macmillan, 1988.

Dillman, Caroline Matheny. *Southern Women*. New York: Hemisphere Publishing, 1988.

Dittmer, John. *Black Georgia in the Progressive Era, 1900–1920*. Urbana: University of Illinois Press, 1977.

Dougherty, Mary Agnes. "The Social Gospel According to Phoebe: The Methodist Deaconesses in the Metropolis, 1885–1918." In *Perspectives on American Methodism*, edited by Russel E. Riche, Kenneth E. Rowe, and Jean Miller Schmidt, 356–70. Nashville: Kingswood Books, 1993.

Douglas, Ann. *The Feminization of American Culture*. New York: Alfred A. Knopf, 1977.

Douglass, Frederick. "The Color Line in America," *North American Review* 132 (June 1, 1881): 568.

DuBois, Ellen Carol. "Harriot Stanton Blatch and the Transformation of Class Relations among Woman Suffragists." In *Gender, Class, Race, and Reform in the Progressive Era*, edited by Noralee Frankel and Nancy S. Dye, 162–79. Lexington: University Press of Kentucky, 1991,

Dye, Nancy S. Introduction to *Gender, Class, Race, and Reform in the Progressive Era*, edited by Noralee Frankel and Nancy S. Dye, 1–9. Lexington: University Press of Kentucky, 1991.

Edwards, Wendy J. Deichmann and Carolyn De Swarte Gifford. *Gender and the Social Gospel*. Urbana: University of Illinois Press, 2003.

Eighmy, John Lee. *Churches in Cultural Captivity: A History of the Social Attitudes of Southern Baptists*. Knoxville: University of Tennessee Press, 1972.

———. "Religious Liberalism in the South during the Progressive Era." *Church History* 38 (September 1969): 359–72.

Eisenstein, Sarah, *Give Us Bread but Give Us Roses: Working Women's Consciousness in the United States, 1890 to the First World War*. Boston: Routledge, 1983.

Ellis, William, *"A Man of Books and a Man of the People:" E. Y. Mullins and the Crisis of Moderate Baptist Leadership*. Macon, GA: Mercer University Press, 1985.

English, Carl Dean. "The Ethical Emphasis of the Editors of Baptist Journals Published in the Southeastern Region of the United States, 1865–1915." ThD diss., Southern Baptist Theological Seminary, 1948.

Epstein, Barbara L. *The Politics of Domesticity*. Middletown, CT: Wesleyan University Press, 1981.

Equal Justice Initiative. *Lynching in America: Confronting the Legacy of Racial Terror.* Montgomery, AL: Equal Justice Initiative, 2015.

Estep, William R. *Baptists and Christian Unity*. Nashville: Broadman Press, 1966.

Evans, Christopher H. "From Militant Methodism to Secular Christianity: The Social Gospel in American Methodist Historical Narratives." *Methodist History* 38, no. 3 (April 2000): 147–61.

———. *The Kingdom Is Always but Coming: A Life of Walter Rauschenbusch*. Grand Rapids, MI: Eerdmans, 2004.

———, ed. *The Social Gospel Today*. Louisville: Westminster John Knox Press, 2001.

Evans, Elizabeth Marshall. *Annie Armstrong*. Birmingham, AL: Woman's Missionary Union Press, 1963.

Evans, Sara M. *Born for Liberty: A History of Women in America*. London: Collier Macmillan, 1989.

Falls, Helen Emery. "Baptist Women in Missions Support in the Nineteenth Century." *Baptist History and Heritage* 12 (January 1977): 26–36.

Farish, Hunter Dickinson. *The Circuit Rider Dismounts: A Social History of Southern Methodism*. New York: Da Capo Press, 1969.

Farmer, Foy Johnson. *Hitherto: History of North Carolina Woman's Missionary Union*. Raleigh: North Carolina Woman's Missionary Union, 1952.

Faust, Drew Gilpin. *Mothers of Invention: Women of the Slaveholding South in the American Civil War*. New York: Vintage Books, 1997.

Ferguson, Charles W. *Methodism and the Making of America*. Austin, TX: Eakin Press, 1983.

Ferguson, Elizabeth A. *Social Work: An Introduction*. New York: J. B. Lippincott, 1963.

Fink, Leon, ed. *Major Problems in the Gilded Age and Progressive Era*. Lexington, MA: D. C. Heath, 1993.

Fishburn, Janet Forsythe. *The Fatherhood of God and the Victorian Family: The Social Gospel in America*. Philadelphia: Fortress Press, 1981.

Fitts, Leroy. *A History of Black Baptists*. Nashville: Broadman Press, 1985.

Fletcher, Jesse C. *The Southern Baptist Convention: A Sesquicentennial History*. Nashville: Broadman Press, 1994.

Flexner, Eleanor. *Century of Struggle: The Women's Rights Movement in the United States*. 2nd ed. Cambridge, MA: Belknap Press of Harvard University Press, 1975.

Flowers, Elizabeth. *Into the Pulpit: Southern Baptist Women and Power since World War II*. Chapel Hill: University of North Carolina Press, 2014.

———. "Southern Baptist Evangelicals or Social Gospel Liberals?: The Woman's Missionary Union and Social Reform, 1888–1928." *American Baptist Quarterly* 19 (June 2000): 106–28.

Flynt, J. Wayne, *Alabama Baptists: Southern Baptists in the Heart of Dixie*. Tuscaloosa: University of Alabama Press, 1998.

———. "Alabama White Protestantism and Labor, 1900–1914." *Alabama Review* 25 (1972): 192–217.

———. "Dissent in Zion: Alabama Baptists and Social Issues, 1900–1914." *Journal of Southern History* 35 (November 1969): 523–42.

———. "Religion for the Blues: Evangelicalism, Poor Whites, and the Great Depression." *Journal of Southern History* 71 (February 2005): 3–38.

———. "Southern Protestantism and Reform, 1890–1920." In *Varieties of Southern Religious Experience*, edited by Samuel S. Hill. Baton Rouge: Louisiana State University Press, 1988.

Fowler, Franklin T. "The History of Southern Baptist Medical Missions." *Baptist History and Heritage* (October 1975): 194–203.

Fox-Genovese, Elizabeth. "Family and Female Identity in the Antebellum South: Sarah Gayle and Her Family." In *In Joy and Sorrow: Women, Family, and Marriage in the Victorian South, 1830–1900*, edited by Carol Bleser, 15–31. New York: Oxford University Press, 1991.

Frankel, Noralee, and Nancy S. Dye, eds. *Gender, Class, Race, and Reform in the Progressive Era*. Lexington: University Press of Kentucky, 1991.

Friedman, Jean E. *The Enclosed Garden: Women and Community in the Evangelical South, 1830–1900*. Chapel Hill: University of North Carolina Press, 1985.

Garrett, James Leo, ed. *Baptist Relations with Other Christians*. Valley Forge, PA: Judson Press, 1974.

Gaston, Paul M. *The New South Creed*. New York: Alfred A. Knopf, 1970.

Genovese, Eugene. "'Our Family, White and Black': Family and Household in the Southern Slaveholders' World View." In *In Joy and Sorrow: Women, Family, and Marriage in the Victorian South, 1830–1900*, ed. Carol Bleser, 69–87. New York: Oxford University Press, 1991.

———. "Toward a Kinder and Gentler America: The Southern Lady and the Greening of the Politics of the Old South." In *In Joy and Sorrow: Women, Family, and Marriage in the Victorian South, 1830–1900*, edited by Carol Bleser, 125–34. New York: Oxford University Press, 1991.

Giddings, Paula. *When and Where I Enter: The Impact of Black Women on Race and Sex in America*. New York: Bantam Books, 1984.

Goodwyn, Lawrence. *The Populist Movement: A Short History of the Agrarian Revolt in America*. New York: Oxford University Press, 1978.

Gorrell, Donald K. *The Age of Social Responsibility: The Social Gospel in the Progressive Era, 1900–1920*. Macon, GA: Mercer University Press, 1988.

Gould, Lewis L., ed. *The Progressive Era*. Syracuse, NY: Syracuse University Press, 1974.

Grantham, Dewey. *Southern Progressivism: The Reconciliation of Progress and Tradition*. Knoxville: University of Tennessee Press, 1983.

Green, Elna C. *Southern Strategies: Southern Women and the Woman Suffrage Question*. Chapel Hill: University of North Carolina Press, 1997.

Hall, Jacquelyn Dowd. "Disorderly Women: Gender and Labor Militancy in the Appalachian South." In *Half Sisters of History*, edited by Catherine Clinton, 180–223. Durham , NC: Duke University Press, 1994.

———. *Revolt against Chivalry: Jessie Daniel Ames and the Women's Campaign against Lynching*. New York: Columbia University Press, 1979.

Handy, Robert T., ed. *The Social Gospel in America, 1870–1920*. New York: Oxford University Press, 1966.

Hansen, Karen Tranberg, ed. *African Encounters with Domesticity*. New Brunswick, NJ: Rutgers University Press, 1992.

Hardesty, Nancy A. "The Best Temperance Organization in the Land." *Methodist History* 28 (April 1990).

———. *Great Women of Faith*. Grand Rapids, MI: Baker Book House, 1980.

———. *Women Called to Witness: Evangelical Feminism in the 19th Century*. Knoxville: University of Tennessee Press, 1999.

Harper, Keith. *The Quality of Mercy: Southern Baptists and Social Christianity, 1890–1920*. Tuscaloosa: University of Alabama Press, 1996.

———. "Southern Baptists and Social Christianity, 1890–1920." PhD thesis, University of Kentucky, 1991.

Harper, William, "Harper's Memoir on Slavery." *The Pro-Slavery Argument: As Maintained by the Most Distinguished Writers of the Southern States*. Philadelphia: Lippencott, 1853.

Harvey, Paul. *Freedom's Coming: Religious Culture and the Shaping of the South from the Civil War to the Civil Rights Movement*. Chapel Hill: University of North Carolina Press, 2005.

———. "The Ideal of Professionalism and the White Southern Baptist Ministry, 1870–1920." *Religion and American Culture* 5 (Winter 1995): 99–123.

———. *Redeeming the South: Religious Cultures and Racial Identities among Southern Baptists, 1865–1925*. Chapel Hill: University of North Carolina Press, 1997.

———. "Saints but Not Subordinates: The Woman's Missionary Union of the Southern Baptist Convention." In *Women and Twentieth-Century Protestantism*, edited by

Margaret Bendroth and Virginia Brereton, 4–24. Urbana: University of Illinois Press, 2002.

———. "Southern Baptists and the Social Gospel: White Religious Progressivism in the South, 1900–1925." *Fides et Historia* 27 (Summer 1995): 59–77.

Hatch, Nathan O.. "The Puzzle of American Methodism." Bartlett Lecture, Yale University, February 9, 1993, 12.

Hesseltine, W. B., and David L. Smiley. *The South in American History*. 2nd ed. Englewood Cliffs, NJ: Prentice-Hall, 1960.

Heyrman, Christine Leigh. *Southern Cross: The Beginnings of the Bible Belt*. New York: Alfred A. Knopf, 1997.

Hickey, Georgina. "Disease, Disorder, and Motherhood: Working-Class Women, Social Welfare, and the Process of Urban Development in Atlanta." In *Before the New Deal: Social Welfare in the South, 1830–1930*, edited by Elna C. Green. Athens: University of Georgia Press, 1999.

Higginbotham, Evelyn Brooks. "The Feminist Theology of the Black Baptist Church, 1880–1900." In *Religion and American Culture*, edited by David G. Hackett, 345–63. London: Routledge, 1995.

———. *Righteous Discontent: The Woman's Movement in the Black Baptist Church, 1880–1920*. Cambridge, MA: Harvard University Press, 1993.

Hill, Patricia R. *The World Their Household: The American Woman's Foreign Mission Movement and Cultural Transformation, 1870–1920*. Ann Arbor: University of Michigan Press, 1985.

Hill, Samuel S., Jr., *Southern Churches in Crisis*. New York: Holt, Rinehart, and Winston, 1966.

Hill, Samuel S., Jr., Charles H. Lippy, and Charles Reagan Wilson, eds. *Encyclopedia of Religion in the South*. Macon, GA: Mercer University Press, 1984.

Hill, Samuel S., Jr., Edgar T. Thompson, Anne Firor Scott, et al., eds. *Religion and the Solid South*. Nashville: Abingdon Press, 1972.

Holcomb, Carol C. "Building a Publishing Empire: The Annie Armstrong Era of WMU, SBC." *Baptist History and Heritage* 47 (Spring 2012): 18–38.

———. "'A Home without Walls': WMU and Reinterpretation of Gender Ideology." *Baptist History and Heritage* 51 (Spring 2016): 37–69.

———. "The Kingdom at Hand: The Social Gospel and the Personal Service Department of the Woman's Missionary Union, Auxiliary to the Southern Baptist Convention." *Baptist History and Heritage* 35 (Spring 2000): 49–66.

———. "Unreliable Allies: Southern Baptist Women and Race." *American Baptist Quarterly* 33 (Summer 2014): 131–157.

Hopkins, Charles Howard. *The Rise of the Social Gospel in American Protestantism, 1865–1915*. New Haven, CT: Yale University Press, 1940.

Hugen, Beryl, and T. Laine Scales, eds. *Christianity and Social Work: Readings on the Integration of Christian Faith and Social Work Practice*. Botsford, CT: North American Association of Social Work, 2002.

Hull, Eleanor. *Women Who Carried the Good News*. Valley Forge , PA: Judson Press, 1975.

Hunt, Alma. *History of the Woman's Missionary Union*. Nashville: Convention Press, 1964.

James, Mrs. W. C. [Minnie Kennedy]. *Fannie E. S. Heck: A Study of the Hidden Springs in a Rarely Useful and Victorious Life*. Nashville: Broadman Press, 1939.

Jaudon, Shirley Dianne. "Attitudes of Southern Baptists Ministers toward Women and Women's Rights." ThD thesis, University of Mississippi, 1979.

Johnson, Charles Price. "Southern Baptists and the Social Gospel Movement." ThD thesis, Southwestern Baptist Theological Seminary, 1948.

Jones, Jaqueline. *Labor of Love, Labor of Sorrow: Black Women, Work, and the Family from Slavery to the Present*. New York: Basic Books, 1985.

Keller, Rosemary Skinner. "Creating a Sphere for Women: The Methodist Episcopal Church, 1869–1906," in *Women in New Worlds: Historical Perspectives on the Wesleyan Tradition*, ed. Hilah F. Thomas, Rosemary Skinner Keller, and Louise L. Queen (Nashville: Abingdon, 1981), 84.

Lebsock, Suzanne D. "Radical Reconstruction and the Property Rights of Southern Women." In *Half Sisters of History*, edited by Catherine Clinton, 110–35. Durham, NC: Duke University Press, 1994.

Lengermann, Patricia Madoo, and Gillian Niebrugge. *The Women Founders: Sociology and Social Theory, 1830–1930*. Long Grove, IL: Waveland Press, 2007.

Leonard, Bill. *God's Last and Only Hope: The Fragmentation of the Southern Baptist Convention*. Grand Rapids, MI: Eerdman's, 1990.

Lerner, Gerda. "The Lady and the Mill-Girl: Changes in the Status of Women in the Age of Jackson." *Mid-Continent American Studies Journal* 10 (1969): 5–15.

Letsinger, Norman. "The Status of Women in the Southern Baptist Convention in Historical Perspective." *Baptist History and Heritage* (January 1977): 37–43.

———. "The Women's Liberation Movement: Implications for Southern Baptists." ThD thesis, Southern Baptist Theological Seminary, 1973.

Levering, Harriet S. "A Sketch of Miss Annie." *The Window of Y.W.A.* (March 1935): 9–32.

Levering, Rosalind Robinson. *Baltimore Baptists, 1773–1973: A History of the Baptist Work in Baltimore during 200 Years*. Baltimore: Baltimore Baptist Association, 1973.

Lincoln, Eric C., and Lawrence H. Mamiya. *The Black Church in the African American Experience*. Durham, NC: Duke University Press, 1998.

Lindley, Susan. "'Neglected Voices' and Praxis in the Social Gospel." *Journal of Religious Ethics* 18 (Spring 1990): 75–102.

———. *"You Have Stept Out of Your Place": A History of Women and Religion in America*. Louisville: Westminster John Knox Press, 1996.

Link, Arthur S. "The Progressive Movement in the South, 1870–1914." *North Carolina Historical Review* 23 (April 1946): 172–205.

Link, William. *The Paradox of Southern Progressivism, 1880–1930*. Chapel Hill: University of North Carolina Press, 1992.

Littlejohn, Carrie. *History of Carver School of Missions and Social Work*. Nashville: Broadman Press, 1958.

Loveland, Anne C. *Southern Evangelicals and the Social Order, 1800–1860*. Baton Rouge: Louisiana State University Press, 1980.

Luker, Ralph. *The Social Gospel in Black and White*. Chapel Hill: University of North Carolina Press, 1991.

Mandle, Joan D. *Women and Social Change in America*. Princeton, NJ: Princeton Book, 1979.

Martin, Patricia Summerlin. "Hidden Work: Baptist Women in Texas, 1880–1920." PhD diss., Rice University, 1982.

Martin, Sandy. *Black Baptists and African Missions: The Origins of a Movement, 1880–1915*. Macon, GA: Mercer University Press, 1998.

Mather, Juliette. *Light Three Candles: History of Virginia Woman's Missionary Union*. Richmond: Virginia Woman's Missionary Union, 1973.

Mathews, Donald G. *Religion in the Old South*. Chicago: University of Chicago Press, 1977.

Maxwell, Melody. *The Woman I Am: Southern Baptist Women's Writings, 1906–2006*. Tuscaloosa: University of Alabama Press, 2014.

May, Henry F. *Protestant Churches and Industrial America*. New York: Harper and Bros. Publishing, 1949.

McBeth, H. Leon. *The Baptist Heritage: Four Centuries of Baptist Witness*. Nashville: Broadman Press, 1987.

———. "Perspectives on Women in Baptist Life." *Baptist History and Heritage* (July 1987): 4–11.

———. "The Role of Women in Southern Baptist History." *Baptist History and Heritage*. 12 (January 1977): 3–25.

———. *A Sourcebook for Baptist Heritage*. Nashville: Broadman Press, 1990.

———. *Women in Baptist Life*. Nashville: Broadman Press, 1979.

McDannell, Colleen. *The Christian Home in Victorian America, 1840–1900*. Bloomington: Indiana University Press, 1986.

McDowell, John Patrick. *The Social Gospel in the South: The Woman's Home Mission Movement in the Methodist Episcopal Church, South, 1886–1939*. Baton Rouge: Louisiana State University Press, 1982.

McGill, Ralph E. *The South and the Southerner*. Boston: Little, Brown, 1963.

Meeker, Ruth Esther. *Six Decades of Service, 1880–1940: A History of the Woman's Home Missionary Society of the Methodist Episcopal Church*. Cincinnati: Steinhauser, 1969.

Miller, Robert M. *American Protestantism and Social Issues, 1919–1939*. Chapel Hill: University of North Carolina Press, 1958.

Mitchell, Broadus, and George S. Mitchell. *The Industrial Revolution in the South*. Baltimore: Johns Hopkins Press, 1930.

Mobley, Kendal. *Helen Barrett Montgomery: The Global Mission of Domestic Feminism*. Waco, TX: Baylor University Press, 2009.

———. "'What a Chasm There Is between Us': Charlotte Hawkins Brown and White Protestant Progressives, 1901–1952," in *Baptist History and Heritage* 42 (Summer/Fall 2007): 42.

Morantz, Regina Markell. *Sympathy and Science: Women Physicians in American Medicine*. New York: Oxford University Press, 1985.

More, Ellen Singer, and Maureen A. Milligan, eds. *The Empathetic Practitioner: Empathy, Gender, and Medicine*. New Brunswick, NJ: Rutgers University Press, 1994.

Newman, Harvey C. "The Role of Women in Atlanta's Churches, 1865–1906." *Atlanta Historical Journal* 24 (1980): 17–30.

Pivar, David J. *Purity Crusade: Sexual Morality and Social Control, 1868–1900*. Westport, CT: Greenwood Press, 1973.

Porter, J. W., ed. *Feminism, Woman, and Her Work*. Louisville: Baptist Book Concern, 1923.

Prescott, Stephen. "The Social Gospel and the American South: An Historiographic Appraisal." In *Perspectives on the Social Gospel Papers from the Inaugural Social Gospel Conference at Colgate Rochester Divinity School.* Texts and Studies in the Social Gospel 3. Lewiston, NY: Edwin Mellen Press, 1999.

Pruitt, Lisa Joy. *A Looking-Glass for Ladies: American Protestant Women and the Orient in the Nineteenth Century*. Macon, GA: Mercer University Press, 2005.

Queen, Edward L. *In the South the Baptists Are the Center of Gravity: Southern Baptists and Social Change, 1930–1980*. New York: Carlson Publishing., 1991.

Rable, George C. *Civil Wars: Women and the Crisis of Southern Nationalism*. Urbana: University of Illinois Press, 1989.

Raley, J. Michael. "'On the Same Basis as Men': The Campaign to Reinstate Women as Messengers to the Southern Baptist Convention, 1885–1918." *Journal of Southern Religion* 7 (2004).

Rauschenbusch, Walter. *Christianity and the Social Crisis*. New York: Macmillan, 1907.

Richey, Russell, Kenneth E. Rowe, and Jean Miller Schmidt, eds. *Perspectives on American Methodism*. Nashville: Kingswood Books, 1993.

Riley, Glenda. *Inventing the American Woman: A Perspective on Women's History*. Arlington Heights, IL: Harlan Davidson, 1987.

Robert, Dana. *American Women in Mission: A Social History of Their Thought and Practice*. Macon, GA: Mercer University Press, 1996.

Ruddick, Sara. *Maternal Thinking: Toward a Politics of Peace*. New York: Ballantine, 1989.

Ruether, Rosemary Radford, and Rosemary Skinner Keller, eds. *Women and Religion in America*. Vol. 2, *The Colonial and Revolutionary Periods*. San Francisco: Harper and Row, 1983.

Scales, T. Laine. *"All That Fits a Woman": Training Southern Baptist Women for Charity and Mission, 1907–1926*. Macon, GA: Mercer University Press, 2000.

Schneider, A. Gregory. *The Way of the Cross Leads Home*. Bloomington: Indiana University Press, 1993.

Scott, Anne Firor. *Natural Allies: Women's Associations in American History*. Urbana: University of Illinois Press, 1992.

———. "Progressive Wind from the South, 1906–1913." *Journal of Southern History* 29 (February 1963): 53–70.

———. *The Southern Lady: From Pedestal to Politics, 1830–1930*. Chicago: University of Chicago Press, 1970.

———. "Women's Perspective on the Patriarchy in the 1850s." In *Half Sisters of History: Southern Women and the American Past*, edited by Catherine Clinton, 76–92. Durham, NC: Duke University Press, 1994.

Scott, Anne Firor, and Andrew M. Scott. *One Half the People: The Fight for Women Suffrage*. Philadelphia: Lippincott, 1975.

Scully, Randolph Ferguson. *Religion and the Making of Nat Turner's Virginia: Baptist Community and Conflict, 1740–1840*. Charlottesville: University of Virginia Press, 2008.

Sharpless, Rebecca. *Fertile Ground, Narrow Choices: Women on Texas Cotton Farms, 1900–1940*. Chapel Hill: University of North Carolina Press, 1999.

Simkins, Francis B. *The Everlasting South*. Baton Rouge: Louisiana State University Press, 1963.

———. *A History of the South*. 3rd ed. New York: Alfred A. Knopf, 1963.

Sims, Anastatia. "Sisterhoods of Service: Women's Clubs and Methodist Women's Missionary Societies in North Carolina, 1890–1930." In *Women in New Worlds*. Vol. 2, edited by Rosemary Skinner Keller, Louise L. Queen, and Hilah F. Thomas. Nashville: Abingdon Press, 1982.

Sklar, Kathryn Kish. *Catharine Beecher: A Study in American Domesticity*. New Haven, CT: Yale University Press, 1973.

Smith, Hilda. "Feminism and the Methodology of Women's History." In *Liberating Women's History*, edited by Berenice A. Carroll, 368–84. Urbana: University of Illinois Press, 1976.

Smith, Timothy L. *Revivalism and Social Reform in Mid-Nineteenth-Century America*. New York: Abingdon Press, 1957.

Smith, W. J. J. *A Centennial History of the Baptist Women of Texas, 1830–1930*. Dallas: Texas Woman's Missionary Union, 1933.

Smoot, Pamela. "African American Baptist Women: Making a Way Out of No Way." *Baptist History and Heritage* 42 (Summer 2007): 19–33.

Sorrill, Bobbie. *Annie Armstrong: Dreamer in Action*. Nashville: Broadman Press, 1984.

———. "Southern Baptist Laywomen in Missions." *Baptist History and Heritage* (July 1987): 21–28.

Sosna, Morton. *In Search of the Silent South: Southern Liberals and the Race Issue*. New York: Columbia University Press, 1977.

Spain, Rufus B. *At Ease in Zion: A Social History of Southern Baptists, 1865–1900*. Nashville: Vanderbilt University Press, 1967.

Stanton, Elizabeth Cady, et al., eds. *History of Woman Suffrage*. 6 vols. New York: Fowler and Wells, 1889–1922.

Storey, John. *Texas Baptist Leadership and Social Christianity, 1900–1980*. College Station: Texas A&M University Press, 1986.

Sullivan, Regina. *Lottie Moon: A Southern Baptist Missionary to China in History and Legend*. Baton Rouge: Louisiana State University Press, 2011.

Sumners, Bill. "Bridge Builders: Baptist Women and Race Relations at the Turn of the Twentieth Century." *Journal of African American Southern Baptist History* (June 2004): 72–81.

———. "Southern Baptists and Women's Right to Vote, 1910–1920." *Baptist History and Heritage* (January 1977): 45–51.

Taylor, William R. *Cavalier and Yankee: The Old South and American National Character*. Garden City, NY: Anchor Books, 1963.

Thompson, James J., Jr. *Tried as by Fire: Southern Baptists and the Religious Controversies of the 1920s*. Macon, GA: Mercer University Press, 1982.

Torbet, Robert G. *A History of the Baptists*. Valley Forge, PA: Judson Press, 1963.

Turner, Elizabeth Hayes. *Women, Culture, and Community: Religion and Reform in Galveston, 1880–1920*. Oxford: Oxford University Press, 1997.

Vail, Albert L. *Mary Webb and the Mother Society*. Philadelphia: American Baptist Publication Society, 1914.

Valentine, Foy D. *A Historical Study of Southern Baptists and Race Relations, 1917–1947*. New York: Arno Press, 1980.

Vickers, Gregory. "Models of Womanhood and the Early Woman's Missionary Union." *Baptist History and Heritage* (January 1989): 41–53.

———. "Southern Baptist Women and Social Concerns, 1910–1929." *Baptist History and Heritage* (October 1988): 3–13.

———. "Woman's Place: Images of Womanhood in the Southern Baptist Convention, 1888–1929." Master's thesis, Vanderbilt University, 1986.

Walker, Melissa. "Shifting Boundaries: Race Relations in the Rural Jim Crow South." In *African American Life in the Rural South, 1900–1950*, edited by R. Douglas Hurt, 81–107. Columbia: University of Missouri Press, 2003.

Warnock, Henry Y. "Modern Racial Thought and Attitudes of Southern Baptists and Methodists, 1900–1921," PhD thesis, Northwestern University, 1963.

Washington, James Melvin. *Frustrated Fellowship: The Black Baptist Quest for Social Power*. Macon, GA: Mercer University Press, 2004.

Watkins, Rees. *The House of Happiness: A Ministry of Love*. Richmond, VA: Woman's Missionary Union, Auxiliary to Richmond Baptist Association, 1981.

Weatherford, Carolyn. "Shaping of Leadership among Southern Baptist Women." *Baptist History and Heritage* (July 1987): 12–20.

Weaver, C. Douglas. *In Search of the New Testament Church: The Baptist Story*. Macon, GA: Mercer University Press, 2008.

Welter, Barbara. "The Cult of True Womanhood, 1820–1860." *American Quarterly* 18 (Summer 1966): 151–74.

Wheeler, Marjorie Spruill. *New Women of the New South: The Leaders of the Woman Suffrage Movement in the Southern States*. Oxford: Oxford University Press, 1993.

Whisenhunt, Donald W. *A Student's Introduction to History*. Boston: American Press, 1993.

White, Blanche Sydnor. *Our Heritage: History of Woman's Missionary Union, Auxiliary to the Maryland Baptist Union Association, 1742–1958*. Baltimore: Woman's Missionary Union of Maryland, 1959.

White, Charles Edward. *The Beauty of Holiness*. Grand Rapids, MI: Francis Asbury Press, 1986.

White, Ronald C., Jr. *Liberty and Justice for All: Racial Reform and the Social Gospel, 1877–1925*. San Francisco: Harper and Row, 1990.

White, Ronald C., Jr., and C. Howard Hopkins. *The Social Gospel: Religion and Reform in Changing America*. Philadelphia: Temple University Press, 1976.

Williams, Joyce E., and Vicky M. MacLean. *Settlement Sociology in the Progressive Years: Faith, Science, and Reform*. Leiden: Brill, 2015.

Wilson, Charles Reagan. *Baptized in Blood: The Religion of the Lost Cause, 1865–1920*. Athens: University of Georgia Press, 1980.

———., ed. *Religion in the South: Essays.* Jackson: University Press of Mississippi, 1985.

Wilson, Mark Robert. *William Owen Carver's Controversies in the Baptist South.* Macon, GA: Mercer University Press, 2010.

Wolfe, Margaret Ripley. *Daughters of Canaan: A Saga of Southern Women.* Lexington: University Press of Kentucky, 1995.

Wood, Ann Douglas. "Mrs. Sigourney and the Sensibility of Inner Space." *New England Quarterly* 45 (1972): 163–81.

Woods, Robert A., and Albert J. Kennedy. *Handbook of Settlements.* Philadelphia: New York Charities Publication Committee, Russell Sage Foundation, 1911.

Woodward, C. Vann. *Origins of the New South, 1877–1913.* Baton Rouge: Louisiana State University Press, 1951.

———. *The Strange Career of Jim Crow.* New York: Oxford University Press, 1966. First published 1955.

Wynes, Charles E. *Forgotten Voices: Dissenting Southerners in an Age of Conformity.* Baton Rouge: Louisiana State University Press, 1967.

Yance, Norman A. *Religion Southern Style: Southern Baptists and Society in Historical Perspective.* Perspectives in Religious Studies Series. Danville, VA: Association of Baptist Professors of Religion, 1978.

Yohn, Susan M. "'Let Christian Women Set the Example in Their Own Gifts': The 'Business' of Protestant Women's Organizations." In *Women and Twentieth-Century Protestantism,* edited by Margaret Lamberts Bendroth and Virginia Lieson Brereton, 213–35. Urbana: University of Illinois Press, 2002.

Young, Elizabeth Barber. *A Study of the Curricula of Seven Selected Women's Colleges of the Southern States.* New York: Teachers College, 1932.

Zimmerman, Jane. "The Penal Reform Movement in the South during the Progressive Era, 1890–1917." *Journal of Southern History* 17 (November 1951): 462–92.

Index

Page numbers in italics indicate figures or tables.